The Community Junior College

SECOND EDITION

The Community Junior College

JAMES W. THORNTON, Jr.

SAN JOSE STATE COLLEGE

John Wiley & Sons, Inc.

NEW YORK   LONDON   SYDNEY

Preface

Since the first edition of *The Community Junior College* appeared in 1960, significant trends have continued in the establishment and operation of junior colleges. Several states for the first time have adopted general enabling legislation authorizing public junior colleges. Enrollments have increased even more rapidly than those in other segments of higher education. Occupational curriculums to provide preparation for technical and semiprofessional work have increased in frequency, as skilled trade courses have begun to decrease slightly. Multicampus districts are appearing in centers of population, and faculty members have worked out formal patterns of participation in policy making. In the fall of 1965, the time seemed ripe for a fresh look at the aspects of junior college education that were analyzed in the first edition.

Accordingly, letters were addressed to some twenty professors of higher education who had been using the first edition as a textbook in their courses in junior college education in colleges and universities in all sections of the country. The professors were asked, in the light of their experience with the first edition, to suggest ways in which a revision might make it more useful. All of their suggestions have been considered seriously, and most of them have been incorporated into this revision. Two of the respondents recommended major revisions and additions, so far-reaching as to involve in effect the preparation of an additional volume dealing with matters of administration and construction of community junior colleges. Although these topics deserve treatment, I feel that they are inappropriate for this introductory discussion, one that is directed principally toward the preparation of prospective teachers and administrators of junior colleges and toward lay persons interested in understanding or in establishing junior colleges. Certainly a debt of gratitude is owed to the friends and colleagues who gave so generously of their time and insights; but the responsibility for the limitations of the book rests with me.

Every chapter has undergone extensive rewriting, and all of the tabular material is new. The last two parts, dealing with curriculum and with emerging issues in junior college education, have been completely revised to reflect the rapid and far-reaching developments since 1960. In addition, suggested readings at chapter ends and the bibliography have been reworked so as to eliminate older, less important or inaccessible references, and to include some of the intensive studies published since 1960.

I sincerely hope that the second edition may continue to serve as a useful and pragmatic introduction to the principles and practices of that uniquely American educational development, the community junior college.

James W. Thornton, Jr.

San Jose State College
July, 1966

Preface to the First Edition

Several states have recently completed studies of their forthcoming needs for opportunity for higher education. In almost all these reports, the establishment of community junior colleges is suggested as one part of the solution of the problem of rapidly rising college enrollments. It seems likely, therefore, that the next few years will see a rapid increase in the number of community junior colleges, the number of their students, and the number of their instructors.

The January 1960 issue of *The Junior College Directory* names 677 junior colleges of all types with enrollments totaling 905,062. The total full-time equivalent for instructors was 24,022. It is entirely possible that another decade will see as many as 800 colleges, with 2,000,000 students and at least 40,000 full-time equivalent instructors.

Adequate preparation of these new instructors is one of the most pressing of our many educational needs. The problem appears even more acute when it is realized that fewer than one-tenth of present junior college teachers have had any specific introduction to the nature, purposes, and philosophy of the community college before they began teaching in it. Most of them have been recruited from the ranks of high-school teachers.

In reporting these facts, Koos suggests that the preparation of teachers for community colleges should include study of (1) the philosophy and place of the junior college, (2) organizing and administering junior colleges, (3) the junior college curriculum, (4) the psychology of post- or late-adolescence, (5) student personnel problems in junior colleges, (6) methods of teaching in junior colleges, and (7) apprentice or practice teaching.

It is the purpose of this textbook to provide graduate students with a basic introduction to the first three and the fifth of Koos' categories. This preparation should prove equally appropriate for prospective teachers and administrators of community colleges, many of whom will be employed, as in the past, without much previous study of the junior college. This book should be helpful in providing them with either formal or informal opportunities to achieve a sound understanding while they are employed. In addition, some school administrators and interested lay persons will find the book helpful in establishing a community junior college in their own districts.

The book has been planned with these several groups of readers in mind. Part I considers the place of the community junior college in relation to all of American education and concludes with a statement of the commonly accepted purposes of the institution. Part II then traces the steps involved in the organization and operation of the college from its legal establishment to the registration of students. Part III treats of the curriculum of the community junior college, listing in detail the courses commonly offered and the limitations and special problems obtaining in each area. The final chapter proposes a comprehensive definition of "community junior college" and considers some of the next steps and basic issues involved in its realization.

Pending the development of that definition, a word about terminology is in order. "Junior college" is an inclusive term for post-high-school educational institutions which offer a two-year curriculum in addition to other educational services. Depending on the nature of control, these institutions are classified as public or private junior colleges. The term "community junior college" implies an interchange of services with the supporting community, and the offering of occupational and adult education in addition to university-parallel courses. In this book, "college" refers to four-year degree-granting institutions, unless the context quite clearly indicates that the term is used as an abbreviation for "junior college." "Junior college" includes any of the institutions listed in *The Junior College Directory*. "Community junior college" refers to those institutions, mostly under public control, which offer an expanded program of education developed in consideration of existing needs of the local community.

To some extent the community junior college is still an institutional ideal, offering the most inclusive educational program of all junior college categories. While existing public or private junior colleges may provide any or all of the several services offered by the community junior college, many of them do not offer the complete program ascribed ideally to the community junior college. Where it is necessary in this book to report facts about public or private junior colleges as reported by other writers, the terminology of the original authors is retained.

A problem often discussed in junior college literature is the appropriate classification of the junior college. Is it the "capstone of secondary education," as suggested by its earliest advocates, or is it rather a facet of American higher education? Actually either categorization is unfortunate if it results in compressing the junior college into a preconceived pattern, and thereby stifling creativity. The community junior college is not just secondary education, deserving the epithet "glorified high school." Nor is it only higher education, as described by the phrase "decapitated college." It is an indigenous American educational institution developed to perform needed functions, some of which are shared by the high schools or by the colleges, and some of which are its own unshared responsibilities. There are junior colleges that have been nurtured by high schools and others that have developed from four-year colleges; but the community junior college, as the present volume demonstrates, need not be confined to either category nor limited in its service by its parentage.

Many obligations have been incurred during the preparation of *The Community Junior College,* some of them as impossible to identify as they are to repay. Among those persons whom it is possible to thank, however, are two colleagues who were most helpful in providing up-to-date information for several chapters of the book: Edmund J. Gleazer, Jr., Executive Director of the American Association of Junior Colleges, for making available the fifth edition of *American Junior Colleges,* prior to its publication in April 1960; and Leland L. Medsker of the Center for the Study of Higher Education, University of California, for permission to read and quote from his important study, *The Junior College: Progress and Prospect.* For general background, I am indebted to Malcolm S. Mac Lean, Basil H. Peterson, and B. Lamar Johnson; each will recognize the points at which he has contributed. I wish to express special appreciation to Donald C. Bridgman of Orange Coast College, Leland L. Medsker, and Cyrilla Thornton for reading and criticizing the entire manuscript, and to May C. Duignan of San Jose City College, who read and criticized Chapter 17. Appreciation is also extended to the several authors and publishers who gave permission to quote copyrighted material; specific acknowledgment is accorded each quotation.

James W. Thornton, Jr.

San Jose State College
April 1960

Contents

I

Backgrounds of the Community Junior College

1

Issues in Higher Education

The community junior college is one part of a sprawling complex of American institutions which offer education beyond the high school. Many uncoordinated influences have led to the establishment of different but often competing kinds of opportunity for higher education. Americans' appetite for learning has been such that students and financial support have been forthcoming for universities private and public, professional schools, liberal arts colleges, institutes of technology, land-grant colleges of agriculture and mechanical arts, theological seminaries, teachers colleges, normal schools, vocational institutes, and junior colleges. Institutions which were originally established to achieve one purpose have expanded to include other purposes, until accurate classification of American colleges and universities is almost impossible.

During the last third of the twentieth century, American higher education will face rapid increases in enrollments and increased urgency of its multifarious tasks. New kinds of education are required of a much greater proportion of the population than ever before. An acquaintance with some of the issues which confront all of higher education is basic to understanding the nature and function of the community junior college. Several of these issues are discussed briefly in Chapter 1.

3

A. Definition of Purposes

Two opposing views of the nature and purposes of higher education in America have been elaborated over the past quarter century. Subcategories of each philosophy are found, particularly in detailed suggestions about methodology and choice of subject matter, but nearly all the fundamental proposals for the future course of the American college can be assigned to either the rationalistic school or the realistic.

The rationalists number among their ranks such authoritative writers as Robert Hutchins, Jacques Maritain, Mortimer Adler, the authors of *General Education in a Free Society* (*55*),[1] Mark Van Doren, Byron Hollinshead, and many presidents of private liberal arts colleges. The realists, in turn, can refer to the President's Commission on Higher Education, James B. Conant, T. R. McConnell, Malcolm S. MacLean, Sidney Hook, John S. Diekhoff, and many presidents of public universities, land-grant colleges, and community colleges (*68*:Ch. II; *16*).

The *rationalist position* assumes

. . . that the distinctive factor in man is his rationality, and the cultivation of man's reason is the sole aim of education, or, of life itself. Since the reason is a separate entity, cut off by definition from its social and physical origin, and is everywhere the same, education must be everywhere the same. The values and truths which are universal are to be found in the texts of the Western tradition, and the reason, which has its own proper business in thinking and in perceiving abstract ideas in their true relation, can discover truths which are intrinsic in the universe by the application of intellectual effort to the correct texts. (*68*:28) `

An adaptation of the same philosophy substitutes for the "texts of the Western tradition" the study of more recently developed subject matter in physical sciences and the humanities. Both varieties see college education as nonvocational, nonprofessional, and nonspecialist. Both depend upon lectures, demonstrations, discussions, and reading as their basic methods.

As a consequence of this concentration upon the content of higher education, the rationalist sees the college as a comparatively fixed and static institution. The student who is "college material," in the sense that he thrives on the program of studies set before him, will succeed. According to this view, on the other hand, those who are not attracted

---

[1] The italic numbers in parentheses refer to items in the bibliography. Numbers after the colon indicate the pages on which a quotation appears.

to such studies or who fail in them have proved themselves not to be college material.

In any case,

. . . the distinguishing mark of the educated person is intellectual power. Hence, the primary aim of higher education is the development of intellectual power. Any other aim is secondary and can be tolerated only to the extent to which the attempt to achieve it does not interfere with the effort to achieve the primary aim. Such an aim as adjustment to the environment is not merely secondary, it is wrong; it would prevent education from putting forth its noblest effort. . . . (77:111)

In modern America, the traditional curriculum espoused by the rationalists creates a dilemma. The social demands for higher education are constantly increasing, but only a very limited proportion of the population possesses the kind of ability and interest to profit by the rationalist pattern of education. Hence the rationalist must espouse an elite concept of higher education, seeking to prepare only "leaders," or he must seek to dilute the content and the difficulty of his limited subject matter in order to make it palatable to greater numbers.[2]

The *realist position*, on the other hand, emphasizes the aphorism that the verb "teach" has an indirect object, the learner, as well as a direct object, the subject matter. Since American economy both permits and requires a larger proportion of the population to aspire to education beyond the high school, the realist rejects both the ruthless selectivity of the rationalist and his static concept of the curriculum. Instead, he feels that knowledge should be useful to society and to individual citizens. He

. . . tries to arrange an educational environment in which it is possible for the individual to find his own way toward full development. . . . Decisions as to what should be taught and the way it should be taught are made by reference to the usefulness of the knowledge in everyday life. Knowledge is conceived of, not as an end in itself, but as a means to a more abundant personal life, and a stronger, freer social order. (68:37)

The realist, then, conceives of men as sharing common needs— as citizens, as individuals, as members of families. He feels that there are common purposes for the education of all for these responsibilities. Yet he realizes that these common purposes will be achieved in differing degrees by men of differing abilities and that different patterns of educational experiences may well lead men toward the same ob-

[2] In the wry comment of Diekhoff, those who propose a limitation of enrollments always assume that they will be among the chosen: "It is only for others that we wish the bliss of ignorance" (35:3).

jectives. He feels that education consists in progress toward a goal rather than solely in the achievement of it. At the same time, the realist sees beyond the likenesses of men to their differences, and so he attempts to establish differentiated courses of specialized nature to train men for their occupations. The graduate schools of the universities, the professional and technical colleges, and the community junior colleges of America have developed in harmony with the realistic analyses of the nature of man, the nature of American society, and the purposes of education. The President's Commission on Higher Education expresses the realist position as follows:

It is a commonplace of the democratic faith that education is indispensable to the maintenance and growth of freedom of thought, faith, enterprise, and association. Thus the social role of education in a democratic society is at once to secure equal liberty and equal opportunity to differing individuals and groups, and to enable the citizen to understand, appraise, and redirect forces, men, and events as these tend to strengthen or to weaken their liberties.

In performing this role, education will necessarily vary its means and methods to fit the diversity of its constituency, but it will achieve its ends more successfully if its programs and policies grow out of and are relevant to the characteristics and needs of contemporary society. Effective democratic education will deal directly with current problems. (70:Vol. I, 5).

Commenting on this Report, Hutchins expresses the rationalist's reaction to the realistic approach to educational purposes as follows:

It is confused, confusing, and contradictory. It has something for everybody. It is generous, ignoble, bold, timid, naive, and optimistic. It is filled with the spirit of universal brotherhood and the sense of American superiority. It has great faith in money. It has great faith in courses. It is antihumanistic and anti-intellectual. It is confident that vices can be turned into virtues by making them larger. Its heart is in the right place; its head does not work very well. (77:107)

    Thus the lines of the debate are drawn. On the one side stand those who believe that the major object of higher education is to transmit an established culture to those innately qualified to receive it. On the other are ranged those who believe that the curriculums of higher education are defined by the needs and the worthy interests of the American people. The dilemma is summarized by Francis H. Horn:

How can the colleges and universities provide graduates prepared for the thousands of specialized tasks which must be carried on in our technological civilization, and at the same time prepared for the demanding responsibilities of intelligent and informed citizenship—including satisfying personal living—in our democratic society?

I suggest that it is time to end this current battle of the books of liberal and vocational education, general and specialized knowledge, culture and training. We must . . . recognize first that the individual and society need both types of education; second, that the problem, both for the student and for the college is the right relationship between the two; third, that the relationship will not be the same for all individuals . . . or for all institutions . . . ; and fourth, that the diversity of curricula and schools within American higher education resulting from these different approaches to the relationship of liberal to vocational education is a matter of strength, and efforts to force a common pattern . . . must be resisted. (75:312)

B. Increasing Enrollments

"What is new in the present situation is a sharply accelerated rate of growth in enrollments coupled with a severe shortage of qualified teachers—a combination which threatens to cause a progressive deterioration of quality at all levels of education over the next two decades" (151:7). The prediction was made in 1955. Halfway through the two-decade period, the statement is still accurate.

Table 1 shows the trend in degree-credit college enrollments in America in recent years. The growth demonstrated is especially remarkable, since the decade of the 1930's saw an annual decrease in the number of births; yet, as these age groups progressed through college in the 1950's, greater numbers and proportions enrolled each year, except during the Korean conflict. In the fifteen-year period from 1949 to 1964, enrollments almost doubled (96% total increase).

Table 1. Total Opening Enrollment of Degree-Credit Students in Relation to Population Aged 18–21: Selected Years, 1939 to 1964 [a]

Fall	Total Enrollment	Population, 18–21	Enrollment as Per Cent of Population 18–21
1939	1,365,000	9,545,000	14.3
1949	2,445,000	8,990,000	27.2
1954	2,447,000	8,437,000	29.0
1959	3,365,000	9,182,000	36.6
1964	4,988,000	11,700,000	42.7

[a] **Source:** *Health, Education, and Welfare Trends,* 1965 Edition. Washington: Government Printing Office, 1965 (66).

Such an increase in college enrollments seems to indicate

(1) that students are persisting in college longer—the rate of withdrawal before graduation is lessening;

(2) that a greater number of older persons (beyond the usual collegiate age of 18–21 years) are enrolling;

(3) that a greater proportion of the so-called "college-age youth" are enrolling in degree programs.

The growth from these reasons is only a foretaste of the enrollment increase to come. During the decade 1940–1950, the birth rate ceased its previous decline. For the first time in the history of the nation, the rate of population growth turned up sharply. Population grew twice as rapidly as in the previous decade, partly because of longer life expectancy, but mainly because of an unprecedented rise in births.

This high level of births has persisted. During the 1930's, births each year numbered between 2,000,000 and 3,000,000. During the 1940's, the annual rate rose to more than 3,000,000 births annually. In 1954 and every year since, about 4,000,000 births have been recorded. Whether the birth rate levels off or decreases in the future, children already born will require almost a doubling of facilities for higher education between 1965 and 1980 (*151*:8). In effect, America must build as many college facilities between 1965 and 1980 as have been built between the landing at Plymouth Rock and 1965! This fact is one of the reasons for the recent growth in interest in the establishment of community junior colleges.

Another aspect of the problem of numbers concerns the availability of college teachers. The Fund for the Advancement of Education summarizes the problem as follows:

> The rise in enrollments confronts American schools and colleges with a staggering problem of finding enough good teachers. . . .
>
> The colleges and universities will have to add more teachers in the next 15 years than in all previous history combined. . . . If the present student-teacher ratio of 13 to 1 is to be preserved, *for every 10 college teachers now employed, somewhere between 16 and 25 new ones will have to be found between now and 1970*. . . . The real question is: Can we get enough *good* teachers? (*151*:17–19)

C. Adult Demands for Schooling

But the increase in the number of full-time students is only the more obvious aspect of growth. In another expression of its faith in schooling, the American public has become during the last quarter century a nation of students. Remarking that "one of every three adults in the United States is engaged in some kind of continuing education during any single year," the President's Committee on Education Beyond the High School defines the field as follows:

Adult education should serve the aspirations of the more mature for literacy, for learning new and more remunerative skills, for a higher degree of culture, for understanding the social, physical, and economic environment, for fulfilling the role of responsible citizenship in a Nation and world having complex problems, and for enriching the leisure time which is steadily growing as a result of automation, shortened work-weeks, and earlier retirement. (*139*:62–66)

A part of the need for adult education is indicated by levels of education of the American people. In the 1960 census, almost 40% of the adult population had less than an eighth grade education; 8.3% of this group had completed less than four years of school. In the same year, only 7.6% of adults had graduated from college: the Nation included more *functional illiterates* than it did college graduates. Yet, most of the social studies such as civics, economics, sociology, problems of democracy, and international relations are usually taught only above the elementary school.

The Report of the President's Commission on Higher Education points out that

. . . the population of the United States is becoming increasingly an adult one. . . . The increasing tempo of change in our technology is another factor which is increasing the demand for adult education. . . . Increased technical efficiency has also made possible a drastic reduction in hours of work. . . . [Specialization of work] has changed the kinds of activities in which individuals need to engage during their leisure hours. . . . The complex interrelationships of labor and management require trained leadership and understanding. . . . A further element in the need for expanding adult education is that adults desire to learn. (*70*:Vol. II, 59–61)

Of course, it might be argued that this need is not truly a need for further college study. Yet,

the colleges and the universities are the best equipped of all the agencies, from the standpoint of resources, to undertake the job. Education on a near adult level is their business, and they have, in some measure at least, the necessary teachers and facilities. . . . The colleges and universities should elevate adult education to a position of equal importance with any other of their functions. . . . The principal obstacle to acceptance of the program, nonetheless, is the limited concept that higher education holds of its role in a free and democratic society. (70:Vol. I, 96–97)

Hutchins agreed with the Commission that the education of adults needs continuing attention:

The Commission is on sound ground when it urges the extension of the educational opportunities open to adults. Many adults have had no education, including great numbers who have graduated from college. Education is a process which should go on through the whole of life. Many disciplines, and they are among the most important, will not give up their secrets except to those who have had experience with the issues which the disciplines raise. The education of youth is a waste of time if youth is to have no future. Unless we can educate those who control the world today, it seems most unlikely that youth can have a future. (77:108)

In this area of adult education also the community junior college is in a position to contribute importantly. It is located in the home community of the adult student, and it has the staff and the facilities to carry on effective adult education.

D. Encouraging the Able Student

In spite of the steady increase in college enrollments, many able young people do not go beyond high school. According to one estimate, about 40% of the ablest one-fourth of American young people enter college; and many of these will not graduate (62:30–40). In a period when there is a shortage of trained professional workers in almost every area of national life, this wastage of more than half of the ablest minds of the population is a serious handicap to society. Much attention has been paid to the problem of eliminating from college those who are unfit to profit from the experience. This problem in reality is of minor importance; most students who lack ability or preparation eliminate themselves even without applying for admission to college. The serious social challenge is that of stimulating able high-school graduates to desire further education and of removing the barriers which now keep them from pursuing it.

Havighurst and Rodgers estimate that 20% of the ablest quarter of youth are prevented from attending college because of financial considerations (64:161). Various proposals have been advanced to overcome this barrier. The college-loan provisions of the National Defense Education Act are an example, as are the many scholarships made available by States, private foundations, and individuals. At the present ratio between costs of college attendance and amounts of loans, however, these measures will not make it possible for very needy youth to attend college away from home. A generous scholarship of $600 must be applied on college costs which average more than $1600. Loans, on the other hand, must be repaid; a young woman will hesitate to accept a loan which may act as a deterrent to marriage, which she may come to value above education. Young men similarly are reluctant to assume a burden which may consume a major part of their earnings during the first several years of their working life. The community junior college helps to remove some of the financial barriers to higher education.

An even more serious cause of failure to seek higher education is lack of desire. Havighurst and Rodgers summarize the nature of this motivational factor:

> Practically all of the superior youths who do not continue their education beyond high school are children of people who have less than a high school education. These families participate in a culture which has little personal contact with higher education. They value a job and an earning career highly for their young people. . . . While these people have come to look favorably on a high school education for their children, they do not regard college as really within the reach of their aspirations or their financial means. (64:162)

Two comments may complete this summary presentation of the problem of motivation of the able student. Many such youths have abilities which are not traditionally valued by the college; either they are not attracted to the college or they leave it because nothing in the curriculum seems to have value or meaning for them. On the other hand, the social groups that now do not desire or aspire to college at one time in our history could not read or write; at a later period, they withdrew their children from school at 10 or 12 or 14 years of age, although now they "look favorably on a high school education." If we can provide early identification and guidance of talented young people, local opportunities for higher education at minimum cost to the student, and curriculums clearly relevant to the demands of modern times, many more of these able students will be encouraged to complete two or four or even more years of college. The value to the nation of such an outcome would far exceed its cost.

E. Maintenance of Standards

Closely related to the definition of purposes and the accommodation of increasing numbers is the maintenance of standards of student achievement in college during the years ahead. Some writers feel certain that an increase in the numbers of students in college must certainly result in a lowering of standards. In fact, this has already happened, they proclaim, and they label those who propose further expansion of higher education as anti-intellectual, irrational, and illogical. These criticisms arise from certain basic assumptions which are not usually clarified by the critics.

"Greater numbers mean lower standards" is a logical conclusion only if we assume

(1) that we cannot get teachers enough to maintain standards,

(2) that at present all college students are chosen solely on the basis of highest college aptitude and that we could get more students only by dipping more deeply into the lower levels of the aptitude pool,

(3) that "success in college" must have a single traditional meaning.

The first fear has a very real basis. Unless college teachers are enabled to use their abilities more effectively, and unless an active program of recruitment is instituted even at the expense of increasing salaries, we may find that the nation is faced with a serious shortage of teachers.

The second assumption is clearly in error. In the preceding section, evidence was cited to show that two-fifths of young people in the upper quarter of tested ability were not in college. Obversely, this figure indicates that three-fifths of the "superior" quarter, or 15% of the total age group, are in college. But figures of enrollment in institutions of higher education indicate that present enrollments (of all ages) are equal to 39% of the population in the 18–21 age group. Obviously, some of these must come not from the upper quarter but from high average and low average intelligence groups.

Figure 1 indicates the nature of the distribution of intelligence (as measured by the Army General Classification Test) among the population as a whole and among college graduates. It is evident that a significant number of college graduates have been drawn from the group of low average intelligence. The shaded area of the chart indicates also that a great many able individuals do not graduate from college. Certainly there are enough young people of above average intelligence not now in college to add significantly to present enrollments—if, as mentioned in Section D, they had the desire and the finances for more schooling—without lowering the average intelligence level of the college student.

The Committee does not agree with those who argue that, in order to preserve quality, colleges must sharply restrict enrollments to some-

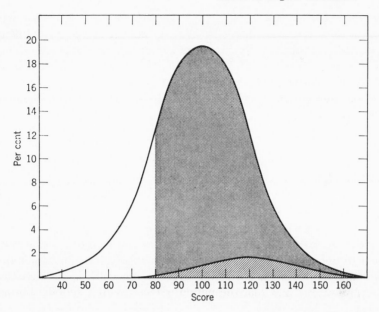

Figure 1. Distribution of intelligence (in terms of scores on the Army General Classification Test) for the United States population is shown by the upper curve; for college graduates, by the smaller curve. The area between the curves at the right represents the part of the population that is intelligent enough for college work but that does not go to college. After Fletcher G. Watson, "A Crisis in Science Teaching," *Scientific American*, 190:27–29, February, 1954. Shading added (*161*:27).

thing like their present level by steadily boosting admission standards. . . . No matter where institutions set their admissions standards, the number of qualifying applicants by 1970 will be at least twice the present level. It should be remembered that college enrollments have already [1957] doubled since 1940 even though the college-age population is smaller and admission standards have been tightened in many institutions. (*139*:9–10)

For 1965, enrollments were four times those of 1940, and twice as large as those considered by the President's Committee on Education beyond the High School.

In the main, however, those who seem certain that increased numbers must entail decreased standards adhere to the rationalist philosophy described earlier. To them, "college" means only exposure to history, world literature, natural sciences, mathematics, foreign languages, and similarly abstract disciplines. If this is the true and only meaning of "college," increasing proportions of youth in college, even increasing proportions of very able youth in college, will probably mean a lowering of standards. For some able persons have little interest, little aptitude, little desire, and little need (as they see it) for scholarship in these areas.

There is an enduring need in any society for the scholar in the humanities, but not all college-educated persons need to be scholars in the humanities. Modern technological society also needs trained and able businessmen, engineers, lawyers, physicians, managers, farmers; it requires trained and able technicians, craftsmen, homemakers. Their education is different; it is not, economically, socially, academically, of a "lower level" or of a "debased standard." The problem of standards arises when ill-considered attempts are made to achieve too many diverse aims within a single curriculum. The community junior college can assist in the preservation of standards by offering a variety of excellent curriculums for the existing variety of worthy objectives.

The definition of standards should involve thoroughness, understanding, and depth in the study of a body of knowledge important and appropriate to the individual and to his society. In this light, differential calculus is not in itself of a higher level than accountancy, nor physiology of a higher level than electronics. The true measure of the stature of an educational institution should be the number of young people it prepares well for their roles in life and not the number who fail to graduate.

F. The Diversity of Institutions

Higher education in America has accepted a dual purpose—to meet the educational needs of its students and to meet the need of America for educated citizens and workers. Because of the rapidly expanding proportions and absolute numbers of youth seeking higher education, this dual objective cannot be met conveniently by any single kind of institution. As a result of constantly emerging needs, which established institutions were unable or unwilling to satisfy, an almost chaotic variety of colleges and universities has been established in America. In a recent year, the American educational establishment included (122:4 and 7)

155 universities with	2,332,135 enrollment
1,401 all other four-year colleges	2,458,424 enrollment
682 two-year institutions with	1,176,852 enrollment [3]
2,238 total with	5,967,411 enrollment

[3] *The Junior College Directory* for the same year (1965) listed 771 junior colleges. In this listing, some of the junior colleges are not classified as two-year institutions.

It seems that there is a sufficient variety of institutions to meet the needs of higher education. Careful study both nationally and in every state will be required to make sure that each existing institution is utilized to the best advantage, that new institutions are established with regard for the optimum location of each kind of institution and to their effective interrelationships. Certainly, it seems that it will be most difficult to establish a sufficient number of new post-high-school institutions in the near future; those that are established should be carefully and soundly established.

A further problem arising from diversity is that of mutual understanding and cooperation. A determined effort on the part of workers in every kind of college to understand the functions of their own institution and of the others will lead to more effective cooperation of all in the interest of the students and of society. In addition, intense effort is needed to help adults and youth understand the purposes of the various available institutions. In this way students may be helped to make more appropriate choices of colleges and thus to improve the quality and the extent of their education.

In all institutions, specialized education must be joined with education for personal and social development. It is not a question of one kind or the other; the student and his society need both.

To make sure of its own health and strength a democratic society must provide free and equal access to education for its youth, and at the same time it must recognize their differences in capacity and purpose. Higher education in America should include a variety of institutional forms and educational programs, so that at whatever point any student leaves school, he will be fitted, within the limits of his mental capacity and educational level, for an abundant and productive life as a person, as a worker, and as a citizen. (70:Vol. I, 67)

The community junior college is the most recent addition to this family of post-high-school educational institutions. As yet, it has failed to achieve from its elders full understanding or complete cooperation. Part of this failure derives from the multiplicity of its functions. The community junior college does indeed offer two years of conventional higher education to some of its students. Yet it is not only a lower division. It adds to the college transfer curriculums other courses adapted to the "mental capacity and educational level" of its students. This inner diversity of program and purpose is one of the most valuable aspects of the community junior college; at the same time, it increases the difficulty either of fitting the institution neatly into the established pattern of higher education or of relegating it to the category of secondary education.

G. Adequate Support

In a period when rapid monetary inflation is combined with greatly expanded enrollments, financial problems are inevitable. One of the most lucid analyses of this situation has been published by the Educational Policies Commission; the summary presented here is based principally upon that study (39:Ch. 7).

Since 1930, the proportion of the gross national product that has been spent on higher education has varied from 0.56% in 1930, to 1.13% in 1959–1960. The increase in dollars is more apparent than real, however, because of monetary inflation, the increase in research grants, and the great increase in enrollments. The expenditure per student, expressed in dollars equivalent to 1930 dollars, actually decreased.

In addition, there were two very marked shifts in the percentage distribution of current expenditures among the several functions of higher education. The percentage of current expenditures allocated to organized research rose from 3.5% in 1929–1930 to 18.5% in 1959–1960. On the other hand, the percentage allocated to resident instruction (i.e., faculty salaries) dropped from 44% to 32% in the same period. The net result has been that

. . . serious erosion has occurred in the real incomes of American college teachers relative to other professional groups and to wage earners generally. . . . The plain fact is that the college teachers of the United States, through their inadequate salaries, are subsidizing the education of students, and in some cases the luxuries of their families, by an amount which is more than double the grand total of alumni gifts, corporate gifts, and endowment income of all colleges and universities combined. (139:5–6)

It seems likely that expenditures for higher education must double once more before 1975 if our colleges are simply to maintain the quality of education which they have been providing.

Barring depression and war, the United States can afford to spend what is needed to expand and improve its enterprise in higher education during the coming decade of decision. . . . To finance higher education will not be at all easy, but it is not impossible. The expansion of higher education is feasible; proponents of expansion are planning within terms of economic reality. (39:127)

Among the means suggested to finance the needed expansion are increase in the state contributions to higher education, marked increase in alumni and corporate regular annual contributions to higher education, increase in the ratio of students to college instructors from an estimated 13:1 at present to approximately 20:1, and more economical administration and utilization of all physical plant facilities. "As a people, we must couple this information with the will to act on it, or face the consequences of inaction. Failure to meet the total cost will adversely affect American youth either by an outright denial of, or an inferior substitute for, genuine educational opportunity" (*139*:87).

H. The Community Junior College as a Part of Higher Education

The junior colleges of America are intimately concerned with all the problems of higher education. They have become full partners in the enterprise and will bear an increasing share of each of the burdens. In addition, however, they must meet several problems which are peculiar to themselves.

Some of these problems arise from their comparative newness in the field of higher education. Their total function and the full scope of their responsibility are not yet entirely clear to their own administrators. It is not surprising, then, that they are misunderstood, even mistrusted, by some of the faculties of other institutions, who have had no opportunity to learn of the present achievements and future potentialities of the junior college. One of their problems is that of *interpretation*—helping educational workers in the schools and other colleges to understand their place in the total educational enterprise. In addition, it is essential that they help the prospective student and the citizenry in general to understand emerging educational needs and the programs that are being developed to meet them.

It is clear that these newer educational programs must be developed with great care. The community junior colleges especially must develop a wide variety of curriculums, but each must combine demanding standards of student achievement with responsible and effective guidance and all reasonable fiscal economy. If unnecessary or trivial courses are organized, if students are enrolled in such haphazard fashion that they then withdraw in great numbers, if instructional standards are allowed to deteriorate—then the community college shall have forfeited its right to a share in the achievement of the most majestic educational ideal ever attempted by a nation. By their success in this high endeavor, on the contrary, these institutions can contribute significantly and enduringly to the preservation and enhancement of American democratic institutions.

Selected References

Butts, R. Freeman. *The College Charts Its Course.* New York: McGraw-Hill Book Co., 1939.

Educational Policies Commission. "Higher Education in a Decade of Decision." Washington: National Education Association, 1957.

Henry, Nelson B. (editor). *General Education.* The Fifty-first Yearbook of the National Society for the Study of Education, Part I. Chicago: University of Chicago Press, 1952.

Horn, Francis H. "Liberal Education Reexamined." Harvard Educational Review, 26:303–314.

"Nature and Needs of Higher Education." The Report of the Commission on Financing Higher Education. New York: Columbia University Press, 1952.

Sanford, Nevitt (editor). *College and Character.* New York: John Wiley and Sons, 1964.

"The College Scene," Special Supplement in *Harper's Magazine,* 223:119–182 (October, 1961).

The President's Commission on Higher Education. "Higher Education for American Democracy." New York: Harper and Row, 1948.

The President's Committee on Education Beyond the High School. "Second Report to the President." Washington: Government Printing Office, 1957.

2

New Economic and Social Needs for Higher Education

The community junior college did not emerge and grow to adulthood in sixty years simply because a few college and university presidents thought that such schools were needed. Most of the people who work to establish, pay for, and attend the community junior colleges have never heard of the philosophers of the movement. Instead, they see a pressing and immediate need in their own local community for educational opportunities which are not afforded by their secondary schools or by available colleges or universities. They hear that a nearby community or state has solved similar problems by establishing a junior college. So they investigate, become convinced, and initiate appropriate action to establish such a college for their community.

But what are the economic and social needs that have led so many communities to develop community junior colleges? Why have constantly increasing numbers of American youth demanded more post-high-school education? What trends seem to indicate a continuation and intensification of these educational demands? This chapter indicates some of the educational consequences of recent technological and cultural developments.

A. The American Economy

One of the basic characteristics of America and one of her most important natural resources is her technology—the ability to make use of materials and processes both to develop more materials and processes of production and to provide a constantly increasing flow of consumer goods. At the time of its discovery and settlement by Europeans, the continent had all the wealth—in metals, in arable land, in petroleum and timber and soil and waterpower—that it has now. Actually, since a prodigal nation has wasted so much of its natural wealth, there were more of all these resources then than there are now. Yet the land supported fewer than a million Indians, at a bare subsistence level. Now the same land supports 200,000,000 in a manner to arouse the envy of the wealthiest kings of history; within a very few years it will support over 250,000,000.

This increase in numbers of people and this rise in the standard of living are made possible by enormously complicated and interdependent techniques of production. These techniques free persons from drudgery so that they may achieve a high level of schooling; at the same time, the techniques could not operate without a high degree of literacy on the part of the citizenry. The community junior colleges and American technology have developed together most rapidly within the space of a single human lifespan. Both also are on the verge of further extension. A review of a few of the more impressive technical achievements will provide a setting for a description of some recent social changes in the United States. In the light of both the economic achievements and the social position, it will be possible to understand more clearly the reasons for the community junior college and the directions of its further development.

Power. The most dramatic technical development of our day is one with great power for evil as well as for good—the controlled release of atomic energy through the processes of fusion and fission. Limited at present to changes in elements at both ends of the periodic table, such reactions can be started in theory with any of the elements. The hydrogen in a cubic mile of seawater could provide enough energy for 300 centuries at the 1960 rate of use—if its release could be controlled. In addition, any of the elements existing in the earth's crust might be similarly transmuted—so that the day is in sight when electric power from atomic generators will be so easily available that it will not be worthwhile to meter it. In case, however, the problems of creating inexpensive power from atomic energy are not solved rapidly, there is promise of the practical availability of solar power before supplies of stored organic fuels are exhausted. The consequences of unlimited low-cost power are beyond imagination. Purification of ocean water for human use, electrified highways, truly automatic homes, liberation from the tyrannies of weather—

these are only a few of the probable developments which await only an economical source of power in great quantity.

Transportation. Another aspect of technology concerns the use of engines for transportation. The modern automobile and the airplane have made travel pleasant, rapid, and convenient. They have expanded man's communities and they have shrunk his world. They have brought new dimensions of production and recreation, as well as new hazards, to human life. Other applications of the engine are equally important— the tractor in farming, the bulldozer in mining and in road building, the truck and trailer in the rapid and economical distribution of goods. The tonnage of earth moved in any state in a single year's roadbuilding would surpass the weight of all the pyramids, yet Americans do not marvel, but only complain at the detours. The internal combustion engine, its manufacture, its fueling, its upkeep, and the roads to make it usable constitute one of the basic elements in American manufacturing, distribution, and consumption.

Agriculture has changed to the extent that one agricultural worker now feeds himself and fourteen others whereas in 1900 he fed himself and only seven others. Yet he accomplishes this increase with fewer hours of work and fewer acres. Part of the increased production is attributable to the substitution of machinery for horses as a source of power so that 63 million acres of farmland formerly needed to grow feed for work animals now can be used to produce marketable products. At the same time, new techniques of soil conservation and fertilization have improved the farmland of the nation. Hybridization of poultry, meat animals, and field crops has resulted in greater yields in almost every segment of farm production.

Automation. In industry as well as in agriculture new processes and new machines have combined to increase the hourly productivity of labor, thus providing both greater leisure and higher real wages.

With increased output per worker and per man-hour, we have been able as a nation to consume an ever larger volume of goods and services, while producing and distributing them with less and less effort. Indeed, average working hours were cut so sharply after 1900 that, despite a more than two-fold increase in private employment during the next half-century, total man-hours worked in private employment rose only 40 percent . . . output per man-hour gained so rapidly that by 1950 total production was about three-and-a-half times as great as in 1900. (34:739)

Developments since 1950 promise to carry this shift in the ratio of capital investment to manpower even further, with additional increments in the standard of living. The use of automation in mass production factories eliminates much of the drudgery of material handling and machine setup. Human muscle power is a most expensive form of energy, costing in the neighborhood of $30 per kilowatt-hour, as compared with only a few cents for electric power. Any process that can substitute mechanical energy for human energy is not only economical but contributes also to a higher standard of living as well as to the ease of life. There are serious philosophical problems involved in this proposed elimination of muscular work, yet it seems unlikely that people will continue to demand the opportunity to perform arduous physical labor simply because they feel that they need the discipline of perspiration.

Research. In scientific research, recent progress has been astounding. Edison tried 3000 substances in his search for a material suitable for a light-bulb filament. Now, materials are almost literally created to meet needs—whether the need is for a heat-resistant ceramic, a crease-resistant fabric, a lightweight insulator for frozen foods, a malleable alloy, or a cheap but indestructible plastic for childrens' toys. One major American industry is said to plan its future investment and personnel development on the premise that in twenty-five years 90% of its income will be from products not yet invented, whereas three-quarters of its present products will be outdated. The scope of the nation's research effort may be inferred from the fact that annual expenditures for research exceed $15 billion; two-thirds of this amount, or $10 billion, comes from Federal sources.

Pharmaceutical chemistry has kept pace with industrial chemistry. A dozen diseases which scourged America in 1925 have almost disappeared as major factors in public health statistics; pneumonia, tuberculosis, diphtheria, typhoid fever, scarlet fever, syphilis, malaria, and poliomyelitis have been robbed of much of their terror by chemotherapeutic discoveries. Workers have been assured longer lives with greater freedom from pain and from loss of earnings due to illness. Even moods, neuroses, and psychoses are beginning to yield to new chemical tranquilizers, so that both productive work and enjoyable leisure may be increased.

Communication. Techniques of communication have changed in similar fashion. Direct distance dialing, mobile telephones, television transmission by satellite, automatic record keeping and billing, long-distance transmission of news photos, and instantaneous worldwide news reporting all compete for attention. It is no wonder that the amount of adult reading is decreasing annually. It is not fantastic to suppose that within a century the reading of the old-fashioned book will be a lost and useless art, and that the storyteller will recreate the art of Homer—on stereophonic video tape.

Distribution. Technological developments have been barely suggested to indicate the tremendous expansion in knowledge in the past fifty years. The application of this knowledge has resulted also in a new science of distribution, so that the consumer is made to feel in dire need of products which, two months ago, he did not dream existed. The entire process has educational implications. Graduates not only need to master the techniques by which machines are controlled and improved; more imperatively, they need to cultivate the wisdom to use creatively the wealth and the leisure with which machines have endowed them. They need to develop resistance, lest they smother under an avalanche of goods! In addition, unskilled tasks are disappearing from the economy; every worker needs a constantly increasing level of education.

B. Recent Social Changes

The explosive expansion of technology has been accompanied by— in some cases it has caused—equally important changes in the character of American society. Inspection of three or four of the more obvious manifestations will indicate the nature of their influence on higher education. The growth in population, the emergence of new patterns of employment, consumption practices in an economy of abundance, and the rise in the average levels of schooling should demonstrate what has been happening to the quality of human life in recent decades.

Population Changes. The statistics of population growth in the United States are a rich source of insights into recent educational problems. Numerical growth in itself has created real difficulties for the school administrator, as he attempts to provide classrooms and teachers to care for more and more young people every year. Beyond that, changes in the age distribution of the population intensify his problems. Even without elaborate statistical tables, it is possible to summarize some of the more important qualities of America's present population, with estimates of its tendencies over the next twenty years. (34:Ch. 3; 63:Ch. 13)

The American population doubled in size every thirty years from 1800 to 1920, when it reached 106 million. By 1960 it had attained 180 million, a gain of 70% over 1920. If the same rate is maintained, the population by 1980 will reach 217 million; there are indications, however, that it is increasing at a more rapid rate. Because of a drop in the death rate (from 17.2 annually per 1000 in 1900 to 9.3 in 1961) and a rise in the birth rate over that of the 1930's (18.7 per 1000 population in 1935; 23.3 in 1961), the composition of the population is changing. The proportion of the population under 19 years of age decreased from 44.2% in 1900 to 34.3% in 1940 and increased to 38.4% in 1960. Persons over 65, on the other hand, have increased from 4.1% of the population in 1900 to 9.3% in 1960, while the average age of the population rose from 22.9 years to 30.3. A white male child born in 1900 would expect, on the average, to reach his forty-eighth birthday. In 1961, his life expectancy was almost 68 years. For females, life expectancy at birth has gained even more—from 51 years in 1900 to 74.5 in 1961 (*66*:13, 87). During the course of the century, the "working population," aged 15 to 64, remained fairly constant at about 62% of the population, although it rose to 68% in 1940.

A second characteristic of the American population is its mobility. Economic opportunity pulls people from the farms toward the cities, and from the center of the nation toward the oceans. Increasing urbanization makes necessary higher levels of literacy. In addition, it points up the problems of interdependence, since every state in the nation must educate large numbers of its youth for life and work in other states. Some of the states suffer a continual drain of manpower through these processes of migration.

The Labor Force. During the same period, 1900–1960, the percentage of females in the labor force grew. In 1900, 18.8% of the labor force was female; in 1940, 25.2%, and in 1960, 35.7%. In the 1960 census, married women living with their husbands accounted for almost two-thirds of the female labor force. School-age children seem to exert relatively little influence on the working status of married women. The median age of working women was 39.7 in 1960.

Other changes in the working proportion of the population will be seen to have educational implications. The proportion of young men in the labor force (aged 20–34) has declined slightly, partly because of increased college attendance. The employment of boys 10 to 15 years of age has almost disappeared as a factor in the labor force.

The same thing has happened in the case of the older men. Although they form a greater proportion of the population, a smaller proportion are in the labor force. In 1900, 64.9% of men over 64 were in the labor force; in 1960, only 47.6%. The labor force has grown in absolute numbers; because of the shift of women into gainful pursuits outside the home, it has also grown in proportion to the total population. This shift, of course, follows on the gradual elimination of human muscle as a major factor in production and on the development of industrial products to replace the food preparation and preservation and clothing manufacture performed by the housewife of 1900.

Along with these shifts in the labor force have come changes in the distribution of workers to the various occupational groups. Table 2 bears out the observation that the socioeconomic status of the nation's labor force is rising rather rapidly. The trend is definitely upward—definitely away from heavy, arduous, unskilled manual labor, and definitely toward more highly skilled manual pursuits and intel-

Table 2. Percentages of Gainful Workers and Persons in the Labor Force, 1950 and 1963 (in thousands) [a]

Group	Gainful Workers 1950, %	Labor Force 1963, %		Net Change, %
Professional, technical, and kindred workers	7.5	12.6	+	5.1
Farmers and farm managers	7.3	3.5	−	3.8
Managers, officials, and proprietors, nonfarm	10.8	10.9	+	0.1
Clerical and kindred workers	12.8	15.3	+	2.5
Sales workers	6.4	6.3	−	0.1
Craftsmen, foremen, and kindred workers	12.9	12.6	−	0.3
Operatives and kindred workers	20.4	18.2	−	2.2
Private household workers	3.2	3.5	+	0.3
Service workers, except private household	7.8	10.0	+	2.2
Farm laborers and foremen	5.0	2.5	−	2.5
Laborers, except farm and mine	5.9	4.7	−	1.2
Total labor force	100.0	100.1		

[a] Derived from U.S. Bureau of Census. *Statistical Abstract of the United States, 1963.* (Eighty-fourth edition.) Washington: Government Printing Office, 1963, p. 231.

lectual pursuits. These developments are caused in part by increase in popular education; in turn, they require the development of new post-high-school programs to prepare workers for the more skilled and more intellectual pursuits.

It was suggested in the first section of the chapter that many social, technological, and economic developments are inextricably interwoven and linked in a serial cause-and-effect relationship. It is difficult and perhaps unnecessary to ascribe specific consequences to specific antecedents. Whatever the causes, it is true that population growth and changes in the labor force have been accompanied by an increase in the standard of living; per capita disposable income rose from $1240 (in 1962 dollars) in 1929 to $2052 in 1962; the work week declined from fifty hours in 1920 to thirty-eight in 1962. The demands for entertainment, for adult education, for all kinds of consumption, grew in like fashion. The ideal of universal education was increasingly realized, as the percentage of 14- to 17-year-olds enrolled in secondary schools rose from 11% in 1900 to 94% in 1963, the graduates from high school grew from 6.4% of the 17-year-olds to 71%, and the number of students enrolled in college rose from 4% of the 18–21 age group in 1900 to 40.4% in 1963 (*143*:14, 56, 75).

C. Educational Implications of Social Changes

Higher Levels of Skill. Havighurst and Neugarten point out that the upper socioeconomic classes have not reproduced themselves in America, and that in order to fill the vacant positions in society and in industry, about one out of eight persons must move up one step in the social scale during his lifetime (*63*:424). This proportion is further increased by the progress of technology and the need for more and more responsible workers.

There may actually be no workers on the production floor of tomorrow's push-button factory. There are practically none today in a power-generating station or an oil refinery. But at the same time incredibly large numbers of men will be required behind the scenes in new, highly skilled jobs as machine builders, machine installers, repair men, controllers of the machinery and of its performance and as "programmers" to prepare and feed information into the machine. In addition, large numbers of highly educated men will be needed in new jobs as designers of machinery, draftsmen, system engineers, mathematicians, and logicians. Finally, large numbers will be needed for new managerial jobs requiring a high ability to think, to analyze, to make decisions, and to assume risks. And this increase both in the numbers of managers and in the demands made on them may well be the largest of all the social impacts of automation. (*36*:26)

Thus technology has created a demand for more people in positions of greater responsibility, requiring more educational preparation. It is the task of higher education, including the community junior college, to satisfy this demand.

Foreign Travel. Another kind of educational need arises from the new ease and rapidity of travel and communication and from America's leadership in international affairs. Aside from military service and the Peace Corps, it has been estimated that within the very near future one-fourth of our college graduates will spend some part of their working life in foreign countries. Obviously, this degree of mobility also requires that more people be trained to understand foreign cultures, to withstand foreign climates, and to speak foreign languages. In addition to the required occupational skills, this aspect of modern employment requires a completely new kind of general education.

Community Life. Baker Brownell sees the trend toward urbanization as evil and accuses education of being a disintegrative force, draining people away from the smaller communities and into the larger cities (13:8). To the extent that the charge is true and to the extent also that the trend is a bad one, an additional educational responsibility is identified. Instead of contributing to the further erosion of small communities, the colleges—and especially the community junior colleges—should develop programs which encourage young people to remain in and to contribute to their home communities.

Personal Development. The human effects of technological progress are not entirely good. It is true that less labor and more mental exertion are required by much modern work. At first glance this may seem to be an unalloyed gain. Yet much of modern work causes strain and mental fatigue and is of such a repetitive nature that it is monotonous and boring. A double educational task arises from this fact—to provide students with the opportunity to cultivate broad interests, including some muscular tastes and skills, and to develop programs of adult education which stimulate the imagination and challenge the abilities of these workers. In this way education can help people to achieve the full benefits of the new technology.

The Custodial Function. A less idealistic, but nevertheless real, consequence of the developments in technology is the emerging custodial function of the college. It is true that the age of first full-time permanent employment for men has risen to about twenty-two years. It is true that the crime rate is higher in the 18–20 age group than in any other. These facts suggest to some thinkers the need for useful educational programs, both to prepare youth for employment and for a higher quality of living and to occupy them wholesomely rather than destructively. Brownell wittily describes the process thus:

> Many educators and others are suggesting that college days be extended still further and that larger numbers of young people be included in them. Thus numbers of persons would be removed from productive life, and the employment problem, supposedly, would be ameliorated. The implications are obvious: create more parasites so that the host will have a fuller employment supporting them. Thus a dog gets busier as the fleas increase (13:6).

Brownell ignores the key word in the discussions of the custodial function, "*useful* educational programs." Several writers point out the high dropout rate from college and the fact that some able high-school graduates do not desire higher education as evidence that greater numbers of young people should not, or could not, achieve more education. In a static society of vintage 1850, their conclusion might be acceptable. In the light of the facts about population and the developments in technology presented earlier in the chapter, this attitude is indefensible. It is not too much to say that unless colleges and community junior colleges can develop *useful* educational programs and meaningful instructional techniques, civilization may decay simply for lack of humans competent to control it.

D. Obstacles to Increased Enrollments

There has been a remarkable increase in the amount of schooling attempted in America over the last half century. No nation in history has ever attempted mass education to such an extent; much less has any nation been confronted with the increased need which lies ahead. College enrollments have grown since 1900 from 4% of the college-age population (18–21) to 43%—although this number conceals the facts that many of the students counted are well over 21 years and that more than half of those who begin a college education drop out before completing it. Responsible analysts suggest that even more youth should be encouraged to attend colleges, although there are formidable obstacles in the way of further enrollment increases.

One of the most important barriers is cost. A 1957 study published by the Office of Education indicates that the total cost of attending a public college rose from $747 in 1940 to $1493 in 1957–1958, and that the cost in private colleges similarly doubled, from $1023 in 1940 to $2047 in 1957–1958.

It was the cost of living at college rather than educational costs that made it so difficult for low-income families to finance attendance of a son or daughter at most colleges. Living costs consumed five-sixths of the average budget of students who attended public colleges and two-thirds of the budget of those who attended private institutions. (74:25–29)

Moreover, evidence of charges in state institutions revealed that "the States are abandoning the philosophy of public tuition-free higher education which has meant so much in building the American way of life, in striving for ever greater and greater equality of opportunity, and in providing the educated manpower for our rapidly expanding economy" (74:64).

Thus there are seen to be three aspects of the developing problem of higher education.

1. It is necessary to plan curriculums which will prepare students for new technological tasks and which will be available to greater numbers of students with wider ranges of abilities than earlier college student bodies exhibited.

2. Guidance plans are needed which will assist students and their parents in learning about the nature of higher education, the kinds of positions which require higher education, and their own abilities and interests. With this information, the student will be more able to choose wisely both an occupational goal and the educational path to it. Such guidance, of course, must be an integral part of the secondary school program, beginning in junior high school and continuing until the student has adopted a realistic set of life goals.

3. In addition, students must be helped to overcome the financial barriers to college attendance by means of adequate scholarship and loan plans and opportunities for part-time work, as well as by the establishment of community junior colleges to provide low-cost local opportunities for higher education.

Havighurst and Rodgers suggest an equation by which it is possible to predict the likelihood that a student will go on to a post-high-school institution of learning. According to this equation, *probability* equals *mental ability* plus *social expectation* plus *individual motivation* plus *financial ability* plus *propinquity* (64:137). This chapter has indicated that recent social and economic developments in America have tended to increase the value of each of the factors in the equation and so to increase the probability that a greater proportion of our population will seek higher education than ever before. While innate *mental ability* is not increased by education, it may either be left fallow and unproductive or intensively cultivated. One effect of the rise in percentage of American youth entering and graduating from high school is that more of them have at least minimum qualifications for higher education. When only 6.4% of 17-year-olds graduated from secondary school, as in 1900, it was obviously impossible for 32% to enter college; when 71% complete high school, as in 1965, they may not be brighter, but their probability of college attendance is greatly enhanced.

So also with *social expectation.* When a pioneer society exalts muscular prowess and scorns intellectuality, youth will aspire to physical strength. At present the pressures of prestige, pay, national need, peer-group values, family ambition, and the demands of employers all point toward longer and longer periods of pre-employment education. These factors have led to the graduation of 70% of all youth from high school. Over the coming years they will increase the probability that many more of those graduates will attempt to gain a college education. *Individual motivation* can also be increased by these factors. Specifically, the chance to qualify for better positions has always been a strong motive for college attendance, even though it is deplored by some college professors as an unworthy aim. If adequate educational guidance is added to this economic pressure, the quality of individual motivation will increase the probability of college attendance.

Recently an experiment was conducted among Massachusetts high school students of equal intelligence, half of whom were given guidance and half of whom were unguided. Twenty-seven per cent of the guided group became honor students, while only 10 per cent of the unguided received such distinction in high school. After graduation, 53 per cent of the guided group and less than 36 per cent of the unguided group were admitted to institutions of higher learning. (23:16)

Financial ability to attend college can be increased by scholarships, but even more by the establishment of local community junior colleges. Not only do these institutions help to solve the problem of costs, but they also increase the factor of *propinquity* in the probability equation. All the recent developments in the American scene point toward a further rapid development of all higher education, and especially of the community junior colleges, over the next several decades.

Victor Cohn sounds a sober warning which makes an excellent epilogue for this chapter:

A changing world is certainly coming, but a happily changing one will require American wisdom, morality, humility, and generosity.

A number of things, let us recognize, could distort our society's rosiest progress. The United States could lose its scientific leadership and, in the world's present struggle for power based on technological might, be quickly engulfed. The world, now half-starving because of overpopulation and underdevelopment, could sink into chaos before science and development catch up. World regimentation could prove necessary to organize and feed a 1999 world of 4 to 5 billion people, or a year 2050 world of 7 to 10 billion. World nuclear war could so set us back that we might never regain the increasingly complex technology that we already need to wrest energy from the earth. Worst of all, in war or peace we could forget the dignity of the individual. (22:168)

Selected References

Boren, Claude B. "Why a Junior College Movement?" *Junior College Journal,* 24:345–357, February, 1954.

Brownell, Baker. *The College and the Community.* New York: Harper and Row, 1952.

Cohn, Victor. *1999—Our Hopeful Future.* Indianapolis: The Bobbs-Merrill Co., 1954.

Dewhurst, J. Frederic and associates. *America's Needs and Resources.* New York: The Twentieth Century Fund, 1955.

Drucker, Peter. *America's Next Twenty Years.* New York: Harper and Row, 1957.

Harris, Seymour E. *Higher Education in the United States: The Economic Problems.* Cambridge, Mass.: Harvard University Press, 1960.

Havighurst, Robert J. and Bernice L. Neugarten. *Society and Education.* Boston: Allyn and Bacon, 1962, Chapter 13.

Hollis, Ernest V. and associates. *Costs of Attending College.* U.S. Office of Education Bulletin, 1957, No. 9. Washington: Government Printing Office.

Mac Lean, Malcolm S. and Dan W. Dodson. "Educational Needs Emerging from the Changing Demands of Society." Chapter II in *The Public Junior College.* Nelson B. Henry (editor). The Fifty-fifth Yearbook of the National Society for the Study of Education. Chicago: The University of Chicago Press, 1956.

3

Philosophical Bases of the Community Junior College

In the brief course of its growth as a part of the American school system, the community junior college has accumulated very few outworn traditions. Its development alongside, rather than within, the main stream of secondary and collegiate education may have saved it from some of the defects of both types. At any rate, the individual colleges and the movement as a whole have maintained a high degree of adaptability and flexibility; they are characterized by a willingness to recognize and to provide for new educational needs. Some critics profess to find in this adaptability a sign of weakness, a lack of well-defined direction. For this reason it is important to state clearly the basic principles on which community junior colleges are founded.

A. General Principles

Junior colleges of all types are integral parts of the entire American educational enterprise. It is true that they have come into existence quite recently, but so have other portions of the school system—our entire sequence of educational opportunities is in many ways an indigenous development. Some parts have been copied from other countries and adapted to American conditions; other parts, such as the liberal arts college, the land-grant college, the public high school, and the junior college, are uniquely American. They share many common philosophical principles.

The first of these principles is that a democratic society cannot exist wholesomely without a well-educated citizenry. As the nation was established, it seemed to the founding fathers that two or three years of schooling would suffice to teach the citizens reading and ciphering and thus guarantee the perpetuation of constitutional government. Even so little schooling for all citizens in those days represented an impossibly idealistic goal. Yet learning, like avarice, grows by what it feeds on. And so each move to extend the learning of the American people has led to a demand for more educational opportunity and to the means to satisfy that demand. Almost three-quarters of our younger people now complete the twelve-year course and graduate from high school. The next and inevitable step is universal availability of public education through the fourteenth year, as a safeguard to the democratic ideal. The worldwide political responsibilities of the United States, its complicated technological economy, its ideals of social as well as political democracy, the serious problems arising from population growth, the lengthening of life expectancy—all of these point to a social need for more and more education for more and more people.

Throughout our history, this social purpose of education has been paralleled by an individual purpose. The nation was founded on the concept of the worth of the individual; it follows that every effort must be expended to help each person make the most of his abilities. To this end, "The American policy should be to give higher education to each individual somewhat in proportion to his natural ability and thus provide higher cultural education for every occupation to the extent that the expenditure can be justified in terms of the needs of the community, both economic and cultural" (137:1). This point of view recognizes that many able young persons are denied education beyond the high school because they cannot afford to leave home to attend college. In addition, it emphasizes the fact that there are varieties of valuable abilities which need development. The local community junior college, with little or no tuition charges and with a broadly diversified instructional program, complements the work of the high school, the technological institute, the college, and the university. It attempts to provide appropriately for the education of all citizens who desire and can profit by further study. In this way, American communities have moved to create opportunity for citizens of all varieties of high ability, of all social and economic classes, to develop their talents for the service of society and for their own self-interest.

It follows that the community junior college must be much more than the lower half of a college or a university. It is true that the junior college duplicates one of their functions: it does provide lower division, preprofessional or prebaccalaureate courses of parallel scope and quality for similar student bodies. Here the similarity and the duplication end. The colleges and universities accept those who complete appropriate lower-division study on their own campuses or in the junior colleges and carry them with ever-increasing specialization toward the bachelor's degree, the master's degree, and the doctorate. The community junior college, meanwhile, welcomes other students who do not need or desire advanced degrees. It studies its community continually to learn the educational needs of its constituency and provides any course of two years or less that will accomplish socially desirable results. "The junior college is designed to serve the *whole* population; the industrial types of students are no more entitled to the exclusive attention of the junior college than is the college-preparatory or the pre-professional group" (*167*:366). This multiple function is difficult for some persons to understand; the difficulty is compounded by the limitations of some existing public junior colleges. Yet many institutions serve several purposes. The university educates poets, artists, engineers, and physicians without questioning its own competence in each field. In exactly the same fashion, the community junior colleges provide both traditional and newly developed courses of study—for both kinds are needed by their students.

Because of the breadth of their purposes, few community junior colleges should aspire to four-year status. A true community junior college, basing its offerings on known needs of its region, will find that it has an exacting and rewarding task; it has an individuality and a prestige which its faculty would not willingly jeopardize for the opportunity to become a four-year college of more limited scope.

B. Admission Policy

The basic admission policy of many community junior colleges is starkly simple: "Any high school graduate, or any person over 18 years of age who seems capable of profiting by the instruction offered, is eligible for admission." Such a welcoming policy is required by the roles of the community junior college in American education. One of its primary functions is to give substance to the ideal of equal opportunity for appropriate education for all citizens. In carrying out this obligation, the community junior college is keenly aware that it is not possible to predict college success with anything approaching perfect accuracy; hence it plans to provide a chance for any applicant who, after competent counseling, insists that he would like to attempt a given course. It does not, of course, guarantee that every student will succeed. Its purpose is to make sure that every person is granted the opportunity to succeed or to fail by his own efforts. The responsibility for choice, for success, for failure, should rest with the student, not with a standardized test nor with the decision of an admissions counselor.

Such a policy recognizes also that the most precious resource of the nation consists of the numerous and varied abilities of its citizens. Many of these abilities, however, remain at present undeveloped because of the dearth of opportunity for their cultivation. In addition, many of the young people who cannot meet the restrictive admission standards of some four-year colleges are precisely the ones who most need further education. Often, of course, they are also the ones who will resist most vigorously any attempt to expose them to it—but not always. In increasing numbers, because of the maturity gained in military service, because of the example of their peers, because of rebuffs in the labor market, able but previously unmotivated young people are joining the ranks of the "late-bloomers." They come to realize their need for more education and go in search of it. Such people are fortunate, at any age, if they find an institution willing to let them prove themselves and succeed or fail by their own efforts.

While such a welcoming admission policy will attract some few applicants who are totally unfit for higher education, they do not constitute a really serious problem. Like the Biblical seed scattered upon the rocks, they have no roots and are quickly blown away. The problem for American society and for individual young people is quite the opposite. It is not necessary to discourage people from seeking post-high-school education. Since so many of the very ablest young people do not now even apply to enter college, the task is rather to convince them of the value of further education. Then every possible artificial barrier must be removed so that they may be enabled to achieve the learning that they have been stimulated to desire. Only by a combination of vigorous recruitment of students and continuing effort to develop appropriate curriculums can the colleges help to ensure an adequate supply of manpower trained in all the skills required by our technology and educated to bear the responsibilities of life in our society (39:29).

The community junior college can render invaluable aid to the senior college in this endeavor. It undertakes the entire burden of occupational training; in addition, it provides the colleges and universities with a steady supply of certified upperclassmen who have proved in the junior college that they can succeed in baccalaureate programs. Under the present organization of higher education, when as many as half of the freshmen withdraw from the colleges and universities before they reach the junior year, this stream of transfer students fills up the vacancies in the upper-division courses. In the future, it is possible that the community junior colleges can do all the education and screening of freshmen and sophomores. Those who now leave the colleges as failures might then, in the community junior college, be helped to find and complete appropriate two-year courses, and the highly talented college and university faculty specialists would be freed to devote their full time to upper-division and graduate instruction, research, and writing.

The welcoming admission policy includes also several categories of adult students. Some are part-time special students; their objectives are mainly cultural rather than vocational. They feel an effective curiosity to know more about their world and so register for classes in day time or in evening sessions, as their leisure permits. Others are moved by advancing technology to bring their occupational skills up to date or perhaps to learn new skills so that they may qualify for advancement in their work. A third group of adults consists of mothers, their children grown to high-school age, who wish to renew their skills in clerical work or to learn a new skill such as teaching or practical nursing. Increasing numbers of such mothers are re-entering the labor force in order to supplement the family income and to prepare for the added expenses to be incurred when the children start to college.

In many communities, the retired senior citizens constitute another important clientele for the adult programs of the community college. Here is a group, freed of the pressures of vocationalism, immediacy, and practicality, who are truly ready for liberal education. They bring to the classroom experience and often wisdom; they seek not credits but learning. Frequently the discussions of one class session provide them a focus of interest and a topic of conversation until the next meeting. Nor can it be argued consistently that, since they do not plan to use their late-won education productively in trade and in industry, they are not entitled to it. Worthy use of leisure time has long been one of the goals of American education, and for many retired persons the organized pursuit of learning for its own sake provides an absorbing interest which keeps them alert.

In the first volume of the *Junior College Journal*, William H. Snyder indicated some of the values of the policy of unrestricted admission when he pointed out that we had provided for the gifted in the university and for the "manually-minded" in vocational schools, but that we had left the average boys and girls to shift for themselves. He suggested that

They need skill in order that they may make a living, but they need sufficient knowledge of the history of the world and the intellectual achievements of mankind to give them the power of orienting themselves to life. They must have both vision and skill, neither of which can be given intensively in the time allotted to junior college but each of which can be given with sufficient scope to enable students to earn a living and to adjust themselves to the progress of the world. (*145:77*)

C. Diversification of Curriculum

Section B suggests that appropriate education should be made available to those who desire it. The suggestion implies that different kinds of post-high-school education may be appropriate for different people.

The community junior colleges believe that nearly all men are educable, that very many men need more education than that represented by their high-school graduation, and that it is economical, for society and for men individually, to attempt to provide effective further education for a sizable proportion of those who need it. The community junior colleges realize that traditional college programs are neither effective nor appropriate for a great many potential students. The community junior colleges themselves have not yet solved entirely the problems of designing courses that will be appropriate, but they have made many excellent starts in that direction. In the process of seeking solutions, they have progressed from the limited programs of the early junior colleges toward the diversified offerings of the community junior college.

An essential step in the elaboration of a community junior college curriculum is the educational and occupational survey. This study helps the faculty decide what courses must be offered. Every community junior college tries to include in its offering those courses required by nearby colleges and universities as preparation for upper-division work in the various fields of study. The survey of these requirements is comparatively simple. The college administrator needs to work with the officers of these institutions to determine accurately what courses must be offered in order to provide fully acceptable preparation for the various baccalaureate specialties. Then he needs to ascertain as accurately as can be done the number of prospective students who hope to transfer to each college and "major" in each field. It may become apparent, for instance, that no student will desire to prepare in the community junior college for transfer to the university school of architecture. In that case, the college is justified in omitting from its offerings those courses that prepare for architecture and for no other major. If only one or two students express a need for such specialized lower-division courses, they may be advised to transfer to the university before their junior year, to attend a nearby community college which offers the courses, to take the courses through correspondence study, or perhaps to enter the university directly from high school. The small community college must not try to offer every possible course in its early years but only those which can be economically and prudently justified. As it grows, it can employ faculty to enable it to expand its offerings year by year. It is for this reason that recent state studies of the need for community junior colleges usually recommend that the contributing area of new colleges be large enough to provide 200 or 300 students at the beginning with fairly rapid growth toward 500 students or more in prospect.

In developing its occupational courses, the community junior college depends upon continuous study of the locality. Several possibilities for occupational courses may be suggested by interested individuals. The decision to offer certain ones and delay others can be justified only by careful and intensive study of the community. The administrator will need to ascertain annual employment and turnover in each field, pay scales, growth trends in the industry, training requirements, equipment needed for a course, extent of student interest, and the attitude of employers and workers toward a college training program in the occupation. In addition, he will find that the series of interviews through which he learns these facts will provide him with excellent opportunities to explain the college to citizens of his community and thus to enlist support for the entire enterprise.

The educational needs of the part-time adult student are likely to be satisfied by a more fluid organization than those of the occupational student; probably also the request for an adult course will develop more rapidly and be satisfied more often with a short-term class. Whereas the periodic survey of the educational and occupational needs of the entire community should concern itself with the needs of adults as well as of youth, this periodic effort must be supplemented by continuous sensitivity to suggestions for new adult offerings. Only by this process of constant scanning of the community can the community junior college administrator accomplish his task of providing for the post-high-school educational needs of his community.

Before establishing any course—transfer, occupational, or adult—the administrator will want to inform himself about practice in other colleges similar to his own. This is not to suggest that he will expand his curriculum only by imitating others; he cannot escape his responsibility for the creative solution of his problems. On the other hand, it would be foolhardy for him to ignore the experience of others when he might so easily profit from their successes and avoid their errors.

D. *The Responsibility for Guidance*

It follows from the two principles of generous admission policy and diversified curriculum that students will find it difficult to choose courses appropriate for their abilities and their opportunities. While college faculty members sometimes feel that they could very successfully assign students to the proper courses, experience shows that this procedure is not usually effective. In a culture which values the concept of individual responsibility and personal freedom, we must protect as far as we can the student's right to choose for himself and to take the consequences of his choice, right or wrong. But such insistence on student choice is a travesty of freedom unless the student has adequate information about the nature and purpose of the several available curriculums, about his own personal and educational qualities, and about employment opportunities for those who complete the various courses. The provision of this information is the task of the guidance program.

Perhaps the most difficult long-range task of the guidance counselor is that of informing the student and the population at large about community junior college offerings. Semiprofessional college education is a comparatively recent development which requires explanation, and many students are misinformed about the success of junior college transfers in four-year college study. If the student is to choose his college course wisely, he needs to have accurate information and interpretation presented to him—and to his parents and to his high-school teachers—time and again. Only by such repeated exposure can young people and their parents overcome the stereotypes that lead them to ascribe value only to the four-year degree, to consider community junior college occupational education as the equivalent of trade-school training, or to esteem the local community junior college as an institution of last resort. Students, parents, and high-school teachers must be helped to learn the growing importance of the community junior college in American higher education by visitation and by exhortation over a period of years. If the preparation for college enrollment consists only of a catalogue and a letter to parents handed to high-school seniors during the last month of high school, they will make many unfortunate mistakes in registration. Too often such mistakes lead to withdrawal from college and abandonment of higher education where complete and careful counseling might have led to a successful college experience.

For effective occupational and educational choice, students also need accurate information about themselves. To some extent, this self-information is a task of the high school. Yet many students enter college either with exaggerated ideas of their intellectual stature or seriously underestimating their powers. Either mistake can lead to waste of effort and the development of a partially educated and unhappy citizen instead of an effective, well-educated one. The counseling service therefore collects information about the students from previous school records, from their own application forms, from tests, from their college instructors, and from observation. It is an important responsibility of the counselor to interpret this information tactfully but conscientiously to the student in order to assist him in reaching decisions about his future education and career choice.

In the course of educational counseling, many problems will come to light that interfere with the student's optimum achievement. Personal or family worries, inadequate study skills, slow reading, substandard health, lack of finances, neurotic or psychotic tendencies, and excessive outside work are only a few of the problems that come to a junior college counselor's attention during an academic year. He will not solve them all; that is not his function. He will try to assist the student to find effective sources of help and to encourage him to make use of them. It happens quite frequently that such information makes the difference for a student between withdrawal from college and successful completion of a course.

E. Standards of Teaching

The community college philosophy places great stress on excellent teaching. As early as 1921, Koos attempted a comparison of the quality of teaching as he observed it in colleges and universities and in junior colleges. He concluded that "A conservative interpretation of the data presented would be that classroom procedure in junior colleges is assuredly on at least as high a plane as is instruction of freshmen and sophomores in college and universities" (90:219). It has been pointed out since that time that the chief function of the junior college instructor is always his teaching, whereas the university faculty member is expected to concentrate on research and publication in addition to teaching. The nature of the student body of the community junior college would seem to emphasize the importance of instructional technique. In comparison with freshmen and sophomores in the colleges and universities, the students tend to be older, they cover a broader range of abilities, and their background of secondary school study is more often undistinguished. It is fair to say that they are able to learn but are relatively unpracticed. Under good instruction they can succeed admirably, whereas pedestrian teaching would be more likely to discourage and defeat them than it would the more highly motivated freshmen and sophomores in the universities.

The alliance of the community junior colleges with the public schools in most states recognizes the importance of pedagogic technique and tends to encourage the development of good teaching. It has been pointed out that the community junior college teacher in some states is required to earn a teaching certificate, whereas university lower-division teaching is often carried on by graduate students who are largely preoccupied with their own degree programs. The small size of classes has been mentioned also as one of the conditions that favors good teaching in the community junior college. It is doubtful, of course, whether small classes can be continued in any institution under the increasing pressure of numbers.

Whatever present facts may be—and meager evidence tends to indicate that community junior college teaching is at least equal to that in other institutions of higher learning—it is true that teaching is the prime function of the community junior college and deserves every encouragement. Careful preparation and selection of teachers and encouragement to employed teachers to be constantly alert to improve their classroom effectiveness are essential elements in discharging this obligation. Experimentation will be needed in the coming years to devise ways to maintain inspired teaching even as class sizes are forced upward by the combination of a scant supply of teachers and a plentiful supply of students. Universities may become great through research, through publication, through opportunities for graduate study, but the community junior college can attain its local renown and the affectionate esteem of its alumni only through the effectiveness of its educational program. Either it teaches excellently, or it fails completely.

F. Standards of Student Achievement

Four principles have been discussed in the earlier sections of this chapter—that the community junior college should welcome all citizens who desire education, that it should develop a variety of educational opportunities to meet their needs, that it should organize guidance services to assist the student to find his way among the wealth of opportunity, and that its very nature requires it to provide excellent teaching. It might be possible to conclude, superficially, that nothing was left for the student but to submit himself docilely to the college services as in a barber chair. Nothing could be further from the truth.

Under the best of auspices, education requires intensive personal effort. The community junior college does attempt to provide the best of auspices but only in order to remove unnecessary and distracting obstacles to learning. The student in any curriculum of the community junior college must be required to achieve. If the college has carried out its part as indicated in the first four principles, the student has no excuse for inadequate achievement. The principle of the admission policy guarantees that the student will be admitted to studies in which he has an interest and for which he has completed stated prerequisite study. It does not promise to keep him in college; that further privilege can be earned only by acceptable accomplishment of the objectives of his study.

Perhaps it is a misunderstanding of this point that causes some four-year college people to express concern about community junior college standards. Since the community junior college admits and graduates people who could not possibly succeed—who would not want to succeed—in university courses in arts, sciences, history, mathematics, or foreign languages, these observers conclude that the community junior college gives credit for substandard academic performance. This conclusion derives from a limited definition of higher education.

Standards of student accomplishment are defined by the degree of attainment by the student of the objectives of the course in which he is enrolled. If the junior college transfer student is enrolled in a second-year course in German, his knowledge at completion of the course should be fully equal to that of the university student with the same grade. The accomplishment of transfer students in their upper-division college work in universities and colleges all over the country demonstrates that their preparation for further study is in fact equal to that of the "native" college students of similar ability (88:180–181). The community junior college courses, in these cases, are equivalent in content, method, and accomplishment to those in the university.

On the other hand, many community college students are enrolled and achieve a high standard of performance in courses that do not parallel any university course. The fact that an automotive mechanics student might fail organic chemistry does not indicate low standards in the course in mechanics. If he understands thoroughly the operation and repair of the many mechanisms of the modern automobile, he is an "A" student in that subject; on the other hand, the "A" student in chemistry might be quite unwilling to do excellent work in mechanics. The student in any subject who does not achieve the objectives of that subject should receive a substandard rating—"F" or "E" or "D" in the usual currencies. If possible, the failing student should be assisted to discover a course in which his talents and interests qualify him to succeed. If his talents and interests are so limited that this is impossible or if the offerings of the educational institution do not include such a course, the student might as well leave, and this is equally true under these conditions, whether he is enrolled in a university or in a community junior college. The chief difference is that the more diversified (lower-division) program of the community junior college is somewhat more likely to include an alternative curriculum which will be appropriate for many students.

In 1955, the faculty of Orange Coast College adopted definitions of course grades which were intended to be applicable in every subject, from archaeology to physical education, physics, and zoology. The several definitions seem to provide a realistic statement of standards, in accordance with the principles explained above:

The "A" student has been consistently superior in all phases of the course. He has shown initiative, efficiency, self direction, and growth.

The "B" student ably satisfies all the requirements and demonstrates substantial mastery of the course materials.

The "C" student completes acceptably most of the assignments, including attendance and participation. The lack of distinction in his work may result from differing combinations of factors such as ability, motivation, health, and work load.

The "D" student has profited meagerly from the course due to a variety of reasons and should not proceed to advanced work.

The "F" student has failed to accomplish the minimum requirement of the course. (*123*:47)

Such then are the principles underlying the community junior college: to make higher education available to qualified students of all ages, all social classes, all varieties of ability; to develop a sufficient variety of curriculums to meet the educational needs, at this level, of the community and of the individual students; to provide counseling and guidance services to help students choose appropriately from the available offerings; to devote concerted attention to effective teaching; and then to require the highest standards of achievement of its students. To the extent that the community junior college makes these principles realities, it will justify its growing importance in the structure of American education.

Selected References

Anderson, Hurst R. "Are Junior Colleges on the Wrong Path?" *Junior College Journal,* 15:249–252, February, 1945.

Fields, Ralph R. *The Community College Movement.* New York: McGraw-Hill Book Co., 1962.

Greenleaf, Walter J. *Junior Colleges.* U.S. Office of Education Bulletin, 1936, No. 3. Washington: Government Printing Office, 1936.

Lounsbury, John L. "Junior Colleges Are *Not* on the Wrong Path," *Junior College Journal,* 15:368–371, April, 1945.

Seashore, Carl E. *The Junior College Movement.* New York: Holt, Rinehart and Winston, 1940.

Singer, C. Gregg. "Junior Colleges Are on the Wrong Path," *Junior College Journal,* 15:67–70, October, 1944.

Snyder, William H. "The Real Function of the Junior College," *Junior College Journal,* 1:74–80, November, 1930.

Ward, Phebe. *Terminal Education in the Junior College.* New York: Harper and Row, 1947.

Weersing, Frederick J. "Misconceptions Regarding the Junior College," *Junior College Journal,* 1:363–369, March, 1931.

Zook, George F. "The Past Twenty Years—The Next Twenty Years," *Junior College Journal,* 10:616–623, May, 1940.

4

Historical Development of the
Community Junior College

The emergence of the junior college as an established element of the American system of education over the past sixty years provides an excellent case study in the sociology of institutions. Only a handful of two-year colleges existed anywhere in the world in 1900. Yet by 1964 the United States harbored 700 of them, with over 1,000,000 students. This rapid growth can be attributed to three main factors, although a good many subsidiary explanations can be found.

First, of course, there was the idea. The penetrating educational statesmanship of a succession of university presidents and deans stimulated discussion and gave the first impetus to the establishment of junior colleges in several areas of the nation. These ideas, in turn, could not have become real, except for the constant increase in economic wealth in the United States. The rising productivity which enabled the country to support more students in college required at the same time a constantly increasing supply of workers with the education to control and to improve the productive apparatus. Both the idea and the economic possibility, however, might have been fruitless in higher education, had it not been for that social phenomenon known as "The American Dream"—the belief inbred in every stratum of society that education is a social and individual good and that society is obligated to provide as much of it as any individual desires and can profit from. The junior college is one of the practical results of the interaction of these forces.

The present-day community junior college has evolved in three

45

major stages. The first and longest lasted from 1850 to 1920. During that period the idea and the acceptable practice of the *junior college,* a separate institution offering the first two years of baccalaureate curriculums, were achieved. Next, the concepts of terminal and semi-professional education in the junior college, which had been described earlier, gained widespread currency with the foundation of the American Association of Junior Colleges in 1920. By the end of World War II in 1945, this idea was an established part of the junior college concept. The changes in post-high-school education brought by the war emphasized a third element of responsibility, service to the adults of the community, and so the period after 1945 has seen the development of the operative definition of the *community junior college.* Finally, the rapid growth in college enrollments during the 1960's seems to emphasize once more the transfer function of the junior college, and to bring increasing recognition of its importance as a part of the system of higher education.

A. The Evolution of the Junior College, 1850–1920

In the realm of policy, several names are associated with the early development of the idea that the first two years of the American liberal arts college were truly not collegiate at all but belonged more appropriately to the secondary schools. These leaders felt that if the college and the university could be freed from the necessity to provide these capstone years of secondary education, they might then become, in the words of Henry A. Tappan, "purely universities without any admixture of collegial tuition" (*150*:44).

At his inauguration in 1869 as President of the University of Minnesota, William Watts Folwell echoed the idea of Michigan's President Tappan:

How immense the gain . . . if a youth could remain at the high school or academy, residing in his home, until he had reached a point, say, somewhere near the end of the sophomore year, there to go over all of those studies which as a boy he ought to study under tutors and governors! Then let the boy, grown up to be a man, emigrate to the university, there to enter upon the work of a man. . . . [In a footnote to his published address, President Folwell remarked, "That [the proposal] was not openly and vigourously denounced, was due to the fact that it was not understood, or if understood, was not taken seriously."] (*51*:37–38)

Neither Tappan nor Folwell succeeded either in eliminating the "secondary" years of their own universities, or in encouraging the widespread development of extended programs in the high schools. It remained for President William Rainey Harper, in 1892, to separate the first and last two years of the new University of Chicago into the "Academic College" and the "University College." Four years later these titles were changed to "junior college" and "senior college"— perhaps the first use of the terms. In addition, President Harper is credited with strongly influencing the foundation of several of the public junior colleges (notably Lewis Institute in Chicago in 1896 and Bradley Polytechnic Institute in Peoria in 1897) and obtaining the addition of two years to the high school program in Joliet, Illinois in 1901. The Joliet Junior College is thus the oldest extant public junior college.

President Harper, in common with the other statesmen of this early period, conceived of the junior college primarily as a continuation of the high school. He proposed a plan for radical reorganization of the entire public system of education, which was studied at a conference in 1903 and favorably reported by three committees of faculty members from academies and high schools affiliating with the University of Chicago. President Harper's plan involved.

1. The connecting of the work of the eighth grade of the elementary school with that of the secondary schools. (The junior high school.)

2. The extension of the work of the secondary schools to include the first two years of college work.

3. The reduction of the work of these seven years thus grouped together to six years.

4. Making it possible for the best class of students to do this work in five years (15:22).

It is a testimony to the remarkable persuasive powers of President Harper that a committee of elementary school men, another of high-school and academy principals, and a third representing Midwestern universities all endorsed this revolutionary plan. The university committee suggested five arguments against the plan:

1. The high schools were unable to do the work because of the inadequacy of their equipment, the incompetency of their instructors, and the fact that they were already too crowded with their four years of work.

2. Youth, to grow and learn, need the surroundings of colleges and the example of the more mature juniors and seniors.

3. Larger cities, which have universities, would certainly not adopt the plan.

4. The plan would do a great deal of damage to the American college.

5. It would inflict irreparable injury to the pattern of American life.

Nevertheless, the University Committee, with two dissenting votes, endorsed the plan, because it recognized that the first two collegiate years were essentially secondary; the plan would hold "scores, even hundreds," of young men and women for two more years of education; much technical and other special preparation for life work (i.e., pre-professional courses) would be offered; the plan would save expense for the student; and anyway, the plan would be adopted only in those localities where it was needed (15:24–25).

On the West Coast, two eminent spokesmen took up the junior college cause. At Stanford University, President David Starr Jordan reviewed the Chicago developments and ventured a prophecy and a recommendation:

It is safe to prophesy that before many years the American university will abandon its junior college, relegating its work to the college on the one hand and to the graduate courses of the secondary school on the other.

I ask your Board to consider the project of the immediate separation of the junior college from the university or the university college, and to consider the possibility of requiring the work of the junior college as a requisite for admission to the university on and after the year 1913, or as soon as a number of the best equipped high schools of the state are prepared to undertake this work. (146:394)

Spindt reports, however, that a faculty committee disagreed with their president and uttered a complaint that has since been repeated over and over without regard to the evidence. The faculty committee decided that ". . . the successful establishment of six year high schools is a problem of the future. Upperclassmen coming from six year high schools and small colleges with limited equipment and endowment, would not be as well trained or as far advanced as those who begin their college work here" (146:395).

During the second decade of the century, Dean Alexis F. Lange of the University of California focused attention on the need for post-graduate work in the public high schools; it was a theme on which he spoke and wrote at every opportunity. Each of his articles contains at least one quotable passage. Spindt has captured one of the most outspoken expressions of Dean Lange's viewpoint:

The frank recognition of the fact—it is a fact—that the difference between the first two years of college and the high school is one of degree only and has never been anything else, implies the remedy. The first step would be for the University to reduce its "swollen fortune" in freshmen and sophomores by actively promoting their distribution among federated colleges, normal schools, and the six-year high schools that are to be and will be. The second would be to give these grades, in and without the University, teachers specially prepared and experienced in secondary education, and to make the position of such teachers a worthy goal, inclusive of *salary*, of legitimate and worthy ambition and initiative. . . . As for the University a number of its most vexing problems would pass out of existence. (*146*:393)

It is interesting to speculate about the first successful and persistent junior college. According to Bogue, "Research has shown that Lasell Junior College, Auburndale, Massachusetts, offered two years of standard collegiate instruction, as early as 1852" (*10*:2). The University of Georgia in 1859 resolved to abolish its first two years because it was felt that the students coming to Franklin College (the liberal arts division of the University) were entirely too young, and "the foundation of failure, if not of ruin, is laid in the Freshmen and Sophomore years of College life." The plan was begun, but its completion was interrupted by the Civil War, which finally caused the University to suspend operation. After the University reopened in 1866, the plan seems to have been forgotten (*31*:26–63).

A little later, according to Hillway,

The high school at Greeley, Colorado, added an extra year of work (the thirteenth grade) in the 1880's. A few years later, in the 1890's, the University of Michigan admitted into the sophomore class a number of students who had completed five years of study in the Michigan high schools. Nearly all such experiments were eventually abandoned. . . . A group of three Baptist colleges in Texas actually reduced their programs to two years in 1897. (*72*:36)

There seems to be full agreement that the first public junior college established in connection with a high school was that at Goshen, Indiana, later discontinued, and that the oldest public junior college still in existence is Joliet Junior College, Illinois (*40*:13).

The history of the degree granted by the junior colleges is worthy of mention. In 1900, The University of Chicago began to award the Associate in Arts degree to all students who successfully completed the junior college program of studies. In his recommendation to the Stanford University trustees on abolition of the University lower division, President Jordan suggested "that on and after August 1, 1910, in addition to the present entrance requirements, two years, or sixty units, of collegiate work, the equivalent of the requirements for the degree or title of 'Associate in Arts' as granted in the University of Chicago, shall be required for entrance to the University" (146:395).

Thereafter, however, some confusion entered the picture. In its "statement of standards" of 1915, the Association of Colleges and Secondary Schools of the Southern States prohibited the granting of degrees by accredited junior colleges. In 1930, William H. Snyder proposed that the newly established Los Angeles City College grant the degree of Associate in Arts, and the California Junior College Federation in that year passed a resolution asking that the degree be authorized and be conferred upon all the graduates, irrespective of whether they had completed the certificate course or the semi-professional course (145:78). In 1934, however, Campbell reported forty-nine different titles, each granted by at least one junior college. Twenty-six different kinds were found in public junior colleges and forty-one in private junior colleges (18:362–365). In 1956, Colvert reported that "recognition of the associate's degree has gained wide favor in educational circles. It is now authorized in all states where there are junior colleges, with the exception of Virginia, and granted by junior colleges and many senior colleges. . . . The granting of the associate's degree places the official stamp of approval on junior college education as definite collegiate accomplishment" (26:11).

In his pioneering dissertation, published conveniently just at the end of the revolutionary period, McDowell summarized the conditions tending to further the development of the junior college idea. He suggested four main influences. First, the university was moved to encourage the development of junior colleges because of its own rapid growth and unhealthy tendency to large classes, because it felt a need to divide secondary work from that of the university, and because a junior college allows for closer contact with and control of youthful students. Second, the normal schools of that day wished to offer collegiate work in addition to purely pedagogical subjects, so many of them became junior colleges. Third, the extension of the high school seemed to be "an additional step in the evolution of our system of public education." Finally, according to McDowell, there was the problem of the small college, too weak to offer a strong four-year program and practically forced by the developing pattern of accreditation to concentrate its efforts on a more attainable objective (107:22).

The junior college, proposed and initiated both as an extension of secondary education and as an amputation from the university or four-year college, grew and prospered until in 1921 there were 207 such colleges, 70 public and 137 private. In that year, also, the enrollment in public colleges surpassed for the first time that in the private institutions. There were 16,000 students enrolled in all, of whom 52% (8349) were in public and 48% (7682) were in private colleges. In the minds of their administrators, however, these 207 institutions were not secondary schools; they felt that they were truly collegiate, as evidenced by the first definition of the junior college adopted by the newly formed American Association of Junior Colleges in 1922: "The junior college is an institution offering two years of instruction of strictly collegiate grade" (40:3).

B. The Expansion of Occupational Programs, 1920–1945

By 1925, The American Association of Junior Colleges felt impelled to expand its definition:

The junior college is an institution offering two years of instruction of strictly collegiate grade. This curriculum may include those courses usually offered in the first two years of the four-year college, in which case these courses must be identical, in scope and thoroughness, with corresponding courses of the standard four-year college. The junior college may, and is likely to, develop a different type of curriculum suited to the larger and ever-changing civic, social, religious, and vocational needs of the entire community in which the college is located. It is understood that in this case also the work offered shall be on a level appropriate for high school graduates. (40:3)

This concept of occupational education had been enunciated much earlier, and some efforts had been made to include it in the curriculums of the junior colleges. In one of his most quoted utterances, Lange concisely expresses the basic essentials of junior college semiprofessional training. After pointing out that both training for specialized efficiency and general education must be provided, he states,

The junior college cannot make preparation for the University its excuse for being. Its courses of instruction and training are to be culminal rather than basal. . . . The junior college will function adequately only if its first concern is with those who will go no farther, if it meets local needs efficiently, if it enables thousands and tens of thousands to round out their general education, if it turns an increasing number into vocations for which training has not hitherto been afforded by our school system." With characteristic candor, he admits that "It is, of course, an inevitable phase of growth that as yet not one of the junior colleges I know about has fully found itself. (96:471–472)

Dr. Merton E. Hill, who was principal of Chaffey Junior College at the time of which he writes, claims for that institution the probable distinction of offering the first terminal courses in California public junior colleges. In September, 1916, Chaffey was established as a junior college in connection with the high school and offered terminal vocational courses in art, manual training, home economics, commerce, music, library training, general agriculture, farm mechanics, and soils (71:313).

In the same article, Hill cites the growth of terminal courses in junior colleges from 100 in 1921 to 400 in 1925, to 1600 by 1930, and to "over 4000" by 1941. A few years later Colvert presented a similar analysis, quoting several studies. The proportion of terminal courses in relation to all junior college offerings was as follows (27:246):

1917: 17.5%–(McDowell)
1921: 28.0%–(Koos)
1930: 33.0%–(Eells)
1947: 32.0%–(Colvert)

One of the strong advocates of semiprofessional education during this period was President Snyder of Los Angeles Junior (now City) College, founded in 1929 and almost immediately the largest of all the junior colleges. During its first year, Los Angeles Junior College established fourteen terminal semiprofessional curriculums (145:74–80). Although convinced of the need for occupational courses, Snyder saw the total function of the junior college quite clearly. In another article he objected to the "secondary school" characterization of the junior college, saying, "Why not keep it in the American college classification and give to it the standings and traditions which have for centuries been developed in our own distinctly American educational unit, the college?" Furthermore, he pointed out that at least 50% of junior college graduates do not continue their studies and that semiprofessional courses were needed just as much as transfer courses. Yet, "If the junior college is to be really collegiate, it cannot allow itself to become merely a vocational institution. It must have well-established courses which embrace both cultural and utilitarian subjects" (144:236–237).

These trends of thought, leading to the establishment of occupational courses in junior colleges over the nation, firmly established the concept of terminal education. In 1940, the American Association of Junior Colleges announced the receipt of a grant of $25,000 from the General Education Board of New York City to finance a series of exploratory studies in the general field of terminal education in the junior college. As an outgrowth of these exploratory studies, the General Education Board in December 1940 granted an additional sum of $45,500 to support a cooperative study of terminal education in the junior colleges. Four volumes were published under this grant, discussing in some detail the concept of semiprofessional terminal education as a function of the junior college (*42, 43, 45, 160*).

Several influences seem to have contributed to the rapid expansion of occupational education in the junior colleges. The leadership of state agencies for vocational education, set up under the Smith-Hughes Act and related federal legislation, was especially effective in the states that considered the public junior colleges to be part of secondary education. The widespread unemployment of the depression years also encouraged the spread of occupational education; it was realized that specific training beyond the high-school level would give an applicant a competitive advantage in the job market. During the 1950's increasing automation required workers with higher levels of technical skills, and the junior colleges were quick to organize classes to train them.

The Vocational Education Act of 1963 recognized the junior colleges by removing the restriction to courses of "less than college grade" that had appeared in earlier federal vocational legislation, and by concentrating on the training needs of people rather than on preparation for specific occupations. Finally, the emphasis of many of the public junior colleges on a close working relationship with their communities encouraged groups of employers or of workers to request the establishment of additional occupational courses. Through these developments the junior colleges branched into activities which were neither secondary education nor higher education; they began to achieve a separate identity and a unique set of purposes.

C. The Community College Concept, 1945–

Although the addition of college-level occupational curriculums to the lower-division offerings brought an entirely new complexion to the junior college, the institution still had not achieved its full stature as a community college. This development required the further addition of adult education and community services. Once again, this expanded scope of operation had been dimly foreseen by some of the early advocates of the junior college and steps toward its realization had been taken in several cities prior to 1940. The drop in enrollment in day classes after the outbreak of World War II and the nationwide emphasis on training for defense work stimulated the colleges to engage in community activities as a temporary measure. The offerings proved so valuable to so many segments of the population, however, that the colleges continued and developed them after the war, and thus with these offerings completed the development of the community junior college.

In 1930, in the first issue of the *Junior College Journal,* Nicholas Ricciardi gave a definition of the functions of the community junior college which has served as model for several later definitions:

A fully organized junior college aims to meet the needs of a community in which it is located, including preparation for institutions of higher learning, liberal arts education for those who are not going beyond graduation from the junior college, vocational training for particular occupations usually designated as semi-professional vocations, and short courses for adults with special interests. (*131:24*)

In 1936 Byron S. Hollinshead essayed a restatement of the same principles:

That the junior college should be a community college, meeting community needs; that it should serve to promote a greater social and civic intelligence in the community; that it should provide opportunities for increased adult education; that it should provide educational, recreational, and vocational opportunities for young people; that the cultural facilities of the institution should be placed at the disposal of the community; and that the work of the community college should be closely integrated with the work of the high school and the work of other community institutions. (*73:111*)

By 1939, the community junior college concept was sufficiently clarified that an article appeared in the *Journal* entitled "The Junior College as a Community Institution" (*65*). In January, 1940, the first "fundamental principle" of the Commission on Terminal Education was "The Junior College is essentially a community institution" (*41: 245*). When the Report of the President's Commission on Higher Education, *Higher Education in American Democracy,* described the community college fully and favorably, using that term, the full task of these institutions was recognized by all who were concerned with them (*70:*Vol. I, Ch. 4; Vol. III, Ch. 2).

In the words of Hillway,

. . . three major currents have created the modern two-year junior and community colleges: (1) the nineteenth-century efforts to reform American university education; (2) the extraordinary growth in the United States of the various types of adult and vocational education as our economy became increasingly industrialized; and (3) the continuing democratic tendency toward the extension and equalization of educational opportunity for all Americans. (*72:33*)

Thus the concept of the community junior college has been fully developed, and the need for it has been established in all parts of the nation. Within the near future many of the present public junior colleges with partial programs will become true community junior colleges which will provide the full scope of service implied in that title and the institution will spread to all the regions of the land, to serve all the people of the land.

The vitality of the junior college concept may be demonstrated by enrollment data from the *1966 Junior College Directory* (*118:57*). For October, 1965, the *Directory* reports total enrollment of 1,152,086 in 503 public junior colleges; 52% are part-time, many attending classes only in the evening. In the 268 independent junior colleges, enrollments totaled 140,667; of these, only 22% were part-time students. The community junior college is truly making post-high-school education widely available to the people of its community.

On June 30 and July 1, 1920, thirty-four junior college representatives met in St. Louis at the call of United States Commissioner of Education, P. P. Claxton. At this meeting, it was decided to organize a national association, and in Chicago, on February 16–17, 1921, a constitution and a name, "The American Association of Junior Colleges," were adopted. The constitution defined the objectives of the Association thus: "To define the junior college by creating standards and curricula, thus determining its position structurally in relation to other parts of the school system; and to study the junior college in all of its types (endowed, municipal, and state) in order to make a genuine contribution to the work of education" (*8:512*).

Since that time, the Association has served as a spokesman for the interests of junior colleges of all types and has contributed beyond measure to their establishment as an important segment of American higher education. Among its outstanding achievements have been the continuous publication since 1930 of the *Junior College Journal*, the preparation annually of the *Junior College Directory*, and the compilation of the six editions of *American Junior Colleges*, published by the American Council on Education. Association membership numbers 558 colleges, out of the total reported of 694. There are 349 publicly supported member colleges and 209 independent colleges. The Association conducts a yearly convention, stimulates research, provides consultant services, carries on a broad public information program, engages in studies, and publishes bulletins on specific aspects of junior college education. It lists eight major objectives of its services:

1. To make additional, substantial efforts to raise the level of administrative competence in junior college education.

2. To assist in establishment of strong junior college teacher

preparation programs, in-service workshops and institutes, to stimulate experimentation and evaluation in teaching organization and practices, and to find ways of inviting promising people to the field of junior college teaching.

3. To stimulate and assist junior colleges to develop comprehensive curricula where appropriate, with special attention to technical education and community services.

4. To clarify and promote public understanding of the functions of junior colleges.

5. To assist the states in developing sound and orderly systems of junior colleges to serve the major part of the population in each state, and to provide at the national and state levels adequate information regarding the appropriate services of junior colleges so that legislation involving these institutions will be realistic and constructive.

6. To promote more effective relationships between junior colleges and high schools on one hand and senior colleges and universities on the other.

7. To assist in strengthening state and regional organizations of junior colleges and to encourage a closer relationship between their activities and those at the national level.

8. To adopt measures to promote greatly improved student personnel services with particular regard to counseling and guidance.

Selected References

American Junior Colleges. 1940 edition, Walter Crosby Eells (editor). 1948, 1952, 1956 editions, Jesse P. Bogue, editor. 1960 and 1963 editions, Edmund J. Gleazer, Jr. (editor). Washington: American Council on Education.

Bogue, Jesse P. *The Community College.* New York: McGraw-Hill Book Co., 1950.

———. *The Development of Junior Colleges* (pamphlet). Washington: American Association of Junior Colleges, 1957.

Brick, Michael. *Forum and Focus for the Junior College Movement.* New York: Bureau of Publications, Teachers College, Columbia University, 1964.

California State Department of Education, *The Junior College in California.* California State Department of Education Bulletin No. G-3. Sacramento, 1928.

Eells, Walter Crosby. *The Junior College.* Boston: Houghton Mifflin Co., 1931.

Greenleaf, Walter J. *Junior Colleges.* U.S. Office of Education Bulletin, 1936, No. 3. Washington: Government Printing Office, 1936.

Higher Education for American Democracy. The Report of the President's Commission on Higher Education. New York: Harper and Row, 1948.

Hillway, Tyrus. *The American Two-Year College.* New York: Harper and Row, 1958.

Junior College Journal, passim. The early volumes especially (vols. 1 to 10) contain notes on "Ancient History" as a continuing department.

Koos, Leonard V. *The Junior College.* Minneapolis: University of Minnesota Press, 1924.

Lindsay, Frank B. "California Junior Colleges, Past and Present," *California Journal of Secondary Education,* 22:137–142, March, 1947.

McDowell, F. M. *The Junior College.* U.S. Bureau of Education Bulletin, 1919, No. 35. Washington: Government Printing Office, 1919.

Proctor, William Martin (editor). *The Junior College: Its Organization and Administration.* Stanford, Calif.: Stanford University Press, 1927.

Rogers, James F. "A Philosophy for the Junior College with Implications for Curriculum," *Junior College Journal,* 30:125–131, November, 1959.

Sack, Saul. "The First Junior College," *Junior College Journal,* 30:13–15, September, 1959.

Seashore, Carl E. *The Junior College Movement.* New York: Holt, Rinehart and Winston, 1940.

5

Accepted Purposes of
Community Junior Colleges

In the early days of the development of junior colleges, many purposes were suggested for them: some were trivial, some grandiose, some totally unachievable. As numbers of institutions and student enrollments have grown, purposes have become clearer, so that it is now possible to state confidently and to define concretely the major educational responsibilities of the ideal community junior college.

In his 1930 survey of the literature on the junior college, Campbell examined 343 articles about the institution, finding 1411 mentions of purposes—an average of 4 per article. Among the purposes mentioned less frequently were "to exert a good influence on the high school," "to keep local money at home," "fewer social temptations for the student," and "moral and religious training." Campbell grouped the 30 purposes he found in the literature into four major categories—preparatory (for further collegiate study), terminal and occupational, democratization of higher education, and popularizing higher education (17:30).

At about the same time Thomas included an additional function, guidance, while uniting the "democratizing" and "popularizing" functions under one heading. Thomas's categories, then, were (1) the preparatory function, (2) the popularizing function, (3) the terminal function, and (4) the guidance function (152:11–25).

In different terms, Ricciardi agreed with Thomas and Campbell when he concluded, in the first issue of the *Junior College Journal*, that

. . . a fully organized junior college aims to meet the needs of a community in which it is located, including preparation for institutions of higher learn-

58

ing, liberal arts education for those who are not going beyond graduation from the junior college, vocational training for particular occupations usually designated as semi-professional vocations, and short courses for adults with special interests. (*131*:24)

Bogue reports a study by Stanley F. Salwak of the reasons for the establishment of 77 colleges between 1940 and 1953 in 23 states (*11*:247–250). Among the reasons ascribed by the administrators of the colleges, as reported by Bogue, the following were mentioned most frequently:

Youth financially unable to attend existing institutions	47
Opportunities needed for short courses and for two-year terminal curriculums	20
To extend the secondary school upward	23
Increasing need for skilled workers in the community	19
Existing institutions too far away	16
People willing to support such an institution through taxation	16
To extend democracy by lengthening equal educational opportunity	13
To make general education available to all the people	13
Better individual attention resulting in better educational opportunity	11
To fill the gap between end of school and employment	15

After consideration of educational needs arising from the changing demands of society and from individual needs and purposes, the Committee on the Public Junior College of the National Society for the Study of Education concluded that the public junior college has four major purposes: (*a*) preparation for advanced study, (*b*) vocational education, (*c*) general education, and (*d*) community service." In addition, the Committee recognized the necessity for guidance and counseling as a specialized service of the public junior college (*69*:69).

In the light of these and other analyses of the role of the community junior college, as well as of the historical development of the institution, its generally accepted purposes may be discerned to include

1. Occupational education of post-high-school level,
2. General education for all categories of its students,
3. Transfer or preprofessional education,
4. Part-time education,
5. Community service,
6. The counseling and guidance of students.

Each of these fundamental purposes is defined briefly in the remainder of this chapter.

A. Occupational Education

At the community junior college level, occupational education includes courses of two years' duration or less, combining the development of skills required for entry into a locally important occupation with related knowledge and theory calculated to help the student progress on the job. Such courses of study include also the general education calculated to prepare all students to assume responsible roles as citizens, as family members, and as individuals. In many institutions, occupational courses are planned so far as possible with an eye to the rapid changes that characterize the labor market. Emphasis is placed on preparing the student for families of related occupations rather than for a single job; fundamental abilities are developed so as to contribute to the student's adaptability as employment opportunities change.

It is probable that community junior colleges will develop more and more of these programs of two years or less, designed to prepare their students for immediate employment on completion of the program. Several reasons may be adduced for the rapid development of occupational education. The high rate of withdrawal of students from college is one cause for concern. Students of the problem of dropout realize that most of the students who enter junior colleges will not go on to further education, although they classify themselves in most cases as "transfer" students. If those students who terminate their full-time formal enrollment with two years or less of college are to be properly accommodated, the colleges must develop courses of two years' duration which are complete and valuable. Otherwise the withdrawing student leaves with an uncompleted portion of an education and a feeling of defeat rather than of having completed a self-assigned task. Recent employment trends serve to emphasize the need for community junior college occupational education. Not only is the age of initial employment rising, but the nature of employment, as set forth in Chapter 2, requires more and more formal education on the part of the worker.

A further reason for the development of occupational courses arises from the "democratization" or "popularizing" of higher education. As greater man-hour productivity and higher standards of living free a continually increasing proportion of our able young people from the labor market, more of them will seek higher education. For some of these increased numbers, education of practical and immediate value is required. Their need will be met by community junior college occupational courses; if such courses are not available, their need will not be met.

Until recently, there has been some resistance to the establishment of such occupational education, so that even though 70–75% of entering students are in fact terminal students, only about one-third of the course offerings in junior colleges are terminal—and a fraction of these are occupational (*69:80*, 94; *84:96–97*). One reason for this disproportion between educational need and educational opportunity is the feeling that choice of a terminal or occupational program of courses "closes the door" of further study to a student who later decides to work toward a bachelor's degree. This objection is only partly valid. Students who change from occupational to baccalaureate courses are a small minority of all entering students. Occupational courses should certainly be planned to accommodate primarily those students who will graduate and enter the occupation for which they trained. For the student in an occupational program who does decide to attempt a baccalaureate program it should be possible to demonstrate (1) that all his study is of value to him, even though he has to spend more than the conventional four years in earning his bachelor's degree, and (2) that some part of his junior college courses, as they meet the required or elective provisions of his four-year college, will be evaluated appropriately there. Certainly any student in any college who changes his objective in midcourse (as from medicine to engineering, architecture to law, or petroleum technology to geology) will find that he has neglected certain prerequisites of his new course which must be completed before he can go on. The outlook for the future is even more hopeful than the present practice here described. Bethel, after a study of the evidence about the transferability of occupational courses, concludes, "It may be said that there is a growing interest on the part of senior college faculty in seeking means for evaluating junior college graduates for transfer in terms of their aptitudes or their *facility for working with* the activities of the senior college regardless of the particular pattern of subjects they may have taken in the junior college" (*8:8*).

B. General Education

Almost all writers who discuss the functions of the community junior college include the concept of general education as one of those functions, although some of the earlier writers did not use that term. Whereas occupational education, in its many manifestations, is concerned with the differences among students, general education is concerned with their fundamental likenesses. General education may be defined as a program of education specifically designed to afford young people more effective preparation for the responsibilities that they share in common as citizens in a free society and for wholesome and creative participation in a wide range of life activities. It attempts to clarify the focal problems of our times and to develop the intellectual skills and moral habits to cope with them.

The purposes of general education are not new purposes. What is new is the reaction against the overspecialization which characterized many college programs during the first half of the twentieth century. General education does not seek to replace specialization; most of the recent technical advances in our culture have come about because of the high quality of our specialized education. On the other hand, specialization is not a complete education for modern living. General education complements specialization through a recognition that although men differ in their abilities, interests, and accomplishments, they share many characteristics that demand common elements of education.

A partial answer to these newly realized needs has involved attempts to develop new organizations of instruction, emphasizing the utility of the subject matter to the student rather than the totality of the disciplinary field. At first such reorganized courses in any field were offered principally to college students who intended to specialize in some other subject field. More recently, the upsurge of adult and community college enrollments has led to a realization that in fact all persons share certain responsibilities in common and that all persons can profit from opportunities for general education. For this reason the community junior colleges have become aware of their responsibility to include general offerings in their planning for all classes of their students. Adult students and occupational students face the focal problems of our times just as poignantly as those who plan to earn bachelor's, master's, or doctor's degrees.

A good many difficulties have retarded the efforts of the junior colleges in developing complete and coherent patterns of general education for all their students. The transient nature of the student bodies, with their high rate of withdrawal, the externally imposed course requirements which transfer students must fulfill, and the shortage of qualified and interested instructors all hinder the establishment of general education.

In spite of the difficulties and deterrents, the need persists for general education for all categories of students. Some progress has been made toward its solution (*153; 69*:Ch. 7). Further progress will continue as faculty members labor to select and organize experiences that will contribute to more abundant personal life for their students and which stimulate the students to work toward a more stable and more satisfactory society. In the words of Bogue, "general education is one of the constants in basic functions of community colleges. It continues in all communities, for all people, regardless of the ever-changing industrial, business, agricultural, and professional methods or their variations between communities. Unless an institution performs this function well, it cannot claim to be a junior or community college. . . . General education should be at the heart of the community program (9:60).

C. Education for Transfer

Preparation for further study at the four-year college or university is the traditional task of the junior college. It was the primary purpose envisaged by Tappan and Folwell, Harper, Lange, and Jordan. This was the objective adopted by the earliest established junior colleges, both private and public. It is the goal which the junior colleges have accomplished most extensively and most successfully and for the greatest numbers of their students. Yet it is also the source of a considerable amount of misunderstanding of the junior colleges on the part of the universities, the students in the junior colleges, and the general public.

The multiplicity of purposes in the community junior college, only partially clear to workers in other fields, is one source of this difficulty. The community junior college has purposes limited in time, for the most part, to the first two years of study after high school. The university and the four-year college also offer courses appropriate for this range of educational background and for this age group. To this extent the functions of the university and the community junior college overlap. Yet the community junior college is much more than half of a university. While it must achieve the aims of the first two years of university study for some of its students, it has other worthy purposes which are no part of the idea of a university and other worthy students who do not desire and should not work toward the baccalaureate degree.

In its "university-parallel" programs, the community junior college performs many important educational services. It enables many able young people to complete their first two years of college while living at home and thus aids them in conserving some of their funds for upper-division and graduate study. Thus it contributes both to equality of educational opportunity and to the development by some young people of specialized talents which might otherwise be neglected. It helps to fill the junior and senior classes of the four-year institutions, after the inevitable attrition has reduced the size of the classes which entered those colleges two years earlier. It provides, moreover, a tried and tested student body for these upper-division classes. This function is a very important one in a society that needs all the trained talent it can get and that intends to afford every citizen opportunity to achieve his highest potential.

The later academic success of students from the junior college is important in relation to the success of students who entered four-year colleges as freshmen. This question has interested students of higher education since the establishment of junior colleges. Gleazer reports a study by Nall, for example, which compared the success of junior college transfer students with native students at the University of Colorado over the four-year period, 1951–1955. Nall found that by the last semester of the senior year the transfer student in the College of Arts and Sciences had a mean grade-point ratio of 2.61 (C = 2.00) as compared with 2.84 for native students at the same point. In the College of Engineering, on the other hand, the transfer student earned mean grade-point ratios of 3.00 and 3.05, respectively, in the two semesters of the senior year, while the native student earned 2.78 and 2.98 (57).

At Florida State University, Stickler found that

> The total group of all Florida junior college transfer students combined approached the same grade-point averages in the University that they had earned in junior college before transfer. The median and mean grade-point averages were lower in the University but only modestly so (median − .03, mean − .11). . . .
>
> Junior college graduates generally do quite satisfactory work in the University, especially after the adjustments of the first semester have been made. The group of junior college graduates who had been in the University for more than one semester achieved very nearly the same grade point averages in the University as in junior college before transfer. This study shows that junior college graduates as a group did substantially better work than many [native] Florida State University groups (e.g., the student body as a whole, fraternities, the freshman class, the sophomore class, the junior class, all upper-classmen combined, and all under-graduates combined). (149)

Knoell and Medsker reported on the achievement of transfers from junior colleges to a sample of four-year colleges and universities in ten states. All junior college students who transferred in 1960 and who met certain other criteria were included in the study group. Their most general conclusion about success of transfer students was:

Cumulative averages at the four-year colleges were generally lower than the junior college averages but reflected steady improvement following the first-term loss immediately after transfer. The cumulative average at the four-year college for the entire group was found to be 2.34, or C+, compared with a cumulative junior college average of 2.56. Averages for the four semesters after transfer increased from 2.27 for the first term to 2.42 for the second, 2.54 for the third, and 2.68 for the fourth (or last term analyzed). The increases in the term averages were the result of both attrition among the poorer students and improvement on the part of the students who persisted. (88:178)

Several problems persist for community colleges in their exercise of the function of transfer education. Among these, one of the most important is that of developing proper relations with the upper-division institutions. The effective preparation of transfer students must be safeguarded, but too frequently this safeguarding has resulted in unnecessary and hampering restrictions on the right of the junior college to develop its own program for its own students. The question of advanced credit for technical courses is related to effective preparation for further study. Bethel points out that a sizable number of students who complete terminal curriculums then apply for transfer and that evidence is accumulating that such students do succeed in baccalaureate programs (8:8).

A further problem for the community junior college is related to the fact that only a minority of those students who enroll as transfer students actually do transfer. The students who change their intention are among those for whom the occupational and other terminal curriculums of the community junior college are established. Yet it requires major attention of counselors and faculty to identify and reorient such students before they have failed too many courses or have decided finally to withdraw from college.

The definition and maintenance of proper standards of accomplishment in the junior college are further problems associated with their transfer function. Too often standards are defined solely by grade-point averages, without adequate consideration of the selection of students, the quality of instruction, or the purposes of the students or of the community junior college. Junior colleges are rated by some universities on the basis of their "grade-point differential"—a comparison of grade averages before and after transfer. It is true that grades in the junior college are one kind of evidence of the ability of a transfer student to continue college study. Yet it is possible for a faculty to concentrate on this recommending function of their grading policy to such an extent that they neglect their parallel responsibilities for excellent instruction, diversity of educational offerings, and careful guidance of all students. In considering standards the community junior college faculty must remember that preparation for transfer is but one of several important functions. They must not concentrate so singly on success in one endeavor that they fail in several others.

It seems certain that preparation of students for further study will continue to be a major function of the community junior college. It is at least possible that increasing proportions of students will classify themselves realistically as "two-year" or "terminal" students, perhaps reversing the present ratios of transfer and terminal students. Even so, the expected growth in all enrollments in higher education will bring ever greater absolute numbers of transfer students to the junior colleges. It is not inconceivable that before many decades most of American lower-division education, with its implied selection of students for further education, will be completed in the junior colleges. Although such a development would increase the responsibility of these colleges, it might serve to improve their relations with the receiving institutions.

D. Continuing Education

In a civilization where no man's education may be considered sufficient and complete, people of all ages and conditions seek opportunities to continue their education while they work. America is becoming a nation of students, and the community junior colleges are increasingly active in providing courses for the fully employed part-time student. Part-time enrollments in public junior colleges exceed the number of full-time students; the 1966 *Junior College Directory* reports 486,975 part-time students and only 424,676 full-time students (*118:26*).

The category of adult students is difficult to define precisely; it is no longer possible to restrict the program of adult education to the hours after six o'clock, to include in it all persons over 21 years of age, or to assign all part-time students to it. As many as 10% of the full-time students in some community junior colleges are more than 25 years of age; on the other hand, many of the students in evening classes are part-time "college age" persons working toward degrees. It is apparent that the term "adult education" is no longer as limited in meaning as it was when Americanization was the main purpose; the term "continuing education" is a more accurate description of the function.

The need for educational opportunities for persons employed full-time includes both credit and noncredit courses, courses paralleling day-time offerings as well as courses developed especially for this clientele, courses scheduled in day-time (for example, for mothers of school children) or during evening hours, and broadly cultural as well as specifically occupational courses. Under the influence of the Manpower Development and Training Act and the Vocational Education Act of 1963, the involvement of junior colleges in part-time education will surely increase.

Community junior colleges will continue to take the lead in studies of their communities to analyze needs for part-time education. Bogue's 1950 summary of this responsibility is still timely and apropos:

> The Community College is in a strategic position from the standpoint of its basic philosophy, its relation to the community, its facilities either actual or potential, and by clear responsibility to provide for adult education on a far more progressive and inclusive scale than is the case at the present time. It would seem that every college, regardless of its size or method of control, should seek out and encourage adults in the community to improve themselves and their occupational status. (9:229)

E. *Community Services*

The function of community services is the most recently developed of the tasks of the community junior college. Nevertheless, the scope and adequacy of these services determine whether or not the college merits the title of "community" junior college; to an important degree, they determine also the extent of community understanding and support of the several functions of the college. Because of the recency of the concept of community services, the experience of junior colleges in performing them has been limited.

Because the community junior college, in many areas, is the only conveniently available "community of scholars," citizens in all walks of life look to it for such services as scholars traditionally provide. Thus the chemistry instructor may be asked to perform an analysis of soil or water samples for a farmer, the biology teacher to consult on techniques and feasibility of plant hybridization, or the language teacher to translate a letter from abroad. Local civic organizations will look to the community college for speakers and consultants on a variety of problems. Performances of college musical and dramatic groups will be open to the public. Community groups are encouraged to use college dining rooms or classrooms for their meetings. Colleges provide cultural activities such as concert series, subscription dramatic seasons, and lecturers. They organize workshops and short courses for special-interest groups in the community. In a word, the community junior college actively seeks ways in which it can contribute to the intellectual and cultural activity of its communities. As Reynolds suggests,

Community services are provided through an extension of the regular school program in terms of the traditional school day, the traditional locations of the instructional activities, the traditional curriculum, and the traditional concept of students. Community services, moreover, often transcend the traditional definition of education in the sense of teacher-student relationships. In many instances this relationship is entirely absent. (69:142)

F. Guidance

The community junior college functions of occupational education, general education, transfer education, and continuing education will attract students with many different ambitions, with varying backgrounds, with extended ranges of abilities. If such students are to make effective use of the curriculums of the college, they must be assisted in choosing appropriate courses of study. Because of the richness and variety of offerings implied by the multiple purposes of community colleges, unaided selection by the student is almost impossible. The guidance function of the community colleges has been developed to aid the student in making appropriate choices.

The student who is about to embark on a career of college study needs to make many important decisions before he enrolls, or very early in his period of attendance. Each unfortunate choice or omission will delay his attainment of his goal; often his resources of time or money are used up, and such mistakes prevent him from ever attaining it. Wise choices depend upon adequate information, and it is the task of the junior college guidance worker to help each student obtain and understand such information so that his educational choices may be made wisely. Four basic categories of information are essential for educational guidance: data about the student, about educational and personal requirements for occupations, about availability of educational opportunity, and about employment prospects in many fields. When such data are well understood by the student, he can choose his course of study with confidence that it will lead him toward his goal. At the same time, he will be made aware of the fact, which so often comes as a surprise to students, that not all college courses are equally valid for all objectives, and that a radical change of goal may require a radical and time-consuming change of course.

As early as possible, and certainly not later than his first college enrollment, the student should be helped to face reality in the form of some facts about himself. His scores on tests of intelligence serve as predictors of success in further study and in occupations: such scores should be available to the guidance worker and should be interpreted carefully to the student. In like manner, his pattern of interests, his record of previous school work, his family status, his financial resources, his personality, his determination, his ambition, all are relevant to the self-understanding which will help him choose an educational goal and an occupational one.

Facts about the world of work are equally pertinent. Each person may have an interest in several varieties of work and the capacity to succeed at several levels of training within each variety. Occupational trends, moreover, are increasing the opportunities for employment in some fields (for example, college teaching and agricultural business), while diminishing them in others (for example, farming). Patterns of educational preparation for different fields are often a mystery to high-school graduates. The community college is obligated to make available to its students information and interpretation of this sort, so that they may relate their own realistically determined ambitions to the facts of vocational opportunity and choose appropriately from the diversity of offerings at the college.

But the guidance task is not completed when the student has planned his course. Throughout his college career—indeed, throughout life—crises in personal relationships can interfere with a student's success in his endeavor. During the college years, the guidance worker stands by to assist in the resolution of such difficulties. Personal difficulties may concern the student's management of his own perplexities in such fields as vocational choice, finances, health, use of time, efficiency of study, or understanding and acceptance of his strengths and limitations. In other cases, the need for assistance will arise from difficulties with others—classmates, instructors, parents, sweetheart, or wife. Although the counselor must not attempt to be all things to all students, he still must realize that misunderstandings can interfere with a student's achievement; his function is to assist the student in working out his problems, so that the college and the student may move on with their primary task of education.

Because of its greater spread of educational offerings and because of the greater diversity of its student body, the community junior college seems to need a complete and effective guidance service even more than other colleges. There are many important difficulties which have kept these colleges from achieving their goals in this field. Hillway summarizes the difficulties as "(1) the cost of a really effective guidance program; (2) the shortage of adequately trained counseling personnel; and (3) lack of knowledge as to how the student personnel program should be properly organized" (72:148). None of these difficulties is insuperable, once the need is clearly recognized.

Selected References

Bogue, Jesse P. *The Community College.* "Basic Functions of Community Colleges." New York: McGraw-Hill Book Co., 1950, Chapter 3.

Campbell, Doak S. *A Critical Study of the Stated Purposes of the Junior College.* Nashville: George Peabody College for Teachers, 1930.

Clark, Burton C. *The Open-Door College.* New York: McGraw-Hill Book Co., 1960.

Eells, Walter C. *Why Junior College Terminal Education?* Washington: American Association of Junior Colleges, 1941.

Harris, Norman C. *Technical Education in the Junior College: New Programs for New Jobs.* Washington: American Association of Junior Colleges, 1964.

Henry, Nelson B. (editor). *The Public Junior College.* The Fifty-fifth Yearbook of the National Society for the Study of Education. Chicago: The University of Chicago Press, 1956, Chapters 4–8 and 10.

Hillway, Tyrus R. *The American Two-Year College.* New York: Harper and Row, 1958, Chapter VII.

Koos, Leonard V. *The Junior College.* Minneapolis: University of Minnesota Press, 1924.

Knoell, Dorothy M. and Leland L. Medsker. *From Junior to Senior College: A National Study of the Transfer Student.* Washington: American Council on Education, 1965.

II

The Organization of Community Junior Colleges

6

Types of Junior Colleges

Junior colleges have developed in response to various local influences, and are subject to the laws of the fifty states and to the guiding principles of their own governing boards. Their relationships to secondary schools and to colleges and universities vary from region to region and even within the same state. These facts explain some of the diversity of purpose and of organization which the colleges exhibit. Their rapid growth, in number, in enrollment, and in scope of educational program, has made it impossible to classify and to define them simply. Each of the terms used to name them, in this volume as well as elsewhere in the literature, is somewhat unsatisfactory.

The original title was "junior college." In its present usage in the literature, "junior college" has two distinct sets of meanings. In the first sense, it is used as a generic title to cover all the institutions that offer two-year college programs, regardless of what other education any individual college may provide. The term is used in this unqualified sense in the present volume. In its more limited usage, often carelessly contrasted with "community college," a junior college is a two-year college, usually privately controlled, which concentrates primarily on preparing its students to transfer to four-year colleges to pursue the bachelor's degree. In this limited sense, hardly any college in the *Junior College Directory* is a junior college. Nearly all the independent colleges offer some two-year courses of a terminal nature, and a good many of the publicly controlled colleges devote most of their attention to transfer work and offer only four or five occupational curriculums (56:Appendix IV).

In recent years, some writers have objected to "junior college" as a term too limited in its connotations to be applied to a two-year college that fulfills all the functions described in Chapter 5. Because of the expansion of functions, colleges in Alaska, California, Illinois, Michigan, New York, and Texas, for example, have begun to delete "junior" from their titles, although very similar institutions in Colorado, Florida, and Mississippi have retained the word. Even within a state, colleges with similar purposes may disagree on nomenclature, as with Kellogg Community College and Jackson Junior College in Michigan or City College of San Francisco, Fullerton Junior College, and El Camino College in California. The national body has retained the title "American Association of Junior Colleges" as the most inclusive term.

As yet, no fully satisfactory and unequivocal terminology has been offered to substitute for "junior college." Simply to eliminate the word "junior" from titles leads to confusion on the part of the unsophisticated patron, who is likely to ask, "When did you become a four-year college?" The terms "community junior college" and "city college" are beginning to acquire meaning, at least among contributors to the *Junior College Journal;* these titles usually imply the concepts of service to the local community, public support, and two-year programs. Here again, however, misunderstanding is possible. There are community colleges and municipal colleges that offer programs of four years leading to bachelors' degrees; there are privately supported two-year colleges that perform community services. Even the newer terms, therefore, are not entirely unambiguous.

 In most common usage and in the present text, "junior college" includes institutions offering general and specialized education to persons beyond high-school age, either to meet immediately their present educational needs or to prepare them for further study. "Community junior college" is a kind of junior college which is *usually* a public institution, draws *most* of its students from its supporting community, develops programs of study in response to needs of the local community, and is likely to offer a wider variety of courses than the "noncommunity" junior college, which intends to attract students from a much wider geographic area. The phrases "public junior college" and "community junior college" are thus seen to be roughly synonymous, although not identical.

These definitions can be clarified by consideration of some of the existing colleges that they are designed to describe. Junior colleges may be classified conveniently on the basis of their fiscal control as "independent" and "public." Within each of these categories, there are varieties of control and of program. Because the community junior college may be understood fully only by comparison with and contrast to other kinds of junior colleges, the remainder of Chapter 6 presents statistics and descriptions of some of the varieties of colleges within the major classes of "independent" and "public" junior colleges.

A. Varieties of Independent Junior Colleges

The 1966 *Junior College Directory* presents statistical data about 268 independent junior colleges (*118*). They enrolled 140,667 students in all classifications in October, 1965, and employed 10,414 faculty members. Of their students, 46% were full-time freshmen, 26% were sophomores, and 28% were part-time students. These facts indicate, as might be expected, that the holding power for regular students is better in the private junior college than in the public institution, in which the freshmen were more than twice the number of sophomores. The part-time students in independent junior colleges accounted for about one-fourth of the total enrollment, whereas in the public colleges they amounted to more than half of all enrollments.

Geographically, independent junior colleges are found in each of the six accreditation regions of the United States, as shown in Table 3. The majority are found east of the Mississippi, whereas very few have been established in the Western States.

Most of the independent junior colleges are coeducational, although significant numbers enroll only men or only women students. Of all listed private junior colleges, 152 are coeducational, 38 are for

Table 3. Geographical Distribution of Independent Junior Colleges, 1965 [a]

Accrediting Regions	Number of Independent Junior Colleges	
New England	32	
Middle States	76	
Southern	87	
Eastern United States		195
North Central	64	
Northwest	3	
Western	6	
Midwestern and Western United States		73
Total		268

[a] **Source:** Author's tabulation from the 1966 *Junior College Directory* (*118*).

men, and 78 are for women. Most of these colleges are denomination-ally controlled, although a strong minority are listed as "nonprofit" colleges. The listings in the 1966 *Junior College Directory* (*118*), are grouped in the following manner according to their source of control:

Nonprofit and proprietary	99
Catholic	75
Baptist	24
Methodist	22
Lutheran	12
Presbyterian	7
Other denominational	29
Total	268

In size, the independent junior college tends to be smaller than the average public junior college. Table 4 sets forth the enrollment statistics for the independent junior college. In total enrollment, the median size of the privately controlled institution was 320 students, as compared with an overall median of 840 in public institutions. For full-time students, the arithmetic mean enrollments were 525 in the independent junior colleges and 2313 in the public. The independent colleges enroll a smaller proportion of part-time and unclassified students than do the public institutions. Only one-fourth of all inde-pendent college enrollments are so classified, while more than half of the public junior college students are either part-time or unclassified.

Table 4. Distribution of Size of Enrollment in Independent Junior Colleges, 1965

Enrollments	Number of Colleges
1–99	50
100–199	39
200–299	38
300–499	62
500–999	46
1000–1999	22
2000–2999	5
3000–9999	6
Total colleges	268
Median enrollment	320
Mean enrollment	525

Source: Condensed from the 1966 *Junior College Directory* (*118*).

The independent junior college is an integral and necessary part of the entire American enterprise of higher education. By its nature, it does not concentrate so intently on service to the local community and part-time adult students as does the public junior college. For these purposes it typically substitutes distinctive aims that can best be achieved within the framework of limited enrollments, residential campuses, recruitment of students from a wide geographical area, and concentration on excellent achievement of a limited set of educational objectives. In addition, the privately controlled junior college is sometimes better able to carry on experimentation in the development of special curriculums or improved techniques of instruction. It can, because of its limited enrollment, afford more opportunity for guidance and counseling and for informal association of students with faculty members than can the larger, nonresidential public community college. Bogue summarizes these specialized opportunities of the independent junior college by pointing out that

The good colleges, however, will do their share to pioneer new ideas, to maintain freedom from group pressures, to demand that personal achievement shall match native ability, to enrich educational experiences through college community living, to emphasize the development of the whole person, to teach and exemplify democratic values and a high degree of flexibility in dealing with the problems of individual students. Moreover, the residential college, in contrast to the purely local community college, can lift its students into regional and even national association and thereby contribute to the breakdown of tendencies to provincialism. The faithful performance of these functions, however small in comparison to the total educational program of the nation, will contribute significantly beyond any measure of numbers or magnificence of plants. (9:120)

The experimental opportunity of the private college has been well realized at Stephens College in Columbia, Missouri, until 1965 a non-denominational junior college for women. Under the leadership of James M. Wood and W. W. Charters, Stephens College pioneered in developing a curriculum based on the life activities of women. *American Junior Colleges* (Sixth Edition) presents a succinct description of some of the salient features of the curriculum.

College bases program on belief that the first 2 years after high school are crucial in the lives and development of young women. Offers varied out-of-class programs of cultural and social opportunities, feeling that environment and associations make significant educational contributions. Features include radio station and closed circuit television station operated by students; summer seminars in Western Europe; legitimate theater on campus; opera workshop; advanced language laboratory. College also sponsors many conferences for its staff. (56:293)

An example of a more traditional program in a private nondenominational junior college for women may be found in Monticello College at Alton, Illinois. Founded as Monticello Female Seminary in 1835, the College was recognized as a junior college in 1917. *American Junior Colleges* (Sixth Edition) describes its present program:

Transfer liberal arts program emphasized. Strong activities and field trip program to use opportunities offered by nearby St. Louis. Honors program designed to give superior sophomore students unusually broad background in liberal arts as well as extended experience in independent research and writing. Intercultural transfer program offers 2 years at Monticello followed by 2 years at major university outside continental United States. (56:175)

The curriculums offered to the 367 young women enrolled (1965) included among others, liberal arts, sciences, home economics, medicine, music, nursing, political science, psychology, teaching, and several specializations in business fields.

The private junior college under religious auspices may be fairly represented by Norman College at Norman Park, Georgia, under control of the Missionary Baptist Church. The exhibit in *American Junior Colleges* (Sixth Edition) describes Norman College as "a community college with Christian philosophy; size makes possible individual attention. Strong programs in Christianity, for ministers and religious education majors; education, business administration, secretarial science, nursing. Offers American Culture Program with emphasis on American way of life" (56:152).

The examples cited are of private junior colleges that appeal to students from all over the country. Some privately controlled junior colleges, on the other hand, are intimately related to their communities and offer programs which meet, in most instances, the suggested definition of a "community junior college." Such a one is New Haven College in Connecticut. The *Catalogue,* 1963–1964, points out that "New Haven College has seven divisions, each of which serves a special function. They are: The Engineering Program, the Cooperative Program, the Arts and Science Program, the Evening Credit Program, the Division of Special Studies, the School of Executive Development, and The Reading Center."

Several of the community programs are of four-year duration. Although the major emphasis of the College had been on the junior college level, in 1965 it changed its classification to "four-year col-

lege." The Engineering Program, the Evening Credit Program, and the School of Executive Development offer four-year curriculums. The Cooperative Program alternates periods of full-time study with periods of employment in business and industry; the Arts and Science Program is a two-year curriculum, primarily intended as a terminal course, although most courses are transferable. The Reading Center provides reading training for persons of all ages.

In 1965, New Haven College enrolled 2673 students of whom 1198 were classified as full-time, and 1475 were part-time or special students (*122*:24).

New Haven College, therefore, demonstrates that a privately controlled junior college can, if it wishes, develop all the characteristic services of a community junior college. From its beginning it has responded appropriately to the educational needs of the New Haven community in a variety of pioneering and unusual ways. It offers few curriculums specifically designed to prepare students to transfer to upper-division work; it has taken the lead in developing cooperative and work-study programs; it offers courses such as Personnel Administration, Law of Commercial Paper and Bankruptcy, Non-ferrous Metallurgy, Methods Engineering, or Advertising and Sales Promotion to qualified students, without distinguishing artificially between those who have or have not earned degrees or between those who desire credit or ignore it. The college demonstrates the basis of the contention of Lawrence L. Bethel, formerly its Director, that the only meaningful distinction in junior colleges is not by type of control but by type of purpose: that is, "(1) the community junior college which seeks to serve any local community need at the collegiate level not being met by other educational institutions of the community; (2) the special junior college which selects the areas of instruction in which it will operate" (*8*:3).

In discussing the aims of junior colleges, Noffsinger summarized the purposes of the private institutions in order of importance; the examples cited indicate that they are still appropriate: "(1) moral and religious training; (2) semi-professional training; (3) terminal education; (4) popularization of higher education; (5) affording attention to the individual; (6) offering of work meeting local needs; (7) preparatory work acceptable to colleges and universities" (*119*:401).

B. Varieties of Public Junior Colleges

The 1966 *Junior College Directory* lists 503 publicly controlled junior colleges, which enrolled 1,152,086 students in the previous year

(*118*). These colleges accounted for 65% of all junior colleges listed; their enrollments were 89% of all junior college students of all categories. A total of 50,072 instructors and administrators staffed the public institutions. Of the students enrolled 29% were classified as full-time freshmen and only 12%—less than half as many—as full-time sophomores. An additional 35% of all students were part-time freshmen and sophomores. The extent of community service of the public junior colleges is indicated by the fact that 52% of all enrollments are either part-time or unclassified students. More than half of all public junior college enrollments, then, are part-time and adult students; of the regularly classified students, two-thirds are classified as freshmen. These facts indicate that for many of their students, the public junior colleges are not in fact two-year colleges even though their organized curriculums are usually designed for completion in two years.

The median enrollment of the public junior colleges, as noted previously, is about three times as large as that of the private junior colleges. Yet in both types there are wide variations in size, as shown by the distribution of enrollments in Tables 4 and 5. Small classes and opportunities for students to know instructors, two advantages claimed for the junior college, undoubtedly exist in the 89 private junior colleges and the 20 public junior colleges which enroll fewer

Table 5.   Distribution of Size of Enrollment in Publicly Controlled Junior Colleges, 1965 [a]

Enrollments	Number of Colleges
1–99	4
100–199	16
200–299	23
300–499	70
500–999	122
1000–1999	105
2000–2999	50
3000–8999	80
9000 and over	28
Total colleges	498
Median enrollment	1150
Mean enrollment	2313

[a] **Source:** Condensed from the 1966 *Junior College Directory* (*118*). Several newly opened and nonreporting junior colleges are not included in the tabulation.

Table 6.   Geographical Distribution of Public Junior Colleges, 1965 [a]

Accrediting Regions	Number of Public Junior Colleges	
New England	21	
Middle States	72	
Southern	130	
Eastern United States		223
North Central	164	
Northwest	35	
Western	81	
Midwestern and Western United States		280
Total		503

[a] **Source:** 1966 *Junior College Directory* (*118*).

than 200 students each. These advantages may well be somewhat impaired in the 114 junior colleges which enroll over 3000 students. On the other hand, it is possible to question whether the smallest colleges can usually provide the breadth of program and the quality of instruction which a fully adequate community junior college requires.

Geographically, public junior colleges are distributed throughout the areas of the six regional accrediting agencies, but whereas private colleges are concentrated in the Eastern and Southern sections of the nation, public institutions are found more frequently in the Central and Western sections. The distribution by accreditation areas is shown in Table 6.

Nearly all the public institutions are coeducational. There are seven military or technological junior colleges whose enrollment is limited to men, but none of the public junior colleges offers instruction only to women.

Whereas control of the private junior colleges was distributed among religious denominations with about one-third undenominational, nonprofit, and proprietary colleges, the control of the public junior colleges is divided among several varieties of governmental agencies. Some are controlled by a state board, and others are branches of state universities or state colleges. County governments, local school districts, and independent junior college districts are the remaining patterns of control.

Establishment of the junior college as a *branch of a state college or state university* is most common in Indiana, Pennsylvania, and Wisconsin, although two-year branches of public four-year colleges are found also in Alabama, Arkansas, Nevada, Tennessee, Virginia, and West Virginia. The Pennsylvania State University Extension Center at Ogontz is a good example of this general type of branch public junior college. In an introductory statement about the Pennsylvania Extension Centers, Gleazer summarizes their basic functions:

System of campuses organized to carry out all the functions of the Pennsylvania State University. Curricular offerings vary. Some campuses offer only 2-year terminal curricula leading to associate degree in a limited number of fields; others offer the first two years of all, or nearly all, university baccalaureate curricula, and a wide variety of terminal curricula leading to the associate degree. At present the principal full-time programs emphasize work at the freshman-sophomore level. Transfer students enrolled in such programs do not receive a degree from the center, but they may transfer to the main campus or to other institutions after 1 or 2 years' work. (56:386)

In the same volume, the Extension Center at Ogontz reports its curriculums for 1962:

Transfer: Liberal arts; agriculture; business; engineering; home economics; mineral industries, physical education and recreation; physical science; teaching. Terminal including occupational: Business, electrical and electronic technology; industrial technology; mechanical technology (56: 390)

The enrollment at Ogontz Center that year was reported as full-time, 930; part-time, 7; special, 24; noncredit, 812.

The *junior colleges under state control* differ in administration from those which are branches of universities or of state colleges, in that they are more independent of direct control by university administration and faculty. Instead, they are usually governed either by a college board appointed by the governor, with responsibility for only one college, or by a statewide board of regents charged with the governance of several similar institutions. Thus, in New York State, there are 28 locally sponsored community colleges under the general supervision of the State University of New York, and six Agricultural and Technical Institutes that are units of the State University, but each one is independent of other units of the University. In a similar way, a Board of Regents for State Agricultural Colleges controls the eight Agricultural and Mechanical Colleges in Oklahoma. Such institutions are found also in Colorado, Georgia, Idaho, Maryland, New

Mexico, North Dakota, Oregon, Texas, and Utah, as well as New York and Oklahoma. The Agricultural and Technical Institute at Delhi, of the State University of New York, may serve as an example of this variety of public junior college, although in other states they may concentrate on teacher training rather than on agricultural and technical studies. *American Junior Colleges* (Sixth Edition) carries this description of the Institute at Delhi:

> College combines technical-terminal curricula with general studies to provide a well-rounded background as well as occupational training. Emphasizes understanding and ability to direct others. Balances science, mathematics, and theory with practical training related to theory. Teaching method based on learning by doing; emphasis on individualized instruction. Curricula designed to prepare students for group of related jobs rather than one specific job. (56:339)

At Delhi, in contrast to the Extension Centers in Pennsylvania, no transfer curriculums are offered; the terminal curriculums include agriculture, building construction, secretarial, food and hotel technology, and individually planned programs.

In some states, it is usual to find *the county as the basic unit* for control, financial support, and source of students of the community junior colleges. This is the predominant organization in Colorado, Florida, Maryland, and Wisconsin; in some states several counties join together to support a community college, whereas in others the junior college district may be coterminous with a county, although more or less independent of the county government and the county board of education. The chief advantages of the use of the county as the unit of control are that it combines local control with adequate tax base and that it draws students from a relatively large area. In the scope of their offerings, these colleges are similar to other community junior colleges, combining transfer studies with terminal and adult offerings in proportions appropriate to the fiscal resources, the philosophy of the controlling board, the needs of the community, and the scope of other nearby institutions of higher education.

The separate junior college district is patterned in many respects after the traditional elementary or high school district. Elected boards of trustees choose the administrative and the instructional staffs and levy a junior college tax for partial support of the college. This organization is found in many of the California and Texas community junior colleges, as well as in Georgia, Idaho, Mississippi, North Carolina, and Wyoming. The chief advantage of this type of control seems to lie in the fact that the governing board can devote its entire attention to the affairs of the district's junior colleges: it is not responsible for other kinds of higher education or for elementary and secondary schools. On the other hand, there is a possibility that the separate organization may increase the difficulties of articulation with other schools and colleges from which students come to the community junior college and to which some of them transfer. It is true here as with other types of administrative organization that neither the advantages nor the disadvantages are realized automatically; organization may facilitate but not insure worthwhile outcomes.

Local school board control is the pattern of organization that was originally suggested by the early proponents of junior colleges, although in recent years it is becoming less common. In this pattern, the community junior college is controlled by the same board that controls other schools in the community; often it is administered in conjunction with the local high schools, as an integral part of the system of public education. Although several of the following states have other forms of public junior college organization also, colleges controlled by local school districts are found in Arizona, Arkansas, California, Illinois, Iowa, Kansas, Kentucky, Maryland, Massachusetts, Michigan, Minnesota, Mississippi, Missouri, Nebraska, New Jersey, North Carolina, North Dakota, Oklahoma, Pennsylvania, Texas, Washington, and Wyoming. The local school district organization of junior colleges emphasizes that they are an upward extension of the public system of education and tends to facilitate the transition from one school to the next by students. However, it sometimes happens that the community junior college loses out in the competition with elementary and secondary schools for buildings and for current support; then its enrollments and the quality of the education it offers are both reduced unnecessarily. Under ideal conditions of administrative support and community understanding, the unified control of all schools ought to be the most effective pattern. It is nonetheless apparent that some community junior colleges so organized have been unable to attain full community college status.

C. The Four-Year Junior College

Another type of junior college deserves mention, even though very few of this type are now in operation: this is the four-year junior college. The best known and best publicized of these institutions was Pasadena City College. Two monographs devoted major attention to this college (140:89). As one of the first established and the largest of the category, it serves as an excellent example. In brief, the four-year junior college unites the eleventh, twelfth, thirteenth, and fourteenth years under one administration; in Pasadena, it followed a six-year elementary school and a four-year junior high school.

Sexson and Harbeson explained that

The relationships between these years or grades are such as will provide a continuous, unbroken, and uninterrupted educational experience for the student. The content of the curricula of the freshman and sophomore years (grades eleven and twelve) is planned in the light of student needs for the entire four years. They do not justify a graduation, a diploma, or a break at the end of the twelfth or sophomore year as might be inferred by one who thinks of these years as the terminal years of the traditional secondary school. The eleventh-year student (freshman) identifies himself immediately with an institution, with a planned and continuous program, with activities and experiences designed to meet his needs, with a student-body government which serves his social extracurricular needs and provides him with opportunities for citizenship duties and responsibilities. In short, the student finds himself in "college"—an institution that differs sufficiently from the one he has left to provide interest and novelty, but enough like it to protect him from the home-sickness and bewilderment sometimes experienced in passing from the traditional secondary school to the traditional college. (*140*:2–3)

Among the specific advantages of the four-year organization, Sexson and Harbeson claimed that

The four-year unit as organized articulates with the upper high school years whereas the two-year unit is still sharply isolated from the rest of the system. . . . The four-year unit makes possible acceleration of more competent students through the four-year period. Strong students may expect to complete a four-year span in a period of three years. . . . the holding power between the twelfth and thirteenth grades is much stronger than in the two-year junior college situation. (*140*:6)

In spite of the persuasive presentations by its advocates, the four-year organization has been abandoned in Pasadena, as well as in the other California systems of Compton, Napa, Stockton, Vallejo, and Ventura. In Mississippi also, the public junior colleges have reverted to the conventional organization. The four-year junior college, contrary to the expectations of its proponents, is not being extended into new areas. The transition to the more usual organization in Pasadena is explained in these words:

In 1954, as a result of the withdrawal of part of the high school district to form a separate Temple City High School District which remained within the junior college district, Pasadena abandoned the 6-4-4 system and returned to the 6-3-3-2 plan of organization. In the process, John Muir

College, which was a smaller four-year college in the district, was merged with the Pasadena City College to form a single two-year institution for the junior college district. Students and faculty were combined in this transition. (8:112)

Although several factors are undoubtedly involved in the failure of the four-year plan to achieve widespread popularity, two influences predominate. One is the fact that administrators, faculty, and students reject the concept that the junior college is a culmination of secondary education; they want it to be, and to seem to be, a part of the American system of higher education. In the second place, rapidly rising enrollments in high school and junior college years, together with the migration of students between districts, convinced boards of trustees and administrators that more effective and economical schools might be attained through the conventional organization, familiar to patrons and students and other colleges, than through the deviate pattern of the four-year junior college.

Selected References

Bogue, Jesse P. *The Community College.* New York: McGraw-Hill Book Co., 1950.

Fields, Ralph. *The Community College Movement.* New York: McGraw-Hill Book Co., 1964.

Gleazer, Edmund J., Jr. (editor). *American Junior Colleges* (Sixth Edition). Washington: American Council on Education, 1963.

———— (editor). *Junior College Directory, 1964.* Washington: American Association of Junior Colleges, 1964.

Koos, Leonard V. *Integrating High School and College.* New York: Harper and Row, 1947.

————. *The Junior College.* Minneapolis: University of Minnesota Press, 1924.

Martorana, S. V. "Patterns of Organization and Fiscal Support in Public 2-Year Colleges," *Higher Education,* 14:151–157, May, 1958.

Noffsinger, H. C. "One-third of a Century of Progress," *Junior College Journal,* 5:395–404, May, 1935.

Reichert, Stephen B. "The End of the Four-Year College Movement in California," *Junior College Journal,* 29:307–312 (February, 1959) and 29:439–443 (April, 1959).

Seashore, Carl E. *The Junior College Movement.* New York: Holt, Rinehart and Winston, 1940.

Sexson, John A. and John W. Harbeson. *The New American College.* New York: Harper and Row, 1946.

7

Legal and Financial Provisions
for Public Junior Colleges

The public junior college has engaged the attention of state legislatures with increasing frequency since the enactment in 1907 by the California Legislature of the Caminetti Act. This original enactment provided that

The Board of Trustees of any city, district, union, joint union or county high school may prescribe postgraduate courses of study for the graduates of such high school, or other high schools, which courses of study shall approximate the studies prescribed in the first two years of University courses. The Board of Trustees of any city, district, union, joint union or county high school wherein the postgraduate courses are taught may charge tuition for pupils living without the boundaries of the district wherein such courses are taught. (146:391)

In the half century since that time, other legislatures in California and in other states have passed longer and more restrictive junior college laws. In fewer than 100 words, however, this original law includes the principles of permissive rather than mandatory legislation, local control of junior colleges, substantial equivalence of instruction to that at the university, free tuition for residents of the sponsoring district, and the extension of public secondary education into the junior college years.

Martorana's survey of legislation affecting junior colleges after the 1962 sessions of all the state legislatures reveals that

. . . only 12 states remained without general enabling legislation for the establishment of junior colleges (public two-year collegiate institutions

87

whether designated as junior colleges, community colleges, technical institutes, or two-year branches of four-year state colleges and universities) and only eight could be identified that had no public junior colleges. (99:31)

By 1965, only three states had not yet adopted any legislation for junior college establishment.

A. Junior College Legislative Status in 1965

In most of the states, the constitutionality of the public junior college is implied rather than expressed. Thus Simms points out that under Amendment X to the United States Constitution, the responsibility for public schools, having been neither "delegated to the United States by the Constitution, nor prohibited by it to the States," is reserved to the states respectively or to the people. Under this power, only California has made express constitutional provision for junior colleges. According to Simms, at the time of his study in 1948, twenty-one additional states made general constitutional provision for common schools; except for the four Southern states of Florida, Louisiana, Mississippi, and South Carolina, all these states were in the Midwestern or Western regions of the United States. Although public junior colleges in other states have been established without specific constitutional authority,

It appears that the legality of the public junior college under general legislation is definitely established. In those cases questioning the legality of the statutes the courts upheld the constitutionality of those sections providing for the establishment of public junior colleges under general legislation. (142:13)

Because of changes from one legislative session to the next and because of the increasing interest in public junior colleges on the part of state legislatures, no listing of states with expressed categories of laws can remain accurate for long. Martorana provides a tabulation of states with general enabling legislation, accurate to 1962 (99:34). To his list must be added Hawaii, where the legislature in 1964 authorized the Regents of the University of Hawaii to establish a system of community colleges, and Pennsylvania, where enabling legislation was adopted in 1963. Several of the other states that in 1962 did not have general junior college legislation (for example, Arkansas, Indiana, Utah, Vermont, and Virginia) nevertheless have organized one or more public community colleges or two-year extensions of colleges or universities. In 1964, according to the 1966

Junior College Directory (*118*), there were no public two-year colleges in operation in Delaware, Hawaii, Louisiana, Maine, South Carolina, South Dakota, and Tennessee, even though four of these states had legislation permitting their establishment (99:31). Table 7 is taken from Martorana's tabulation (99:34): It is almost certain, however, that additional junior college legislation will be passed in many of the states during each biennium. Martorana and Palmer, in their 1962 survey of legislation, listed twelve states which had authorized new surveys of junior college needs. All of the twelve states making surveys, except Utah, were among those that already had general legislation on the subject.

With detailed legal provisions for the public junior college in such a fluid status, it is almost impossible to present a meaningful description of the present similarities and divergencies in the laws of the several states. Instead, the present chapter includes a discussion of guiding standards for general legislation to provide for the estab-

Table 7. States with General Enabling Legislation for Public Junior Colleges (1962)

State	Date of Enactment First	Date of Enactment Latest	State	Date of Enactment First	Date of Enactment Latest
Alabama	1962	—	Missouri	1927	1961
Alaska	1953	1962	Montana	1939	1953
Arizona	1927	1960	Nebraska	1931	1957
California	1907	1962	New Hampshire	1961	—
Colorado	1937	1962	New Jersey	1946	1962
Connecticut	1959	—	New Mexico	1957	—
Florida	1939	1961	New York	1948	1962
Georgia	1958	—	North Carolina	1957	1961
Idaho	1939	1957	North Dakota	1931	1961
Illinois	1937	1957	Ohio	1961	—
Iowa	1927	1957	Oklahoma	1939	1961
Kansas	1917	1961	Oregon	1949	1961
Kentucky	1936	1962	Rhode Island	1960	—
Louisiana	1928	—	South Carolina	1935	—
Maryland	1961	—	Texas	1929	1961
Massachusetts	1947	1962	Washington	1941	1961
Michigan	1917	1960	West Virginia	1961	—
Minnesota	1925	1957	Wisconsin	1961	—
Mississippi	1928	1960	Wyoming	1945	1961

lishment, control, and support of public junior colleges, with illustrations from existing state laws. Since special legislation to establish individual institutions varies with each individual situation (99:44–45), no attempt is made to discover basic principles underlying this category of state legislation.

B. Legislative Provisions for Establishment and Control

 Lack of uniformity is an outstanding characteristic in present junior college laws. The law of Iowa consists primarily of a permissive statement authorizing the establishment of public junior colleges and makes no definite provisions for their support. This law consists of approximately one-fourth page, and provides that the board of education, upon approval of the State Superintendent of Education and the voters, may establish and maintain one or more junior colleges in the district. . . . In contrast to this the law in California consists of approximately seventy pages of the present school code. Practically every phase in the establishment, maintenance, and operation of public junior colleges is given in detail. The scope of the legislation in the remaining states falls within this range (*142*:94–95).

Specific Restrictions. Martorana has noted, in addition to the variations between the states, a trend toward greater specificity:

Legislation which was enacted during the early years of the junior college movement consisted, in most cases, of mere permissive statements authorizing establishment of public junior colleges. The amendments to the earlier legislation, however, and the more recently enacted laws are much more specific and detailed in structure. As illustrations, the 1951 Oregon enactment stipulates standards and procedures for establishment, relationships to the State Board of Education and the State Board of Higher Education, and tuition charges allowed, as well as other matters; the 1955 Michigan act is also a lengthy and detailed legal document. (8:22)

Students of trends in junior college legislation are in agreement that much recent legislation prescribes procedures for establishment and curricular offerings in too great detail, and that it would be wiser to enact general statements of responsibility and grants of authority to school boards so that they could carry out their educational tasks in the light of their own judgment of local needs. In this respect, the Mississippi junior college law is admirable in its broad definition of function of the junior college. "The law is drawn so as to make available at low cost to the largest possible percentage of the people of every section a high quality junior college education, and to furnish other unique educational services determined by the needs of each community" (*108*:91). The Mississippi law provides for five types of curriculums:

(1) courses of study correlated with those of senior colleges or professional schools, (2) semi-professional and vocational-technical courses on the college level, (3) strictly vocational or trade training courses, (4) short-term curriculums for training for specific jobs subject to the needs of the community, (5) courses, either "college credit" or "non-credit," to serve the needs of the adult population. (*108*:91–92; *156*)

Some states, on the other hand, restrict the junior college to certain varieties or sizes of districts, limit the curriculum to the "first two years of the baccalaureate degree course," or establish statutory limitations on admission and graduation. Consideration of both the variety and the nature of state junior college laws has led several writers to suggest criteria for state legislation about the junior college. In general, the purpose of such criteria is to guide legislatures in drafting or revising junior college legislation. The authors agree that laws should provide for local initiative in the establishment of junior colleges, protected by impartial fact-finding services from the state and by certain minimum standards for state and local support and for prospective enrollment at the junior college. In the words of Young, "Items of general legislation . . . should provide for flexibility . . . Standardization should generally be kept to a minimum. The college should retain local autonomy within the framework of flexible and desirable legal and semi-legal standards and requirements" (*165*:449).

Desirable Provisions. In accordance with this basic principle, it is possible to suggest certain desirable elements of adequate and effective state legislation for the establishment of public junior colleges. Such legislation should include

1. a definition of the junior college,
2. provision for local initiative in the establishment of new junior colleges,
3. provision for a survey of the local area by a designated state agency, to determine whether an adequate college could be established and supported,
4. insistence on acceptance of the junior college proposal by the local electorate,
5. authorization for any varieties of local organization and control which are appropriate to the state and to the locality,
6. allocation of elements of control between a local board and a supervising state agency, and
7. provision for financial support.

The *legislative definition* of the public junior college should be sufficiently broad to enable the responsible local and state authorities to develop the patterns of post-high-school education that will satisfy the developing needs of their communities. At the same time, the definition should set forth the relationships of the public junior college to other levels of education, so that fiscal and supervisory officers may be able to determine whether given practices are or are not authorized under law. For these reasons, it is well for the basic act to include the public junior college within the established framework of education within the state and to express clearly the areas of educational service authorized for the junior colleges. If this is done, much of the legislation already enacted concerning education may be made to apply, as appropriate, to the public junior college; it will be easier to exclude the junior college from certain inappropriate enactments than it would be to attempt to cover every point of inclusion by specific positive legislation.

The Florida statute of 1957 is an example of adequate legislation in this respect. It provides:

Junior colleges may be established in the discretion of the county boards in the manner prescribed by law. The term, junior college, as used herein shall mean an educational institution operated by the county board as part of the county school system and offering (a) a program of general education consisting of classical and scientific courses in the thirteenth and fourteenth grades parallel to that of the first and second years of work at a senior four-year State institution of higher learning, (b) terminal courses of a technical and vocational nature, and (c) courses for adults. (50:Sec. 228.14 [3])

In a later section, a desired exclusion is stated separately: "*PRO-VIDED*, that the county board shall not requisition from the state any textbooks for pupils attending a junior college, nor shall it furnish any textbooks to pupils attending a junior college" (50:Sec. 230.23 [7][b]). Except for similar exclusions, the laws governing the Florida public schools apply also to junior college administrators, teachers, students, and fiscal affairs. To that extent their legal status is clear.

The statute should establish *local initiative* as the usual source of the movement for public junior colleges. Community junior colleges exist by virtue of and in relation to the existing educational needs of their local citizenry. The best guarantee that those needs exist and are recognized locally is the desire of local citizens to assume the burden of establishing and maintaining a public junior college. For this reason, basic legislation should provide for an affirmative vote of the citizens of the area to be served by a new college before its establishment is authorized. In harmony with this principle, the laws of California, Florida, and Illinois, for example, provide that established school boards may initiate the process leading to the creation of a community college. In other states, Arizona, Colorado, Idaho, Montana, and Texas among them, a petition signed by a stipulated number of qualified voters is required to start the establishment procedure of certain types of junior college districts. In still other states, either a local school board or a body of qualified voters may request a study of the need for a junior college—as in Kansas and Michigan. Such a provision tends to ensure careful local consideration of the proposal, and certainly it will help to prevent the establishment of an unneeded junior college in any location.

Local school boards have the authority to establish junior colleges in certain kinds of districts in several states. Because of the dangers of hasty and superficially considered action inherent in this procedure, the basic junior college legislation should *provide for a local junior college survey* to be completed before further action is taken. The original petition, therefore, should be addressed to an appropriate state agency—State Board of Education, State Department of Education, Junior College Commission, or a similar body—which is authorized by law to study the ability of the proposed district to support an effective community college. Some writers suggest very specific conditions concerning, for example, projected minimum enrollment, assessed valuation, minimum population of the district, and high-school enrollment, that must be met before a junior college is authorized (*47; 142*:99–104). The purpose of such recommendations is to ensure the viability of a public junior college established in conformity with them; they become outdated very rapidly, however, and may be so rigid as to stifle initiative. The 1951 junior college law in Oregon, for example, required a school district to have assessed valuation of $20,000,000 in order to establish a public junior college. It failed to provide for adequate state support and did not authorize school districts to join together in establishing a junior college. Since that time revision of the requirements and an increase in authorized state aid has encouraged the formation of seven new public junior colleges (*124*).

Instead of writing the standards into the law, the legislators might provide for an impartial survey of the need for a public junior college in a petitioning district and of the district's financial ability. In this way adequate standards could be protected, together with flexibility to care for special situations and for changing economic conditions.

Several of the states have recently completed studies of all their needs in higher education (*100; 113*:129). In some of the reports of statewide surveys, junior colleges are recommended for specific areas. Such general recommendations should not be accepted as sufficient warrant for the establishment of individual junior colleges. Local surveys are needed also. In harmony with this caution, the Florida Community College Council established three steps in its development of a statewide plan for the establishment of *locally controlled* community junior colleges. The first, embodied in its report, was a statewide examination of the educational needs of all counties. *Step two* involved a local survey to determine the readiness of local people to support a community junior college and to determine the feasibility of locating an institution in that area. *Step three* involves the study and planning necessary before the actual establishment of a junior college (*28*:28).

A *local election* to decide the question of establishing the proposed college should be provided for in the basic law and should follow upon approval by the survey staff of the proposal as it was submitted to them or as revised in the light of their findings. Although some states in providing for such an election require approval by two-thirds (Minnesota) or by 60% (Iowa) of votes cast, a simple majority should suffice to establish the will of the people. In any case, since the taxpayers of the district will send their children to the college and will themselves attend in increasing numbers, and since they will inevitably be asked to support the college through additional taxes, the approval by means of an election requires that they become aware of the nature of the services of the proposed college. An election is thus one step in the interpretation of the college to its community, as well as an essential precondition for its establishment.

In some states, a wide *variety of public school districts* has grown up over the years; in others, recent legislation has served to unify and consolidate districts. Within a single state, one community junior college proposal may be introduced in a single unified district that includes an area and a population sufficient for a flourishing junior college; another may be applied to a region that has only recently become a geographic and economic unit but still maintains the separate elementary districts and union and joint union high school districts that were appropriate in the nineteenth century. For this reason, the basic junior college law should make provision for a variety of kinds of local districts. As Putnam noted, the failure of the 1951 Oregon law to permit two or more districts to unite in forming a junior college made it impossible for several areas to achieve the $20,000,000 assessed valuation required as a minimum tax base for an Oregon junior college (128:344).

Clear-cut allocation of elements of control between a local board and a supervising state agency is another basic element in junior college legislation. Certainly, details of curriculum, admission of students, and graduation requirements should be excluded from legislative enactments. The establishment of general standards for junior colleges is a legitimate function of a state agency; inspection and accreditation of these colleges should accompany the certification of the institutions as eligible for state financial aid. General regulations about admission of students, amounts of study required for graduation, and kinds of courses that may be approved for state support are within the province of the state agency. The determination of which specific curriculums are appropriate to the local area, specific course and quality requirements for graduation, teachers' salaries, and similar matters should be reserved to the local junior college board in much the same way as they are now reserved to other governing boards. Bogue and Burns summarize the relationship as follows:

The relationship of junior colleges to state departments of education rests legally on four functions generally assigned to state departments: (*a*) supervision of the expenditure of funds appropriated by the legislature for public education, (*b*) enforcing standards of teacher preparation included in teacher certification laws or state department regulations, (*c*) certifying teachers for public schools, and (*d*) administering educational programs in agencies of education. (69:236)

Morrison and Martorana summarize their guidelines for state legislation by noting that,

Shortcomings in legislation once created are extremely difficult to correct; much legislative attention and energy (are) consumed in the effort to do so. As a general principle, a State law enabling establishment of 2-year colleges should be phrased in broad, permissive terms, setting forth the basic conditions to be met and procedures to be followed by the agency or agencies authorized to set up and operate these institutions. Specific criteria for establishing a 2-year college and detailed restrictive statements should *not* be included in State laws. (115:71)

C. *Legislative Provisions for Financing*

In 1947, the Committee on Legislation of the American Association of Junior Colleges, in considering "Principles for Guidance in Setting-up of State Laws for the Establishment of Junior Colleges," strongly recommended that such laws provide for free tuition (47:386). This recommendation is in harmony with the thinking of many writers on the subject of the junior college, among them Eells, Proctor, Koos, and Seashore. It recognizes also that important numbers of able high-school graduates are kept from college by financial barriers and that the public community college which charges no tuition can encourage a good many of these students to complete two years of study while living at home. As yet, only a minority of the states authorizing junior colleges have accepted the recommendation for free tuition in their legislation. Martorana found that

. . . contrary to the stated philosophy of most public community colleges that they seek to provide free, or practically free, education, common practice is to charge tuition or general fees of students attending. Only two states (California and Illinois) have specific legal restrictions against charging resident students tuition for attending junior colleges. Eight states specifically authorize (but usually not in dollar amounts) tuition charges for resident students . . . another 16, while not specifying conditions or classifying students affected, provide in broad general phraseology that the controlling board may charge general fees or tuition of students attending the institution. (99:40–41)

For 1962–1963, the Office of Education reported a median tuition in public junior colleges of $113; the medians ranged from $291 in North Atlantic states to $114 in the Southeast; $112 in the Great Lakes and Plains states, and $60 in the West and Southwest (143:99).

It is obvious that such tuition charges cannot bear a major portion of the costs of operating the colleges, and yet it is equally evident that even a moderate tuition charge can make the difference for some young people from indigent families between enrollment at the junior college and failure to enroll. To this extent, tuition charges tend to negate the attempts of a state to provide for equality of educational opportunity for qualified students. In a study of "Costs of Attending College" in 1952–1953, Hollis found that students in all colleges who lived with their parents spent about $1000 each on the average, although such students in public colleges averaged about $800 annual expenditures (74:9). In his concluding chapter, Hollis points out that

As educational expenditures increase with spiraling economic costs, the issue arises as to whether students and the general public shall continue to pay prevailing portions of the cost, or whether one or the other should pay a larger proportion. . . . The simple fact is that the States are abandoning the philosophy of public tuition-free higher education which has meant so much in building the American way of life, in striving for ever greater and greater equality of opportunity, and in providing the educated manpower for our rapidly expanding economy. (74:63–65)

The costs cited by Hollis are annual student expenditures for all items—tuition and living combined. Colvert surveyed the total educational costs in 1954–1955 in the public junior colleges from the standpoint of the institutional budget. He found a regional range in total current costs from $430.36 per student in the North Central region to $516.65 in the Western and Northwestern regions. In addition, he concluded that as a rule, the cost per student decreases with the increase in the size of enrollment, although there are some exceptions (25:396–401). There is evidence that recent total current costs per student range from approximately $600 to $725.

How are these expenditures financed? What trends are discernible in state legislation for the support of public junior colleges? Such legislation may be considered under the three headings of provision for buildings and capital outlay, provisions for state and local sharing of current costs of operation, and provision for tuition charges to students.

Capital Outlay. The cost of providing buildings and equipment for public junior colleges is divided between the state and the local district in a variety of patterns. Although most of the burden is borne by local districts, there is an increasing trend toward state assistance for this category of expenditures. In 1962, 14 of the states provided state funds for junior college capital outlays; 37 states authorized local revenues, from special district tax levies, or from district bond issues. Eleven of these states authorize a combination of state and local funds for capital outlay (99:42).

No specific recommendation about legislation for support of capital outlays for public junior colleges grows out of consideration of existing statutes. In general, it seems clear that some more adequate provision than "use of existing buildings" should be established by law; if the junior college is to be truly a community college, some local responsibility for planning and paying for the buildings would seem to be a wise provision. Also, local conditions may be met more flexibly if the law authorizes the local district to choose either the bond issue or the "pay-as-you-go" special tax method of paying for its share of capital outlays. Beyond this, the determination of proportions of the cost of grounds, buildings, and equipment to be borne by the state and the local district respectively, and of the limitations to be set on the amount of bonding capacity of a local district, depends on the history of such enactments in each state and on the prevailing political philosophy.

Current Costs. In 1948, Simms wrote that "The statutes of nine states provide for state aid for the public junior colleges [for current expenditures]. In two states the statutes specifically prohibit such aid" (*142*:117). In 1956, Martorana reported that thirteen states provided such aid (8:24), and his report on the action of the 1962 state legislatures increased the number to twenty-eight; ten states provided no state funds for current expenditures. There seems to be a definite trend, therefore, toward state participation in the financing of current expenditures of local public junior colleges. Medsker found that "The chief state school officers were fairly unanimous in their opinion that the ideal method of financing is by combinations of state and local effort" (69:263). Medsker pointed out in addition that

Despite the fact that local control and partial local support for a junior-college program may be desirable, its dual nature and its responsibility for serving in the realm of higher education make state support important for two reasons: (*a*) Many local communities cannot afford the entire burden on top of the strain in caring for elementary- and high-school students, and (*b*) it seems just as fair for the state to assist in the support of a segment of higher education carried on by junior colleges as for it to support the same kind of education in four-year colleges or state universities. (69:264)

The nature and proportion of state support differ widely among the states which authorize any state aid for junior colleges. Most of the states extend the fiscal provisions of their support of common schools to the locally controlled junior colleges, with some special definitions of units of attendance or of the minimum foundation amounts. In five states, separate legislation and appropriations provide for the support of public junior colleges in a variety of individual ways. Although no author has been willing to recommend that any single system of state aid be applied to all states, there is apparent agreement on the two principles that (1) generous state aid is essential for the development of a strong system of locally controlled public junior colleges, and (2) support for junior colleges should be distributed in a manner similar to that established for other units of the public school system, including provision for equalization aid to poorer districts if that aid is provided at other levels of the common schools.

Tuition Charges. The President's Commission on Higher Education recommended that public education through the fourteenth year of schooling be made available, tuition free, to all Americans able and willing to receive it, regardless of race, creed, color, sex, or economic and social status (70:Vol. V, 3). To this end, the Commission recommended the development of more "strategically located community colleges and technical institutes." Their ideal has not yet been achieved in most of the thirty-eight states that have enacted statutes to govern the establishment of locally controlled public junior colleges.

Two states—California and Illinois—provide not only that tuition shall be free to residents of the junior college district, but that nonjunior college districts in which students reside may pay to the junior college district the cost of their education. At the other extreme, eight states require the local junior colleges to charge tuition; three of them make tuition a condition to qualify for state aid. These states are Colorado, Connecticut, Idaho, Kansas, Maryland, Mississippi, Missouri, and Ohio (99:40). In sixteen states, tuition is authorized but not required. An example is Florida, which provides "that tuition or matriculation fees may be charged only if and as authorized by regulations of the State board" (50:Sec. 228.16 [4]).

Although present practice in tuition charges varies widely from state to state and even within states, both the philosophy and the functions of the community college require that the cost to the student be kept as low as possible. State laws should therefore permit and encourage local junior college districts to offer tuition-free instruction to district residents. Nonjunior college districts may well be required to pay the costs of instruction in lieu of tuition for those of their residents who attend a neighboring junior college. In this way the opportunities for higher education in America will become more nearly equal.

D. Federal Recognition of Community Colleges

After years of attempting to qualify, in its relations with the Federal Government, both for the privileges and grants available to institutions of higher education and for educational funds appropriated for courses of "less than college grade," the community colleges in 1963 and 1964 finally found their role clarified by Federal enactments that explicitly recognized junior colleges as institutions of higher education.

The Economic Opportunity Act of 1964 authorizes matching grants to junior colleges that take part in the operation of work-study programs for college students from low-income families, as well as for research, training, and demonstrations in the community action plan. The National Defense Education Act Amendments of 1964 extend the forgiveness feature for NDEA loans to junior college teachers, open up fellowships for graduate study to them, and extend support of guidance and counseling programs and of training institutes to higher education.

Most significant, perhaps, are the special provisions for junior college grants embodied in both the Higher Education Facilities Act of 1963, and the Vocational Education Act of 1963, both of which recognize the special contributions and needs of the community junior colleges.

The new Federal relationships of the community colleges open up tempting new opportunities for the expansion of their roles in education and new sources of funds. It is inevitable as well that greater involvement with Federal agencies will beget new legal problems, new patterns of accreditation, and new varieties of community institutions offering post-high-school education.

Selected References

Bogue, Jesse P. and Norman Burns. "Legal and Extra-Legal Influences for Improving Junior Colleges," Chapter XII in *The Public Junior College*. Nelson B. Henry (editor). The Fifty-fifth Yearbook of the National Society for the Study of Education, Part I. Chicago: The University of Chicago Press, 1956.

Colvert, C. C. "Cost per Student in the Public Junior Colleges in the United States," *Junior College Journal*, 27:396–401, March, 1957.

Hackett, Roger C. "Tuition Rates in Public Junior Colleges," *Junior College Journal*, 25:229–230, December, 1954.

Hollis, Ernest V. and associates. *Costs of Attending College*. Office of Education Bulletin, 1957, No. 9. Washington: Government Printing Office, 1957.

Morrison, D. G. and S. V. Martorana. *Criteria for the Establishment of 2-Year Colleges*. Office of Education Bulletin 1961, No. 2, Washington: Government Printing Office, 1963.

Martorana, S. V. "The Legal Status of American Public Junior Colleges," Chapter 4 in *American Junior Colleges* (Sixth Edition), Edmund J. Gleazer, Jr. (editor). Washington: American Council on Education, 1963.

———. "Recent Legislative Proposals Affecting Junior Colleges," *Junior College Journal*, 28:372–379, March, 1958; 30:381–389, March, 1960; and (with James K. Palmer) 32:297–405, March, 1962.

———. "Recent State Legislation Affecting Junior Colleges," *Junior College Journal*, 24:459–471, April, 1954; 26:328–341, February, 1956; 28:307–321, February, 1958; 30:310–326, February, 1960; (with James K. Palmer) 32:316–330, February, 1962; (with Robert F. McHugh) 36:27–36, March, 1966.

Medsker, Leland L. "Financing Public Junior College Operation," Chapter XIII in *The Public Junior College*. Nelson B. Henry (editor). The Fifty-fifth Yearbook of the National Society for the Study of Education, Part I. Chicago: The University of Chicago Press, 1956.

Principles of Legislative Action for Community Junior Colleges. Washington: American Association of Junior Colleges, 1962.

Simms, Charles Wesley. *The Present Legal Status of the Public Junior College.* Nashville: George Peabody College for Teachers, 1948.

"Some Aspects of the Status of Junior Colleges in the United States." A series of reports on individual states in the *Junior College Journal* from Volume 22 through Volume 27 (1951 through 1956).

State Junior College Advisory Board. *Five Years of Progress: Florida's Community Junior Colleges.* Tallahassee: State Department of Education, 1963.

8

Establishing the New Community Junior College

There is in America a select group of junior college administrators who have had the privilege of nurturing a college from the moment of its legal establishment through its growing pains to the achievement of full accreditation. A very few of these, moreover, were active in their communities in urging the original establishment of the local junior college. Their tales of their first offices in barns, in barracks, in hotel rooms, in church buildings, or in momentarily unused corners of high schools and of their seemingly unsurmountable early problems are part of the growing folklore of the junior college movement. An excellent sample of their labors is found in Chapman's story of Cuyahoga Community College in Cleveland, Ohio, as it prepared to open in the fall of 1963 (20).

Gleazer's studies for the American Association of Junior Colleges indicate that there will be a good many more of these innovating administrators:

> . . . Junior colleges are being established at a dramatic rate. During the period 1958 to 1962, 108 new junior colleges were established: 86 public; 14 church-related; and 8 independent nonprofit. . . . To our knowledge 18 junior colleges are slated for opening in the fall of 1963: 15 public; 2 church-related; and one independent nonprofit. Three new junior colleges, all public, are already [July, 1963] organized for opening in 1964. . . . [The American Association of Junior Colleges] sees other indications of tremendous growth. California will have 100 junior colleges by 1975; New York will have 40 publicly supported community colleges, and Florida

will have 35. . . . We can look toward the establishment of 20 to 30 community junior colleges each year. (46:11–12)

The present chapter outlines some of the principles, problems, and procedures involved in bringing a new community junior college through its very earliest stages. The first section will describe the steps from a local realization of the need through the legal authorization of the college; the second will present the work of the first administrative officers of the college in bringing it to the point where the first students may be enrolled in classes.

A. Securing Legal Authorization

Before a community junior college can be inaugurated, someone in the community must realize the need for additional educational opportunity. Such persons are not always educators—they may include newspaper editors, chamber of commerce leaders, PTA members, school boards, or any public-spirited layman, as well as the administrators in high schools or city school systems. Usually, such realization of need is not at first precise and clearly defined. Most leaders do not envisage at the outset the nature of the institution which they feel is needed. The existence of enabling legislation for junior colleges and of a number of successfully operating junior colleges in the state may help to focus attention on such colleges as an answer to the need. In general, however, some perceptive and responsible observer becomes concerned about opportunities for higher education and begins to interpret the need to others at the same time that he searches for an appropriate method of satisfying the need.

The existence of numbers of able high-school graduates who are not in college is likely to be noticed first as one of the evidences of the need for an additional college. Such a condition may arise from any of several causes. Thus, the effects of the depression led to the establishment in 1933 of the Palm Beach Junior College in Florida, and the imminent return of World War II veterans, whose education had been interrupted by military service, contributed to the founding of Montgomery Junior College in Maryland and of Orange County Community College in New York, as well as of some sixty other public junior colleges founded between 1946 and 1950 (53:Ch. 6, 7). In the second half of the twentieth century, the crowding of existing colleges, together with rising tuition costs and increasing need for educated technicians, has caused leaders in many communities to recognize a need for a community junior college. Finally, the factors of local pride and fiscal economy have always played a part in initiating new colleges. If neighboring communities have successful junior colleges to which local students must travel and to which they or the school district in which they reside must pay higher tuition, it is inevitable that sooner or later the desirability of a local junior college will be suggested.

Preliminary Studies. After it has come to the attention of the community that a junior college seems to be needed by young people and that the state has established legal procedures to provide one, several additional factors need to be studied before further action is pressed. Some estimate should be made, first, of the number of students who might be expected to enroll in such a local college. Are there enough annual high-school graduates in the contributing area to assure that the new college will be of adequate size? Are there groups of adults in the community (such as the returning veterans in the period 1945–1950) who will swell the enrollments permanently or temporarily? Is it likely that the number of youth needing education will grow or diminish in the foreseeable future? In various state laws, provision is made for either a minimum school enrollment or a minimum total district population before a junior college may be authorized. Early writers on the junior college, also, have suggested that a minimum prospective enrollment of 100, 200, or 300 students should be in sight to guarantee the success of a new college.

Such specific limitations seem unrealistic. Because so many variable conditions affect the desirability of founding a college, no concrete stipulations can apply to all areas. The need for a limited academic program in a remote area might justify recommending the establishment of a junior college for a prospective 100 or 150 students. In a more metropolitan area, with nearby junior colleges available, it would probably be unwise to plan an additional site unless at least 1000 day students, a comprehensive curriculum, and an extensive adult program were in sight.

Fretwell suggests several conditions which contribute to the establishment of public junior colleges. He points out that the community's need for a college must be realized by someone and translated into effective public *demand* before any action will be taken. This demand will be enhanced by realization that no colleges are available for the youth of the community in reasonable or economic proximity, or that the colleges that do exist are either overcrowded or too costly for many of the able young people who should go to college. An additional element of need is not often apparent to the lay public as they begin to think of higher education: that is, the newly developing need for diversity of educational opportunity beyond the high school for kinds of courses not offered in liberal arts colleges and not appropriate for them (53:126–127).

Opposition. As the idea of a local college is discussed more and more widely, negative arguments are certain to be advanced. The first point brought out by opponents of a junior college for a given community will probably be that of expense. Taxes are already prohibitively high, according to this view; there is not enough money to do an adequate job with the elementary and high-school students, and the public junior college will deprive children in order to pamper young adults. In addition, it may be argued that public education at local expense should end at grade twelve or before; beyond that age, the objection continues, education is of primary benefit to the student and to the state, not to the local community, and should be supported by student tuition and state taxes. If there exists within reasonable traveling distance a college or university of any kind, opponents of the local junior college idea will urge that it can be adapted to serve all the needs. Besides, it will be argued, there is no point in establishing a "partial" and "substandard" two-year institution when it might be possible to achieve a four-year college through state action or some other means. In some proposed districts which included extended areas with several cities of fairly equal size, dissension about the site of the college has been raised in order to divide the constituency and defeat a college proposal (53:Ch. 7).

Gaining Support. Once the idea of a community junior college has been conceived, therefore, two early steps seem absolutely essential to its eventual realization. The first is consultation with the local school administrators and school boards. In this way unnecessary duplication of effort can be avoided; in addition, these sources can supply accurate information about legal procedures for establishing local junior colleges, estimates of probable enrollment, effect of such a development on the tax rate and on the educational opportunity of younger pupils, avenues of approach to other areas which should be included in the junior college territory, and other useful services and consultation. On the other hand, if local school authorities either refuse to support or actively oppose the establishment of a junior college, it will be in some states impossible and in all states unwise to proceed further with the proposal until those attitudes are changed.

The second essential procedure, which should be undertaken early in the elaboration of the plans for college establishment, is a careful presentation of the entire concept of community junior college education and of the possibilities so far apparent locally to the press of the area. Junior colleges have been established in the face of influential newspaper opposition (53:Ch. 5); but the entire process of establishing the need, interpreting it clearly to the electorate, and securing authorization is facilitated if the editors of the region are fully informed of the progress of the idea. For this reason, it may be well to invite a competent authority on the junior college from the state department of education, a university, or elsewhere to meet with the editors and acquaint them with the community junior college concept and its local applicability, so far as it may be determined at this early stage.

State Approval. Although state regulations vary on steps to be followed in the establishment of junior college districts, the legislation surveyed in Chapter 7 indicates that a general basic pattern of procedure is emerging. Informal consultation by employees of the state department of education or other agency may have established the fact that a community junior college is feasible in the area. Following this the first formal action is likely to be a petition, either from a local school board or boards or from a number or percentage of qualified voters, requesting the established state agency to determine whether or not the area under consideration meets the criteria established by law for the approval of a public junior college. In accordance with the principle of local responsibility for public education, it is important that this first formal request be an expression of substantial local interest in the establishment of a college.

Following the receipt of the petition, the state department of education or other legally established office will investigate the likelihood of successful operation of a college in the area. In accordance with specific legal provisions and exercising the responsibility for judgment legally delegated to it, it will survey the assessed valuation, the population, the school population, the availability of other educational opportunity, the economic future of the area, and the attitudes of representative bodies of citizens. On the basis of its findings, it will arrive at one of several conclusions. Such a survey might reveal that no real need exists for a community junior college, that the community could not support one in acceptable fashion, or that the imminent decline of the community would make it unwise to invest in such a college. Again, the survey staff might approve the idea set forth in the petition but recommend changes in estimated enrollment, in preliminary listings of possible courses of study, in suggested site, or in other elements of the original and tentative plan submitted to them. It is more probable, if the preliminary work has been carefully planned and carried out, that the state survey will confirm the conclusions of the local sponsors of the movement and that submission of the proposal to the electors of the district will be approved.

Local Election. After approval by state survey authorities of the original proposal for the junior college, some states allow a local municipal or county school board to proceed with the establishment of the college, either as an adjunct of a high school or on a separate campus (53:94, 119). In other states the local authorities are required to submit the question of establishment to a vote of the people in the area of the new college. This procedure, of course, is slower and more costly. In addition, it may result in defeat of the entire proposal. There are nevertheless several practical advantages to the popular-election procedure. It facilitates public discussion and public understanding of the nature of the college; it brings into the open any latent opposition to the establishment and requires the voters to commit themselves on the proposal before final steps are taken. Thus the new college, when it is established, will be more widely understood and more firmly supported. The citizenry who must support the college and who will benefit by its existence will have had a direct and positive voice in its founding.

Governing Board. Independent community junior college districts must provide for a board of trustees after the voters have authorized the establishment of the district. When a local school board is the sponsoring body of the newly authorized community junior college, this step is not required; even so, the law may provide, as it does in Florida, for the naming of a college advisory board to consult with the president and to approve certain matters before they are acted upon by the legally responsible school board. In other states the laws provide for the appointment or the election of the board of trustees for the independent community college district. Upon their qualification, the first concerns of the new governing board must be to provide funds for the interim operation of the college until local taxes, state aid, and tuition fees are available, to provide space for the initial operation of the college, and to find a competent administrator to direct the development of the college.

B. Establishing the Authorized Community Junior College

Late in July, a president was chosen for a newly authorized community junior college. By mid-August, he had come to the community to begin his work. Before the end of August, an abandoned wartime building had been acquired and reconstruction had begun including a new roof, new exterior sheathing, new interior wallboard, and gallons of paint. At the same time, a dozen faculty members were employed, students were informed of the existence of the institution, and library orders were rushed to publishers. By mid-September, a basic program of lower-division courses was being taught to 180 students, about equally divided between full-time day and part-time evening registrants. The curriculum planning, the gathering of materials of instruction, the development of the college philosophy, and even the design of student record forms were completed at the same time as instruction was being offered. In its second year, the institution more than doubled its enrollment and was able to bring its borrowed building up to presentable status, while embarking on construction of its permanent campus on a nearby site.

Many school administrators would prefer to move more deliberately in preparing for the first year's instruction. The college described was organized separately from its supporting high schools (although under the same superintendent of schools and county board) and so was unable to make use of established facilities and of personnel who had been working together previously. Yet even when a public junior college is created in connection with a high school, a year or more of preplanning is very helpful to faculty, administrators, and students and to the initial quality of instruction (130).

In the separate community junior college district, a period of approximately a year between the legal authorization and the offering of the first full-scale program is not only useful but almost essential. A review of the tasks which must be accomplished will demonstrate the need for time. Again, it must be understood that in some of the organizational patterns for junior colleges, some of these arrangements may have been completed before the employment of the new chief administrator. The complete plan of procedure, however, is best described in relation to the supposition that an administrator is employed for a junior college district which is legally authorized, which has access to taxing power and to some initial appropriation of funds, and which has an enthusiastic board of trustees. Such a district would have no other employees and no property of any kind; the board might have been carrying on its business with borrowed offices and staff (53:76–83, 121). The community has voted for and expects a college to be established but has made no final commitments as to site, staff, or educational program. Since state provisions vary so widely, it is further assumed that money for capital outlays will be provided as needed in the manner appropriate to each state.

Time Schedule. One of the administrator's first concerns must be the establishment of a time schedule for operations, acceptable to his board of trustees, which can also be explained to the public through the press and in speeches. In such a plan, the most important date will be that agreed upon for welcoming the first full-time class to the college. College terms usually open in September; the administrator should, if at all possible, allow himself a minimum of nine months, and preferably a full year, to complete his preparations for that opening. With the target date in mind, he will schedule each of the major tasks that must be completed before then. Among them will be selection and preparation of a site, either temporary or permanent, detailed survey of educational needs of the community, decision on curriculums and courses to be offered, preparation of a catalog, selection of instructors and other college officers, interpretation of the institution to prospective students as well as to the public generally, preparation of a schedule of classes, procurement of books, equipment, and supplies, preopening orientation of the faculty, and registration of students.

A full description of the essential steps and the time sequence factors involved in establishing an actual new junior college is found in Benson's presentation of the use of computers in establishing "critical paths." In Benson's words,

An essential element of the [critical path] method is the necessity for explicitness in planning; it automatically requires the establishment of detailed plans as evidenced by the flow-chart network. The method provides management by objective as well as management by exception. . . . It can be a valuable aid to administrators faced with the task of establishing a new junior college. (46:34; also see 83:Ch. 8)

Site Selection. Usually the studies that led to the legal approval of the college will have included some consideration of possible sites for the first classes. The administrator will find it necessary to become familiar with these sites and to determine what kinds of contractual arrangements are necessary and what physical changes need to be made. Since the provision of facilities, including architectural work, bidding procedures, and actual construction or reconstruction are most time-consuming, this entire process must be one of the first activities of the new president. Junior colleges only rarely offer their first classes in new buildings designed especially for them; local high schools, churches, military buildings, dwellings—any building with sturdy walls and a roof—are used temporarily while a permanent home is being provided. Even though the entire curriculum cannot be foreseen so early in the planning, it is necessary to make concrete arrangements for a home for the college, maintaining flexibility so that adaptation in space assignment may be made as the analysis of educational needs progresses.

The question of a permanent site also requires early attention; enough is known about the requirements of junior colleges to allow decisions to be made on the basis of availability, extent, accessibility, and adaptability of any proposed site even before the final details of vocational and academic curriculums are determined. Some colleges have found that bitter and extended public debate, especially between rival communities, may be aroused over choice between two sites. It is highly important that the new administrator become acquainted as rapidly as he can with the characteristics of each possible site and with the educational advantages and disadvantages of each, so that he may properly evaluate the claims of local boosters for each site and recommend wisely to his board.

Survey of Needs. A general survey of educational needs, of course, was the basis for the establishment of the new community junior college. Yet it will be necessary for the new president to conduct a more detailed investigation as a basis for his later decisions. At the same time, the process of investigation itself can serve as a part of the interpretation of the college to the community and to its prospective students. One part of the survey will be directed at high-school students. From them it is possible to ascertain how many plan to go to college and specifically to the new college, what kinds of courses they think they need, what vocations they have chosen, and what activities they would want to engage in while at college. A good deal of informed judgment will be required both in the design of the questionnaire and in the interpretation of the answers. Certainly an interest of 127 boys in engineering courses, as an example, should not lead to immediate provision for that number of laboratory spaces. Such a study will be useful, even so, in indicating proportions of interest in the several possible fields of study; it serves, as well, to convince all students that the college is about to become a reality and intends to offer the courses they need.

A similar survey must be made of the business and industrial leaders of the communities. Employers, managers, labor union officials, chamber of commerce manager, placement officers, and any other knowledgeable persons should be interviewed about employment trends, training requirements, labor supply, and economic future of their specialty in the region in order that the college interviewer may form some judgment about feasible curriculums for the college. Here again, an opportunity is provided for the college official both to gain useful information and to provide interpretation of the college to its patrons.

After the results of these two surveys are tabulated and presented to the board of trustees, certain tentative decisions will be reached concerning educational opportunities to be offered, both for transfer to four-year colleges and for training for immediate employment. At this point it will be useful to call a meeting of interested adults, including many of those interviewed in the survey as well as leaders in every kind of local organization, to present for their criticism and suggestions the present status of the planning for the college. From such a meeting can come four beneficial results: revision of the educational planning on the basis of discussion in the meeting, informed public support and loyalty to the program, a realization by civic leaders that their advice had been considered and applied, and a list of names of able and interested persons for assignment to the several advisory committees which will begin to help in developing details of curriculums, especially in the occupational fields.

Until this time, all decisions have been tentative and subject to revision. After the survey results have been presented to the college board and to the citizens' meeting, the tempo of events increases. The citizens' meeting may be considered as a "point of no return" in the planning for the college. Decisions reached in the light of all of the investigations to date are final; action on them is required.

Study of other colleges will be helpful at this time. Some of the curriculums adopted are planned to prepare students for transfer to parallel curriculums at nearby colleges and universities. For this reason, consultation is in order with admissions officers and deans of the institutions to which future students seem most likely to transfer, so that appropriate parallel courses may be established. Although the four-year institutions will not agree with each other entirely on course organization, they will probably all agree to accept any course which is equivalent in content and standard to that offered by any one of them. On the basis of study of their catalogs supplemented by conferences with each, decisions can be reached on the minimum essential offerings in each of the subject fields. How many semester courses in which foreign languages? How to arrange the sequence of courses in college algebra, analytic geometry, calculus? What topics in physics? In chemistry? What courses in history? In economics? In sociology? How to determine eligibility for freshmen English? Answers to such questions are preliminary both to publication of the catalog and to employment of faculty members.

Existing community junior colleges should also be consulted at this point. The new institution will not wish to pattern itself identically after a neighboring college even if it is in the same district and under the same board of trustees. Yet the experience of other similar colleges can be invaluable in learning of special techniques, triumphs and failures, successful and unhappy solutions to problems of all sorts. A neighboring college will share solutions to problems of transfer-course organization, of catalog and schedule preparation, of vocational-course equipment and planning, and even of necessary student accounting forms.

Employing Faculty. The preparation of a catalog and the employment of faculty can proceed simultaneously. Once decisions have been reached about the probable number of students in the first year and the scope of the courses to be offered for them, a table of organization can be drawn up to indicate what administrative, counseling, and instructional personnel will be needed, with qualifications and salary scale for each. It is possible that the search for qualified instructors will consume most of the time of the college president for several months. Even though he will know several persons whom he wishes to invite to join him without further search, he will find that in other areas he must interview seven or eight applicants before finding one with whom he is satisfied and who wishes to undertake the burdens of a pioneering venture. In addition, it is entirely possible that the local survey will lead to the decision to inaugurate an occupational curriculum for which it is almost impossible to discover qualified instructors. In such a case, it may become necessary to postpone the offering of the course.

The catalog will serve the entire district as one of the basic sources of information about the college. For this reason it should be prepared carefully, illustrated attractively, printed in quantity, and distributed widely. It is false economy and penurious public relations to prepare an inadequate number of official catalogs. It is especially important in the first year of the college to provide an impression of permanence and substance to all the patrons, and a well-prepared catalog can contribute measurably to this impression. It should present the history, the purposes, the regulations, and the educational offerings of the college in the clearest and most dignified fashion possible.

Equipment. A new independent public junior college, of course, will have no backlog of equipment or of books; everything must be acquired. For this reason, every instructor, as soon as he accepts the offer of employment, should be asked to develop in detail a list of equipment, supplies, and library books that he will need for his courses during the first year. If possible, he should be informed of the total sum available for his courses; in any event, his lists should be segregated to indicate the items that are absoluately essential, those that are highly desirable, and those that could be deferred to a later date. Since many items in the requests of instructors will duplicate each other, it will become almost a full-time job for a competent clerk to keep track of materials already ordered, to make certain that unnecessary duplicates are not ordered, and to distribute the incoming books and materials to the proper recipients.

Informing Students. Simultaneously with the development of other aspects of the college—site, program, faculty, equipment—attention must be paid to the prospective student body. Among the high-school seniors of the district will be many who had planned to go elsewhere to college and some who had given up hope of college because of expense or because they knew of no courses that would meet their needs. Some members of each of these groups must be recruited for the new college; a continuous program of information and interpretation is required. The high-school newspaper can aid in these efforts by announcing the various achievements in developing curriculum, acquiring site, and employing instructors. The cooperation of the high-school principal and teachers of seniors will be very helpful, especially if a program of college aptitude tests or a series of talks to senior classes can be arranged. The distribution of the catalog, the schedule of classes, or a letter to parents of high-school students can be followed by preregistration interviews in the high school before graduation day. Unless the students are informed early and continuously of the progress of the college, they will not be able to plan to attend it. On the other hand, such energetic efforts to inform high-school seniors and to enlist their support during early planning of the college instructional program and of student activities help to create a favorable spirit and a positive enthusiasm on the part of the first students.

In-Service Training of Faculty. The newly employed faculty should be brought to the campus well in advance of the first day of classes. They will need to complete a good many routine tasks which only they can do, such as storage of chemicals or specimens for laboratories or assembling of complicated specialized equipment and arrangement of their classrooms to suit their purposes. Equally important are the orientation sessions by which they become acquainted with each other, with the administration, with the college, and with the community. In these sessions also they can begin to develop agreement on some elements of the college philosophy. Since students will be gathering for final registration in the days before the opening of instruction, the instructors will be needed to help in advising them.

It is apparent from the description of the tasks to be completed in preparing for the opening of a new college that a considerable period of time, at least nine months to a year, is desirable for their successful completion. Certainly their accomplishment would seem to necessitate the employment of some help for the administrator; he will need a purchasing agent or business manager, certainly, and probably a dean of instruction to care for the surveys, the catalog, the schedule, and other details of establishing the instructional program. Colleges have been opened more rapidly and with less professional assistance. Yet if the college is to attain its full educational scope, stature, and quality at the earliest possible moment, it is important that it be thoroughly and soundly established.

Fretwell summarizes the entire founding process in this paragraph:

When the five steps are completed, some people will think that a junior college has been created. It hasn't, quite. True, these are certain of the steps necessary in order to measure need and probable response, meet legal requirements, identify prime movers and citizen supporters, and work out arrangements for facilities, funds, administrators and staff. The new junior college is really in operation, however, only when it is offering a program . . . that really means something to the people it is set up to serve. If the new institution does these things well and continues to merit community confidence and support, it has reached full stature. By then its prime movers will have rendered a lasting service to the community. (69:297–298)

Selected References

Bastian, Mildred E. "How We Created a Junior College District," *Junior College Journal,* 33:10–15, February, 1963.

Chapman, Charles E. "Ohio Joins the Club," *Junior College Journal,* 35:8–12, October, 1964.

Establishing Junior Colleges, A Report of a National Conference. Occasional Report Number 5, Junior College Leadership Program. Los Angeles: University of California, 1964.

Fretwell, Elbert K., Jr. "Establishing a Junior College," Chapter XIV in *The Public Junior College.* Nelson B. Henry (editor). Fifty-fifth Yearbook of the National Society for the Study of Education, Part I. Chicago: The University of Chicago Press, 1956.

———. *Founding Public Junior Colleges.* New York: Teachers College, Columbia University, 1954.

Johnson, B. Lamar. *Starting a Community Junior College.* Washington: American Association of Junior Colleges, 1964.

Peterson, Basil H. and James W. Thornton, Jr., "Building a Functional Program for a Junior College," *Junior College Journal,* 19:119–124, November, 1948.

———. "A Comprehensive Pattern of Vocational Education," *Junior College Journal,* 19:446–451, April, 1949.

Price, Hugh C. "Planning for Public Junior College Development through State and National Surveys," *Junior College Journal,* 20:16–22, September, 1949.

Rawlinson, Howard E. "Preliminary Planning for a New Junior College," *Junior College Journal,* 29:186–190, December, 1958.

9

Administration of the Community Junior College

Previous chapters have described some of the variations in size, in objective, and in legal support and control of community junior colleges. No single chart of administrative organization could include appropriate officers and lines of responsibility for all these kinds of institutions. Even in colleges that are similar in size and type of legal control, local considerations may lead to substantial differences in the names of the various administrative officers and in the grouping of their duties. Moreover, it is important to realize that the arrangement of administrative titles and assignments according to one scheme or another does not in itself achieve any purpose; it merely makes it more convenient for the responsible officers to work harmoniously. The most sophisticated organization will not assure effective functioning of inept or uncooperative staff members, whereas a primitive and haphazard arrangement may yield good results if it is manned by devoted and able administrators. Nevertheless, a clear statement of administrative responsibilities and lines of authority can help to eliminate duplication or conflict of effort and to provide each officer with a secure understanding of his relation to other workers and to the total task of the college.

In spite of the diversity of their organization and control, community junior colleges of all sizes share many common objectives. The attainment of these objectives by the teaching faculty and the students requires leadership, planning, coordination, financing, housekeeping, supervision, and evaluation. It is the task of the administrative staff

116

to carry out these functions in such fashion that the instructional staff may work smoothly, without unnecessary difficulties, and with high morale at the fundamental job of the college—instructing students. The present chapter discusses some of the administrative functions necessary in any type of junior college. A consideration of the purposes and functions of the college board of trustees is followed by discussions of administrative tasks closely related to instruction and of supportive or secondary functions. The final section of the chapter presents a suggested administrative organization for a sizable community junior college which may be adapted quite simply to other varieties of junior colleges.

A. The Community Junior College Board of Trustees

Locally controlled community junior colleges are governed in much the same way as other elements of the public schools. In unified districts, the same board determines policy for all the schools, from kindergarten through junior college; in separate junior college districts, the board of trustees is established to deal only with the problems of the junior college, leaving policies for the elementary and high schools to the appropriate board or boards.

Extension centers of state universities, on the other hand, and junior colleges operated as units in a statewide system of higher education will have only a remote relation to the Board of Regents or the State Board of Control. Although the descriptions of school-board functions found in the literature on public school administration might be adapted to serve as guides to statewide boards of control, they are intended primarily to apply to locally elected boards having responsibility for the operation and control of a single school district. Such districts almost never include more area than one county; frequently they are limited in area to a township, a municipality, or other comparatively small unit. The board members of such a district are therefore residents of the community, acquainted with its people and its problems, and concerned about the optimum development of a program of education for the local people.

According to a yearbook of the American Association of School Administrators, the chief responsibilities of school boards are:

1. To develop and constantly improve the educational program.
2. To provide personnel for staffing the school program.
3. To provide and maintain an educationally efficient physical plant.
4. To secure adequate financial resources.

5. To maintain a two-way contact with the adult community and the schools.

6. To choose the chief executive and work harmoniously with him. (*135:35*)

In the execution of these responsibilities, school boards face many dangers. A board may see itself as an administrative rather than a policy-making body. In this case the superintendent, who should be the professionally trained executive officer of the board, administering the affairs of the district in accordance with the law and the established policies of the board, is reduced to the position of errand boy, with little opportunity to exercise judgment or leadership. At the same time, preoccupation with administrative detail prevents the board from devoting its attention to policy matters and to the development of the educational program. An example may be found within the second responsibility just listed. Some boards attempt to interview applicants for employment and to nominate candidates from their own acquaintances. In the days of the one-teacher rural school, this was a necessary practice; in the choice of a superintendent of schools, it remains one of the board's major responsibilities. In relation to teaching positions, however, the board's responsibility is to establish the number and nature of the positions to be filled for the next year. The superintendent then interviews candidates and recommends to the board those he considers most qualified. If for some reason the board is unwilling to accept any of the recommended teachers, it does not seek a substitute, but requests the superintendent to recommend another applicant. The line between policy forming and its execution is sometimes a fine one, but it must be scrupulously observed in order to realize the values of the uniquely American combination of lay control and professional leadership of the public schools.

An equal and opposite danger, of course, is that the board will relinquish its duties of policy making and evaluation to the superintendent, so that the board becomes in effect only a rubber stamp. Although some critics of school boards have suggested that they be abolished in favor of completely professional management of the schools, most educators and probably most citizens would agree with the point of view of the American Association of School Administrators:

School board members represent the people who own and support the schools. They form a grass roots organization which is closer to the people than to any other form of government. They voice the wishes and aspirations of the parents and the children. They spend the local taxpayers' money and are responsible to their neighbors for the action. They are the trustees of a great public responsibility. (*135:27*)

In the exercise of their trusteeship, the board and the superintendent must work as a harmonious team. The superintendent reports basic information of all sorts that is essential to good policy making and recommends policies which he judges will be effective. The board considers all of these matters in the light of its understanding of the desires of the community, the financial ability of the district, and the basic wisdom of the several board members, and reaches its decision. It is a fundamental concept in many areas of American life that policies thus decided by a pooling of information, experience, and judgment will in a majority of cases be sounder than those arrived at authoritatively by an individual. The executive application of policy to concrete cases often requires immediate decision by the administrator; this is the role of the superintendent. The policy in accordance with which such decisions are made, however, should be elaborated deliberately, cooperatively, and in the light of the best information available; this is the role of the board of trustees.

Among suitable areas for policy making by the board of trustees of a community junior college may be listed

1. the adoption of a statement of the purposes of the college,

2. policies affecting the admission, control, and graduation of students,

3. personnel policies, including employment practices, salary schedules, working conditions, and fringe benefits,

4. development, use, and maintenance of sites, buildings, and equipment,

5. financial procedures in budgeting and expending funds,

6. relations with other colleges and with governmental agencies, and

7. its own procedural rules.

Board Rules. The relationship between school board, superintendent, faculty, and the public may be safeguarded by the adoption and publication of "Board Rules and Regulations" in which policy decisions gathered from minutes of board meetings are codified and if necessary extended. Although in such policy statements it is impossible and probably undesirable to provide for every contingency, the adoption by the board of a compilation of policy decisions as evidence of its present philosophy and practice facilitates mutual understanding and cooperation on the part of all who are concerned with the college. The board and the superintendent should review the rules and regulations periodically with the purpose of eliminating nonfunctional or out-moded provisions and including newly developed policies (*85*).

A *faculty manual* is a useful adjunct to the board rules and regulations. Such a volume sets forth the philosophy of the college, the responsibilities of various officers and faculty members, and established procedures in relation to employment, promotion, expenditures of college funds, relations with students, and similar matters on which instructors need to be uniformly and reliably informed. It too should be adopted by the board as a statement of board policy and revised periodically (*86*). Because the *annual catalog* contains many statements of policy regarding courses of study and student progress, it is important for the board to be informed in advance of the changes of basic policy to be introduced into each annual edition. If it has approved, in advance of printing, changes in curricular descriptions, grading policies, graduation requirements, and other important matters, the board will be able to accept by resolution each successive issue of the college catalog. Such acceptance officially establishes the catalog statements as elements of board rules and regulations.

A public junior college board of trustees which clearly understands its own proper relationships to its community and to its college is a basic element in effective administration. If such a board chooses a superintendent of the college district with similarly clear understanding and develops rules and regulations that clarify the relationships and duties of all employees, smooth running of the entire junior college is virtually assured.

B. Instructional Tasks of Administration

Some aspects of the work of the college administrator have a direct effect on the nature and the quality of instruction in the college. Other administrative procedures may be considered as supporting instruction, but not directly affecting its quality. Among the former, continuing study of community educational needs, use of lay advisory committees, development of the curriculum, selection of teachers, scheduling of classes, supervision of instruction, in-service training of instructors, evaluation, and fostering of student government are considered in the present section. The supportive tasks of administration will be discussed in a succeeding section of the chapter.

Community Surveys. Every junior college serves its own selected clientele and succeeds or fails in the same degree that it understands and provides for the educational needs of that clientele. The community junior college has accepted as its clientele the supporting community and attempts to meet the educational needs, beyond the high school but short of the bachelor's degree, of young people and adults. Such a college is established only after careful surveys of the local community have demonstrated the need for it; its courses of study are elaborated after further detailed investigation of specific curricular possibilities.

But communities change. Educational needs emerge or wane. The junior college administrator must never assume that he has completed his study of his community and that he can establish his curriculum once and for all. Instead, he must provide both for uninterrupted continuous study of his community and for periodic intensive resurveys. Such constant concern provides the basis for the steady development of the college toward more and more adequate educational service. The day-to-day study of community trends will consist in part simply of alert observation of local developments such as the influx of new industries, the overcrowding of the lower schools, the gain or loss of population in the area, and general social or technological changes that require new emphases in the college program. More formally, a sizable district may assign a faculty member to devote part of his time to this continuing search for the facts on which educational decisions may be based. Sometimes a coordinator of vocational education, for example, will be requested to report periodically on such facts as trends in the area, ideas of employer and labor groups about needed offerings, indications of coming needs for more courses or different courses, evidences of satisfaction or dissatisfaction of employers with junior-college-trained employees, and similar data. Such observations are not likely to be well done if they are only by-products of the chief administrator's daily rounds; someone must assume the stated responsibility for them lest they be lost, and their educational meaning with them, beneath the bustling busynesses of operational tediums.

There is much value also in a periodic full-scale resurvey of the community, similar to that completed before the establishment of the junior college. In addition to the information such a resurvey affords for curricular planning, it can provide two very useful results. Instructors who participate in such a survey, gathering statistics, interviewing citizens, visiting offices and factories, will learn about their community in ways that will inevitably help them to become better teachers. At the same time, the citizens and graduates interviewed will gain a new understanding of the purposes of the college and an enhanced regard for the quality of its efforts. Primarily, of course, the purpose of the survey is to provide an up-to-date description of the educational needs of the college communities. It will consider such data as population change, business and industrial activity, occupational distribution and trends, characteristics of present students, follow-up of former students in universities and on the job, forecast of future enrollments, and evaluation of the educational program of the college. Other activities may seem to the administrator more immediately pressing than the careful study of his community, but surely this one is essential and fundamental as a guide and justification for all the other activities of administrators, instructors, and students.

Lay Advisory Committees. In the several specialized areas of the curriculum, additional effective information from the community may be gained by the use of lay advisory committees. Originally formed to assist in the design and development of curriculums in vocational education, such committees in any instructional field are useful adjuncts to administration. Thus a community junior college might well establish lay advisory committees for each of its operating or contemplated vocational and technical curriculums, for several specialties in business, in homemaking, in engineering, in general education, or for any other area where details of the curriculum, placement of graduates, selection of equipment, opportunities for field trips and guest speakers, or any aspect of instruction might be appreciably improved by the practical advice of a group of informed laymen (*81*:314–316). The leadership of these advisory committees will ordinarily be exercised by the junior college administrative staff; they will meet on call to consider reports of progress in developing the program and to advise on methods of improving and extending it. Although advisory committees are always consultative rather than legislative or policy-making groups, the college programs will benefit measurably from careful consideration of their suggestions.

Proposals for added courses and curriculums, of course, will come from instructors and from students as well as from the more formal studies described above. From time to time, also, consideration must be given to the elimination of courses which duplicate other offerings or which are no longer educationally useful or economically desirable. Not all suggestions for the installation of courses will be sound ones; the survey staffs, specialized lay advisory committees, or departmental faculty members may serve well in their respective areas but fail to consider all aspects of a complete curriculum. Such groups are quite unlikely to propose any fundamental re-evaluation of the entire pattern of requirements for graduation, or of general education courses, or of any practices whose effects extend beyond their limited responsibility. For these reasons, after all possible facts and insights have been assembled from all sources, the fundamental responsibility of leadership in the development of the junior college curriculum rests on the administrative staff. If administrative organization and operation stress the importance of this function, the board of trustees, the faculty, and the community will be interested and effective in their several roles. On the other hand, if secondary factors are given priority by the administrative staff, the curriculum will fail to serve well the community's ᴖducational needs.

Teacher Selection. For this same reason, one of the most important tasks of administration is the careful selection of teachers. It is perhaps ironic to speak of selecting teachers in a period of severe scarcity. Yet the difficulty of the task does not excuse the administrator from searching diligently for the best instructors available to him. At each registration period he will gather data that will enable him to analyze past trends in enrollments by courses and to forecast with considerable accuracy his future needs for faculty expansion. He will request the board to approve new positions at the earliest possible moment, so that he may notify placement agencies and begin interviewing candidates. So important is this administrative responsibility that some junior college administrators budget considerable amounts of time and money for travel to interview applicants. In the final analysis, the classroom teacher is the embodiment of the effective college curriculum. He is the most important employee of the college. The administrator who fails to choose good instructors, fails.

Class Schedules. The same registration information that enables the administrator to forecast his needs for additional instructors is useful also in developing the schedule of classes. After a policy on class size in the various instructional areas has been calculated, the number of sections needed is determined by simple division. The scheduling of classes, however, requires perceptive judgment based on a balance of four factors. The most important consideration is the ability of all students who need a given class to fit it into their schedules. When multiple sections can be offered in most courses, this requirement is no problem. When only one section can be offered in each of several important courses, careful cross-checking of curricular patterns will reveal conflicts and ways to their resolution. The conscientious schedule maker will work out a trial student schedule for each of the major curriculums offered by the college, in order to discover cases in which two courses required of the same student in the same semester appear at the same hour in the preliminary draft. The availability of rooms is another factor in schedule making—if the college has only one chemistry laboratory, some of the laboratory sections must be scheduled at unpopular hours. On the other hand, even where there are enough rooms, it is important to arrange for a balanced offering throughout the college day. If fifty classes are offered at one hour and one hundred classes the next to the same student body, the first set of classes will have overlarge enrollments whereas the enrollments in the second set will be comparatively small. Finally, it is important in scheduling to consider as far as possible the convenience of the instructor. A free period before a laboratory class, or two consecutive sections of the same course, or the preservation of a reasonable block of free time for conference, correction, and preparation mean a great deal to the morale of instructors. Schedule making is the delicate art of harmonizing all these factors so that the instructional objectives of the college can be achieved with the greatest effectiveness and with economy of effort and of capital resources.

Many of the tedious tasks of schedule making and schedule checking can be performed by punched card computers. Cosand describes a process through which several "trial runs" even in advance of the opening of a college enabled the administrative staff to be sure of the number and capacity of classrooms needed. In addition, the computer simulation checked the projected schedule to make certain that faculty members were assigned without conflicts and that students in all majors would be able to register for the classes they needed (30:50).

Supervision of Instruction. Supervision of junior college instruction is another administrative responsibility. It is carried on for one reason—to improve teaching and learning. In the pursuit of this goal, it cannot be denied that the administrator who visits classes is attempting to assess the quality of the instruction and learning and that he will base some of his judgments about reemployment of teachers on his observations. It is a mistake, though for the administrator and the teacher to limit their concept of supervision only to classroom visitation, or to assume that its only purpose is evaluation of the teacher. If the teacher and the administrator see themselves as partners in the educational process, class visits will be seen as one method to enable the administrator to serve the teacher better. It is the only way in which the administrator can maintain meaningful contact with classroom problems, gain a first-hand understanding of the full scope of the curriculum, reach a realistic appreciation of his faculty, and come to see the true relationship between the physical environment (the administrator's traditional concern) and the quality of instruction. Such visitation not only emphasizes that the administration is honestly interested in high quality of instruction, but it can also lead to stimulation of a college-wide desire for continuous improvement in an atmosphere of freedom. Supervision has been, in some junior colleges and in an earlier period, authoritarian and threatening rather than helpful. It need not be so; properly understood, it is the soundest approach to improved faculty status. It enables the administrator to speak with confidence and knowledge when he discusses the high quality of junior college instruction.

In-Service Training. Hand in hand with classroom visitation and consultation must go a program of in-service training for faculty members. Few junior college instructors have had the preservice training to help them understand the distinctive opportunities and requirements of teaching in this kind of college. Even those who have had such training can profit from a continuing study of their current problems. It is a responsibility of the administrator to develop plans for experiences which will add to the breadth and depth of faculty understanding and appreciation of their significant role in American education. Participation in the community resurvey has been mentioned as one step in this process of in-service training. Vacation-time workshops, with added pay, can help faculty members within an instructional division seek better answers to problems of the organization of courses and the development of instructional materials. Faculty meetings, before the opening of the term and during it, can be devoted to presentations by instructors of the work and objectives of the several divisions of the college or consideration of descriptive data about students. Addresses by competent outsiders on the topic of their competence—not necessarily junior college topics—can help broaden the horizons of the faculty. It will often be true that a faculty will appreciate and profit more from a presentation by their own colleagues of aspects of a college problem than they will from an "expert" presentation, yet both are needed in a complete program of continuing faculty growth.

Evaluation. Improvement of instruction can be based only on accurate assessment of present status, and although it is very difficult to obtain adequate and accurate evaluative data, some meaningful indicators of quality can be gathered. Standardized examinations are one measure of some of the outcomes of instruction. If the examinations are truly appropriate for the subject matter and for the students tested and if the comparative norms can be accepted as proper bases for comparison, much can be learned from standardized examinations about the effectiveness of the instruction in the community junior college. Because of difficulties both in choice of examination and in interpretation of results, and because the purposes of the community junior college transcend the transmission of information, other kinds of evaluation must be added to that of standardized examinations. The success of transfer students in later study provides an additional indication of the quality of the junior college. Preparation for transfer is only one part of the community junior college program, and certainly the college is not the only factor affecting the success or failure of its transferring students; within these limitations, however, transfer-student success adds to evaluative information.

Less frequently studied is the success of terminal students, employed in jobs for which they trained at the college. A further source of evaluative insight is the student who drops out of junior college before he completes his course. Sometimes he may represent a failure by the junior college and in others a real success. Too few community junior colleges have been able to study thoroughly their withdrawing students, either while they are withdrawing or after a period of time.

Because of the diffuse nature of the adult program with its many constituencies, it is even more difficult to evaluate this aspect of the program. Public opinion is perhaps the most accessible index to college performance in this area; the program is established to serve the needs of adults, who can surely be trusted to judge well whether or not those needs have been satisfied. From whatever source the information is gathered, evaluation serves as a fruitful starting point for improvement; an organized evaluative program is a constant concern of administrators.

Student Government. Student government is also listed as an administrative task closely related to instruction, since student government is fostered in community junior colleges mainly for its contributions to the education of students. Some officer of administration must bear the primary responsibility for helping to organize the student government and for advising the student officers in carrying on their responsibilities and associated functions. In some community junior colleges, the board of trustees formally delegates certain responsibility to the student government. This practice not only clarifies the precise nature of student authority but serves as a reminder of the obligation of the faculty and the board to exercise supervision and at times even a veto power over student government.

C. Supporting Functions of Administration

Land and Buildings. The provision of land and buildings for junior colleges is a major concern in any public district. School administrators, particularly in our growing cities, must plan years ahead to provide adequate sites for their schools and junior colleges before all appropriate acreage is subdivided and built upon and before land costs skyrocket. This problem is intensified for the community junior college by the requirement of sixty to eighty acres for an adequate campus; if sufficient parking space for student automobiles is to be provided, enough land must be added to allow one parking space per student. Foresight is required on the part of the superintendent and of the board if the growing junior colleges in many states are to have suitable sites.

The development of building plans is another time-consuming aspect of the business administration of the college. After forecasts of probable enrollments over a twenty-year period have been determined, it is possible to delineate the specifications for a desirable site. Next, a master plan for campus development must be drawn up by the cooperative effort of faculty, administrators, board of trustees, and architects. Certainly such a plan cannot be correct in all its details, but it is essential to develop a concept of the final state of the college plant if hideous flaws in early buildings and major inconveniences in later developments are to be avoided. The public junior college that can find temporary quarters for its first several years of operation is fortunate. Then the master plan, the plan of finance for buildings, and the detailed plans for each building can be developed carefully and critically, with ample consideration by faculty members as well as by architects and administrators.

Finance. The financing of the community junior college program, as well as the careful budgeting and expenditure of funds, is another area that the instructor may take for granted, although the administrator must spend a major part of his time on it. Publicly supported junior colleges receive stipulated sums from their local communities and from the state. In several states these funds are allocated in accordance with complicated formulas. The average daily attendance of students, the tax effort of the local district, the number of instructional units, the established minimum foundation program, and the indebtedness of the junior college district are some of the factors used in determining state support. In addition, state laws ordinarily require the development of a detailed budget for the expenditure of district funds which must be approved before moneys are allocated; all records involved in the calculation, receipt, and disbursement of funds are subject to audit by designated authority.

Research. Research into all aspects of the college program is another function of administration. Wise decisions require adequate information. The regular assembling of such information will enable college officers to solve easily many questions of daily procedure, while also providing a firm basis for long-range planning in the light of past trends. An example of the scope of such statistical summaries gathered during the course of a single year is found in the *Annual Report of the Superintendent, 1963–1964,* of Orange Coast Junior College District. The *Report* begins with "Student Population," presenting tables on Enrollment Facts, Average Daily Attendance, Growth of the College, Source of Students, Graduates, Characteristics of Students (Semester of Attendance, Major Fields, Hours of Employment per Week, Age Distribution), and similar background information. A section on "Instructional Program" gives a descriptive account of the year's history in the eight instructional divisions, including new courses approved during the year, and efforts and evidence relating to the improvement of instruction. Other major sections of the report include "Research and Evaluation," "Building Program," and "Financial Reports." In each section, data are presented in tabular or narrative form, accompanied by comparisons with earlier years (4). Such a summary serves not only to inform the Board of Trustees of pertinent facts about their junior college, but it also enables the administration to plan effectively for the future in the light of recent trends.

Public Interpretation. The superintendent's *Annual Report* also can help in the interpretation of the junior college to its community, as do the student paper, the annual, the catalog, the football programs, and printed schedules and announcements of specialized curriculums. Printed matter, however, is not the only means of cultivating public relations. Because of the intimate dependence of the public junior college on its local community, a constant stream of information and interpretation is necessary. Every instructor and every student contributes daily to this cultivation of relations, good or bad; in addition, many community junior colleges are adding a full-time or part-time director of public relations. Such an officer seeks to keep the patrons of the junior college fully and continuously informed, so that the college may merit cooperation and support, and the public will make use of its services. Although the administration is responsible for the organized program of public relations, all activities of the college and of its students, faculty, and administrators contribute to the total impression of the college in the minds of the public.

D. Organization for Administration

All the instructional and supportive duties listed for administrators, as well as others too numerous and too intricate for summary discussion, require personnel. Current fund expenditures for higher education in 1961–1962 allocated 10.2% to administration, and 30.8% to instruction. The remainder of current costs included libraries (2.5%), operation and maintenance (7.9%), organized research (20.6%), "other educational and general expenditures" (8.6%), and auxiliary and student aid expenditures (19.3%) (*143*:100).

The appointment of competent officers for these administrative tasks and definition of their responsibilities and their relationships is a major element of the success of the superintendent and the board. Titles of officers will vary in the several types of community junior college organization and control, but in all of them certain tasks must be accomplished. Clear-cut assignment of responsibility can be achieved only through analysis and description of the work to be done. It is on this basis that administrative organization can be developed.

The executive head of a community junior college has four major areas of responsibility. In the smallest junior colleges, he exercises all of them himself; in the largest, he must subdivide and delegate responsibility to such an extent that he will have only indirect knowledge of some facets of the instructional program. In the simplest organization, the junior college president is directly concerned with

1. the board of trustees and the supporting public,
2. financial aspects of the college operation,
3. buildings and grounds,
4. the entire program of instruction.

As the enrollment of students and the number of faculty increase, each of these areas will grow in complexity.

Board and Public Relationships are a responsibility that will never be delegated by the community junior college president. In unified school districts, of course, these are the direct concern of the district superintendent rather than of the college president; here the president manages most of the relations between the junior college and the central office. In separate junior college districts, the president, as the executive officer of the elected board of trustees, will serve as the direct channel of information and policy recommendation from the college to the board. He will add assistants to help him discharge his responsibilities, but not through delegation of authority. He may need to add secretaries to keep board minutes and assist with preparing for board meetings and a public relations officer, possibly an instructor, to prepare press releases and to assist with the interpretation of the community junior college to the people. He will wish to secure the aid of his administrative staff and faculty in developing policies by means of executive councils or faculty committees which can be either permanent or appointed for specific problems. He will encourage all members of the faculty to consider themselves as interpreters of the college to the community; he may request subordinate officers to attend board meetings as resource persons and observers. In the final analysis, however, the president himself represents the community junior college to the board and to the public.

The Financial Operation of the community junior college is the responsibility which the wise administrator will delegate at the earliest possible moment as his college grows. The detailed and time-consuming work required in gathering data for budgets and in accounting for receipts and disbursements would interfere with other necessary work of the president. He will need to keep constantly informed of the state of the finances of the college; he will devote considerable attention to the development and presentation of the budget as an instrument of educational policy; he cannot abdicate his ultimate responsibility to see that the financial affairs of the college are capably and honestly managed. Nevertheless, the day-to-day accounting for income from tax sources, from tuition fees, from the several enterprises of the college or of the student body and their disbursement according to law and the policies of the board will be the responsibility of a comptroller or bursar, who will prepare periodic reports on all financial matters for the information of the president. His subordinates will include accountants and managers of such businesses as the bookstore or cafeteria.

The Physical Aspects of the community junior college are a third area of the administrative responsibility of the president. These matters will be delegated to a business manager, who will be responsible for preliminary analysis of new site needs and building requirements, for the maintenance of existing buildings and equipment, for the procurement of supplies and equipment needed in the instructional program, and for the transportation of students and faculty, if any is provided. The business manager in turn may be aided according to the size of the college by a superintendent of buildings and grounds, a purchasing agent, or a transportation superintendent.

The Educational Responsibility of the president is the most important and complex and requires the most extensive delegation of authority. Two major aspects are student personnel and instruction. A sizable community junior college might well employ a Dean of the College to bear most of the delegated responsibility for the educational program. He would be assisted by a Dean of Student Personnel, who would plan and supervise guidance services, student activities, student government, health services, registration, and records, with such assistance as those tasks required. The Dean of Instruction would participate in recruitment of faculty and care for the development of the curriculum, the preparation of the catalog and the schedule of classes, and the supervision of instruction. The division chairmen, the instructors, and the librarian would be directly responsible to the Dean of Instruction. This task of instruction may be further subdivided according to the functions of education for transfer, occupational education, and education of adults. In general, the educational program should be treated as a unit as far as possible, with unified planning and coordination. Too great a segregation of adult from occupational education and of occupational from general education, either in organization or in physical site, works against both quality and availability of educational opportunity.

The foregoing discussion of administrative organization might be expressed in the form of a chart. Samples of such charts may be found in Bogue (*91:286*) and in Price (*126:19*). Since every community junior college is the unique resultant of its own history, site, personnel, finances, and philosophy, no general chart is presented here. In each institution, the titles and responsibilities of the administrative staff will vary, but the four areas of responsibility must be cared for in every one.

Selected References

Barnhart, Richard E. "Six Characteristics of a Good School Board Member," *Nation's Schools*, 53:82–83, February, 1954.

Bogue, Jesse P. *The Community College.* New York: McGraw-Hill Book Co., 1950, Chapter 11.

Colvert, C. C. "A Study of Official External Influences on the Curriculums of Public Junior Colleges," *Junior College Journal*, 31:210–213, December, 1960.

Cosand, Joseph. "Flying a College on the Computer," *Junior College Journal*, 35:5–8, September, 1964.

Gross, Neal. *Who Runs Our Schools?* New York: John Wiley and Sons, 1958.

Institutional Research in the Junior College. Occasional Report No. 3, Junior College Leadership Program. Los Angeles: University of California, 1962.

Johnson, B. Lamar. *General Education in Action.* Washington: American Council on Education, 1952. Chapter XIV, "Administration: Facilitating General Education.

Kintzer, Frederick C. *Board Policy Manuals in California Junior Colleges.* Occasional Report No. 2, Junior College Leadership Program. Los Angeles: University of California, 1962.

———. *Faculty Handbooks in California Public Junior Colleges.* Occasional Report

No. 1, Junior College Leadership Program. Los Angeles: University of California, 1961.

Kintzer, Frederick C. *Presidents' Reports in American Junior Colleges.* Occasional Report No. 4, Junior College Leadership Program. Los Angeles: University of California, 1963.

Morrison, D. G., Ken August Brunner and S. V. Marotana. *The 2-Year Community College: An Annotated List of Unpublished Studies and Surveys, 1957–61.* Office of Education Bulletin 1963, No. 28. Washington: Government Printing Office, 1963.

Pierce, A. C. "Deans in the Organization and Administration of Junior Colleges," *Junior College Journal,* 21:364–366, February, 1951.

Price, Hugh G. "The Role of Administration in Excellent Teaching," *Junior College Journal,* 24:37–42, September, 1953.

Reynolds, James W. "Administrative and Supervisory Practices for Improving Instruction," *Junior College Journal,* 18:181–190, December, 1947.

School Board-Superintendent Relationships. The Thirty-fourth Yearbook. Washington: American Association of School Administrators, 1956.

The Superintendent As Instructional Leader. The Thirty-fifth Yearbook. Washington: American Association of School Administrators, 1957.

10

Instructors for
Community Junior Colleges

The crucial role of the teaching faculty is implicit in all that has been said about the nature and the mission of the community junior college. Unless qualified instructors are available in sufficient numbers, the purposes of the institution cannot be achieved. Chapter 10 presents evidence on the extent of demand for instructors for the junior colleges, in relation to other demands for teachers. Material descriptive of present junior college faculties is set forth next, followed by data about the conditions under which they work in the colleges, patterns of preparation, and in-service training.

A. The Need for Instructors

The most critical bottleneck to the expansion and improvement of education in the United States is the mounting shortage of excellent teachers. Unless enough of the Nation's ablest manpower is reinvested in the educational enterprise, its human resources will remain underdeveloped and specialized manpower shortages in every field will compound. Unwittingly the United States right now is pursuing precisely the opposite course. Demands for high quality manpower have everywhere been mounting, but colleges and universities have found themselves at a growing competitive disadvantage in the professional manpower market. Our Nation, like the prodigal farmer, is consuming the seed corn needed for future harvests. The ultimate result could be disaster. (139:5)

A publication of the Carnegie Foundation for the Advancement of Teaching summarizes the extent of the need for college and uni-

133

versity teachers in three sets of figures. Estimated enrollments will rise from a present six million to ten million students before 1980; the annual need for college teachers at present ranges between 32,000 and 36,000 per year; and the annual doctoral output of the graduate schools amounts to less than half that number, of whom about 45% are college teachers. At present, the annual supply of fully qualified teachers amounts to about one-fourth of the annual need; and the annual need will grow at least as rapidly as the supply (*49*).

It is difficult to determine the proportion of this need that is attributable to the community junior college. The student-teacher ratio in the junior colleges tends to be higher than it is in the universities and four-year colleges. On the other hand, the increase of legislative interest in the community junior college in several of the states indicates a more rapid increase in the number and in the average enrollments of these institutions than in the four-year colleges and universities. In the fall of 1965, junior college "degree-credit" enrollments accounted for about one-seventh of all degree-credit enrollment; the total faculty in junior colleges numbered almost 50,000 in 1965. At 10% annual replacement, 5000 of the estimated annual need, or about 15%, would be needed to maintain junior college faculty size. Anticipated growth in junior college enrollments could well add an additional 500 to 1000 to their annual teacher needs. In addition, Schultz estimates an annual requirement, nationwide, of about 350 administrative officers for junior colleges (*136*).

All indications considered seem to indicate that the junior colleges are likely to need at least one-sixth, and possibly a greater proportion, of the total numbers of additional college instructors required between now and 1980. At this rate, between 5500 and 6000 new instructors annually would be the junior college share of the estimated annual requirement. Although the total size of this figure may be alarming, in relation to the total full-time equivalent faculty in 1964 of 44,405, it consists of an average of between 7 and 9 instructors annually for each of the existing junior colleges to care for both replacement and growth. Viewed in these terms, the total estimate may seem to be conservative, especially in relation to recent growth in junior colleges in such states as Florida, Washington, New York, Texas, or California.

At any rate, the task of recruiting competent instructors is formidable. Substantial increases in faculty salaries will help to retain present instructors and to attract additional ones. Four further steps are necessary: strenuous recruitment activities, improved preparation of teachers in both preservice and in-service programs, more efficient use of faculty by provision of additional help for nonteaching work, and the continued improvement of the social climate for the academic life. The Educational Policies Commission suggests that five groups of our population are suitable targets for intensive campaigns of recruitment: present students, women, minority groups, older persons, and specialists available on a part-time basis (39:87). Certainly the shortage is sufficiently acute and the task of sufficient importance to justify aggressive and vigorous campaigns to interest able and idealistic persons in preparing themselves for teaching in the junior colleges. It is unlikely that any advance in the technology of communication will relieve the need substantially by providing an adequate substitute for the personal influence of fine teachers on comparatively limited numbers of students.

B. *Qualifications of Junior College Instructors*

What are the qualities of junior college instructors that can help to define the kind of person to whom efforts at recruitment should be directed? Although present practice does not always indicate an adequate standard, a description of junior college teachers presents a helpful point of departure for a discussion of training and recruitment programs. Data are available regarding the extent of academic preparation of junior college faculty members, as well as about some aspects of their attitudes and previous experience.

Degrees Held. Medsker has studied several characteristics of full-time staff members in junior colleges. His figures on degrees earned permit comparison with those reported for all college and university faculty members, as well as with earlier studies of the degrees held by junior college faculties (109:172). Table 8 summarizes the findings of several studies.

Certain comments are appropriate about the distribution of the several degrees. In all cases, some of the faculty members with less than doctorate degrees were working toward the next higher degree. Medsker, for example, reported that 9% of his entire group were working toward the master's degree and more than 10% were approaching the doctorate (109:171). Again, it should be pointed out that the smaller proportion of doctorates held by junior college faculty members is appropriate, because their instruction is limited to lower division. Their number also includes a large proportion of teachers of applied subjects, who will be less likely to achieve a doctorate in their teaching fields. Finally, the comparison of junior college faculty training with that of instructors in colleges and universities shows a remark-

Table 8.   Per Cent of the Instructors in Public Junior Colleges for the Years Designated Who Have the Doctor's, Master's, Bachelor's, and No Degree for Their Highest Degrees [a]

Year and Study	Total Number of Instructors	Doctor's Per Cent	Master's Per Cent	Bachelor's Per Cent	No Degree Per Cent
1918, McDowell	180	2.8	39.5	55.0	2.8
1922, Koos	163	3.0	47.0	47.0	3.0
1953, Colvert and Litton	4,955	6.3	67.5	20.9	5.3
1955, Colvert and Baker	6,985	7.2	68.5	17.9	6.5
1958, Medsker	3,274	9.7	64.6	17.0	6.8
1955, College and university faculty, all ranks	58,719	40.5	49.1	10.4 [b]	—
1955, College and university instructors only	11,646	11.0	62.0	27.0 [b]	—

[a] Sources: The first four studies are set forth in an exactly similar table in C. C. Calvert, "Professional Development of Junior College Instructors" (27:475). Medsker's figures are from (109:172.) The College and University figures are from Fund for the Advancement of Education, Teachers for Tomorrow (151:62).

[b] These figures are for "less than master's degree" faculty members, and include an undetermined number of nondegree instructors.

ably similar proportion of doctor's and master's degrees; the "degree-granting" instructors have a higher proportion of bachelor's degrees and a slight excess of doctorates.

Between 1954 and 1959 the per cent of new teachers entering full-time college service as holders of the doctor's degree declined from 31.4 to 23.8, and in 1963 it stood at 25.4. Over the 10-year span those with one year of training beyond the master's degree increased slightly, from 18.2 to 20.3 per cent, but new teachers with just the master's degree increased from 32.2 to 39.4 per cent. The necessity for accepting many new teachers with obviously insufficient training is shown by the fact that in 1954, 18.2 per cent of the new group had not yet attained master's degree status. This figure went as high as 23.1 in 1957, but has declined to 14.9 in 1963. (117:109)

Whether increasing annual numbers of master's degree graduates will enable the junior colleges to hold their own in the struggle for faculty quality depends in part on the efforts of junior college workers to interpret their need and to encourage able students to prepare for teaching.

Previous Experience. Medsker found that 72% of junior college teachers are men. This finding adds force to the suggestion of the Educational Policies Commission that attempts be made to encourage able women to enter the field of college teaching. Medsker's question on previous experience brought the information that more than 64% of his full-time staff respondents had once taught at either the secondary or elementary school level—mostly, however, in the secondary school (*109:172*). Although previous teaching experience may well serve as a selective device and should help to ensure a high quality of junior college teaching, it is evident that such an exchange of positions contributes nothing to the solution of the teacher shortage which exists at all levels of the educational system. Koos corroborates the other two studies with the report that "last previous positions, for about three-fifths of all, were in high-school teaching, and for only an eighth, college and university (not junior college) teaching." Koos points out, however, that these same facts indicate that most of the junior college teachers "have had no opportunity for systematic consideration in a course of the institution in which they are at work" (*92:468*).

Knowledge about the Junior College. Since teachers are largely recruited from other positions into the junior college, with comparatively little opportunity to study in advance its distinctive purposes and problems, it is appropriate to ask about their understanding of the institution and their attitude toward it. Medsker gathered data on these points also. He found that junior college faculties in general were in substantial agreement with the concept of the two-year college as a part of the system of American post-high-school education and that the great majority of the staff were satisfied with their positions in the two-year college. They believed that the junior college should fulfill several functions, including both preparatory and terminal programs in the same institution; that the quality of instruction in the junior college was equal to, if not superior to, that in the four-year college; and that the junior college should have its own governing board and its own administrative officer, directly responsible to that board. On the other hand, he found sufficient minority dissent on every attitude measured to indicate the necessity for a continuing program of in-service training, particularly about the nature of the junior college, about the characteristics of its students, and about state and national trends in providing opportunity for higher education (*109*: 200–205).

C. Working Conditions in Community Junior Colleges

A basic factor in recruitment of junior college teachers is the comparative desirability of their work. Such factors as total teaching load, salary, extra class duties, sick leave, tenure, and retirement benefits all contribute to the attractiveness of one position in relation to others for which one may be equally qualified. In several of these areas, no national data are available for comparison; in others, fairly definite information has been provided.

Teaching Load. Teaching assignments in public junior colleges tend to approximate fifteen credit hours of teaching per semester, with some variation between twelve and eighteen credit hours.

The use of credit hours as a basis of computing load will lead to variations in the number of classroom hours per week required of instructors in different subjects.

In 1939, Conley studied the junior college instructor and discovered certain facts about his work load that are still reasonably accurate, as confirmed by a limited questionnaire distributed by the writer. Conley obtained responses from 1150 instructors in 15 instructional departments; he used only public junior colleges that employed more than 15 instructors. He found 5 departments (agriculture, art, biological science, engineering, and physical science) in which the usual teaching load exceeded 20 clock hours. It will be noted that in each of these departments there is a high ratio of laboratory hours to lecture classes. In 6 other departments, Conley found average loads of between 16 and 20 hours weekly. In these departments, commerce, home economics, mathematics, natural science, physical education, and social science, it is usual for the scheduled weekly hours to exceed the credit value. In the remaining 4 departments (education, English, languages, and music), 15 hours per week or less were spent in the classroom. The music instructor, Conley explains, may often be required to give individual lessons and lead public performances. In the other classes, the number of papers required and the usual clock-hour credit-hour equivalence account for the lower assignment of scheduled hours (*29*).

In addition, Conley discovered that the average time devoted each week to instructional duties amounts to 35 hours, almost equally divided between classroom and nonclassroom instructional duties. To this 35 hours must be added more than 16 hours per week that instructors spend in other duties—student activities, committee work, administration, and miscellaneous. The total of 51 hours of professional activity weekly is not out of line with the findings of other investigators of loads in colleges, in junior colleges, and in high schools. Hillway, for example, summarizes the situation as follows: "15 hours in the classroom, 15 hours in lesson preparation, and 15 hours in conferences, community meetings, and similar activities" (72:200).

An additional factor in teacher load is the number of different class preparations required of the teacher—especially if the preparations are in unrelated subject fields. Koos, after reporting on class preparations of 1458 instructors in 48 local public junior colleges, recommended that instructors "be equipped to teach more broadly than in a single subject." He found that 45% of his respondents taught in a single subject field, 36% in two fields, 13% in three, and 6% in four or more fields. Although the typical junior college instructor, then, may teach only in his major and minor subject fields, one out of five (19%) must expect to be asked, at least on occasion, to teach in one or two additional fields (93:203). In the fall of 1958, the administrators of 51 California junior colleges reported to the author that they expected that there would be no preparations outside of the major or minor field. It is assumed, apparently, that preparations of courses within a subject field, such as English composition and English literature, are less burdensome than preparations in two fields, such as general chemistry and trigonometry.

Salaries. The need for improved salaries for college teachers has been widely and ably presented. The Educational Policies Commission states

Increase in faculty salaries is the most urgent priority in financing higher education. . . . Competition for highly trained personnel and the high levels of industrial and technical salaries make low academic salaries all the more disastrous. Current faculty shortages plus anticipated faculty needs indicate that faculties a generation from now may be of distinctly lower caliber unless substantial salary increases are provided. (39:130–31)

Even more pointed is the observation of The President's Committee on Education Beyond the High School:

The plain fact is that the college teachers of the United States, through their inadequate salaries, are subsidizing the education of students, and in some cases the luxuries of their families, by an amount which is more than double the grand total of alumni gifts, corporate gifts, and endowment income of all colleges and universities combined. Unless this condition is corrected forthwith the quality of American higher education will decline. (139:6)

In 1957–1958, according to the Research Division of the National Education Association, the median salary in public junior colleges was $7828, and in nonpublic junior colleges it was $5719. These sums represented substantial increases over previous studies by the NEA, but they still represent an inadequate recompense for the quality of preparation demanded of junior college teachers in comparison with other economic groups in the population. In general, the data indicate that public junior college teachers receive median salaries between the medians for college and university assistant professors and associate professors ($7539 and $8969, respectively) (*24*:37).

Tenure and Retirement. The evidence that is available concerning the legal status of teachers in public junior colleges, especially concerning tenure and retirement provisions, indicates that in most states they share in the benefits available to all public school teachers. Simms found little general legislation pertaining directly to public junior college teachers. For that reason, the general school laws pertaining to teacher retirement, tenure, selection, appointment, and conduct apply equally to public junior college teachers (*142*:87).

In a report of an extended study of conditions of work among faculties in 219 junior colleges, Punke stated that tenure is granted

After 1 year in	7 public junior colleges	3%
After 1–3 years in	28 public junior colleges	13%
After more than 3 years in	92 public junior colleges	42%
Not at all in	92 public junior colleges	42%

In 58% of public junior colleges, a teacher who completes his probationary period satisfactorily earns permanent tenure until retirement age, subject only to legally defined standards of good conduct (*127*: 484).

Academic Rank. Approximately 100 junior colleges award academic rank to their teachers; the number has been increasing especially since 1960. There is evidence of considerable lack of agreement among junior college administrators and faculty members on the wisdom of imitating the ranking policies of the colleges and universities. Those in favor of a system of rank argue that it provides a symbol of prestige and permits outward recognition of meritorious service. The titles of assistant professor, associate professor, and professor give status to the teacher in his contacts with the faculty of other institutions and in submitting articles to journals for publication. Rank also recognizes the professional competence of the junior college teacher, and sets him apart from the secondary school teacher. It is a source of strength when he exercises the professorial responsibility of participating in policy formation for his college.

On the other hand, other writers see the introduction of academic rank as a peril. It increases the drive toward specialization that is not appropriate in junior college teaching; it ties the aspirations and the practice of the junior college more closely to the traditional and the academic, rather than to the experimental and the community-centered aspects of its task. The mere fact of rank, it is suggested, will distract junior college faculties from their major task of effective teaching toward the kinds of publication and research that will win promotions (*155* and *67*).

D. Preparation of Instructors

Many descriptions have been written of the ideal personality and preparation of the junior college instructor. To mention only one, Langsdorf suggests five characteristics of the good academic teacher:

1. The academic teacher must love his subject and knowledge in general. . . .
2. The academic teacher should have a fondness for people. . . .
3. The academic teacher must have an awareness of his times. . . .
4. The academic teacher must have an attractive personality. . . .
5. And finally, in summary, the academic teacher must have sufficient depth of preparation to avoid the superficiality of hasty and inaccurate syntheses and the breadth to avoid the sterility and boredom of overspecialization. He should be able to make our culture seem pregnant with unexplored possibilities for every young man and woman. (*182*:15)

Merson has presented a program of preparation that requires two years of graduate study, including a subject-field master's degree, some twelve to fifteen units of study in professional education, and a full semester of supervised internship in a junior college (*69*:220–222). There is no doubt that preparation of this nature would do much to ensure that the new teacher had achieved at least some of the qualities desired by Langsdorf. Yet in a period of increasing demand for college instructors, when the most typical educational level of junior college teachers is the master's degree and when lower levels of training are in prospect, it is unlikely that many candidates will delay employment until they have completed two years of graduate study.

Basic Assumptions. At least for the forthcoming period of severe shortage of teachers, certain realistic assumptions should form the basis of program planning for junior college teacher training. One of these assumptions is that the prospective teacher is not—cannot be—fully trained at the time he receives his credential. Employers should expect that the beginning teacher will continue to learn in his subject field, that the demands of his teaching will force him to achieve greater breadth and depth over the years, and that for several years he should become annually a better teacher and a more mature personality. Personnel practices in junior colleges should be established in the light of this assumption to make certain that growth does continue after employment. Helpful supervision, well-planned programs of in-service training during the college year, and salary schedule provisions that encourage teachers to use their summers to improve their instructional competence can all combine to keep the faculty moving toward ideal competence.

A second assumption that should influence teacher training programs is that the junior college teacher may frequently be asked to teach in two or more subject fields. For this reason every prospective junior college teacher should, if possible, include strong preparation in a second field as part of his program. The student who decides to aim for junior college teaching during his undergraduate days will have little difficulty in achieving this breadth. The credential candidate who has already earned a specialized master's degree may find it more difficult to include such a second subject in his preparation. Colleges and universities, in setting up curriculums that are intended to prepare junior college teachers, must include provision for this breadth as a part of their basic plans.

A third assumption that should influence patterns of preparation is that economy of time is important both for the student and for the employing junior college. The student will be unwilling to invest an additional year in acquiring the highest qualifications; he will desire to qualify for employment as soon as possible, planning to add desirable additional competences later. The junior colleges, facing unprecedented annual needs for qualified instructors, will also press for training programs which balance the claims of ideal competence with those of urgent need.

Curriculum Proposal. In the light of these considerations, it seems that the curriculum for training junior college teachers should be planned to begin with the junior year of undergraduate study. It should envisage steady progress by the student during a minimum period of three years, plus one or two summer sessions if needed, toward completion of the following educational elements:

1. A master's degree in a subject field.
2. A teaching minor, amounting to approximately one-fifth of the student's total college credits, in a field related to the master's degree major field.

3. Courses in professional education to equal about one semester's total, including

a. Educational psychology—junior college student characteristics, principles of learning, guidance, and counseling.

b. A course in history, purposes, status, and problems of the junior college.

c. Methods and techniques of teaching in the junior college, including evaluation.

d. Supervised teaching, or internship, in a junior college.

If some of these courses in education could be included in the undergraduate program, it would be possible to reserve time in the graduate year for supervised teaching, after completion of several graduate courses in the teaching field. A variation of this plan will appeal to candidates who have earned the master's degree before considering junior college teaching. A specially contrived student-teaching experience is followed by a teaching internship in a junior college, in which the full responsibilities of a teacher are undertaken, with salary, for at least one semester with supervision provided on a cooperative basis by the junior college and the teacher-education institution. The seminars that accompany the student teaching and the internship include the material of the education courses required under the more conventional pattern. The credential is awarded upon successful completion of the internship.

Occupational Instructors. The pattern so far presented has concentrated implicitly on preparing teachers of academic and general education subjects. With suitable adaptations, the same principles may guide the preparation of instructors in the vocational and technical subjects that are such an important part of the total program of the public junior college. Since such instructors are more likely to teach in one subject field, not so much stress need be placed on the teaching minor. Instead, a pattern of preparation such as the following might serve to attract able persons from other employment fields to teach these courses:

1. Education beyond the high-school equivalent to the Associate in Arts degree.

2. Successful experience in the occupation to be taught, equivalent to apprenticeship and three years of journeyman experience. In some fields, apprenticeship and journeyman status are not specifically provided, but the principle of extended and meaningful successful experience can be applied.

3. Courses in professional education equal to about one semester's total, and including the same elements as suggested for the master's degree candidate.

Such instructors should be encouraged to improve their formal education as they are able to do so, but in many fields no graduate training program exists that is as effective as employment experience in providing the technical knowledge and skills essential to teaching the junior college technical course.

In-Service Training. If the training curriculum assumes that further growth in teaching competence will be required of the teacher even after he is employed, carefully planned programs of in-service training are needed. Koos has remarked that "It is surprising that the proportion of junior-college teachers who have had the course called 'Junior College,' which should yield for them an understanding of the institution in which they are at work, did not rise to a tenth of the entire group of teachers (94:313). For this reason, precollege meetings of several days duration, for both new and returning instructors, can be addressed to aspects of the junior college in American education. During the year, regular faculty meetings as well as especially appointed committees and intensive workshop sessions may be devoted to topics that concern the entire faculty or subgroups of it. In every case, a workable program must be developed locally, through the cooperation of instructors and administrators, to meet local needs. Its purpose is to assist members of the faculty to understand better some aspect of their work in a junior college, with the ultimate objective of improving the instructional program. Community junior colleges organize their adult programs on the premise that citizens need recurring opportunity throughout life to learn new things, both occupational and avocational. The same principle applies to their instructors.

Selected References

Blocker, Clyde E. and Wendell Wolfe. "Academic Rank in Two-Year Colleges," *Junior College Journal*, 35:21–25, December, 1964.

Colvert, C. C. "Professional Development of Junior College Instructors," *Junior College Journal*, 25:474–478, April, 1955.

—— and H. F. Bright. "Suggested Materials for In-Service Training Programs for Junior Colleges," *Research Bulletin*, American Association of Junior Colleges, Vol. 1, No. 2, 1950.

Conley, William H. "The Junior College Instructor," *Junior College Journal*, 9:507–512, May, 1939.

Eckert, Ruth E. and John E. Stecklein. "Career Motivations and Satisfactions of Junior College Teachers," *Junior College Journal*, 30:83–89, October, 1959.

Educational Policies Commission. *Higher Education in a Decade of Decision.* Washington: National Education Association, 1957.

Jarvie, L. L. "Making Teaching More Effective," Chapter XI in *The Public Junior College.* Nelson B. Henry (editor). Fifty-fifth Yearbook of the National Society for the Study of Education. Chicago: The University of Chicago Press, 1956.

Kintzer, Frederick C. *Faculty Handbooks in California Public Junior Colleges.* Occasional Report No. 1. Los Angeles: Junior College Leadership Program, University of California, 1961.

Koos, Leonard V. "Junior College Teachers: Background of Experience," *Junior College Journal,* 18:457–469, April, 1948.

———. "Junior College Teachers: Degrees and Graduate Residence," *Junior College Journal,* 18:77–89, October, 1947.

———. "Junior College Teachers: Preparation in Education," *Junior College Journal,* 18:332–344, February, 1948.

———. "Junior College Teachers: Subjects Taught and Specialized Preparation," *Junior College Journal,* 18:196–209, December, 1947.

———. "Programs of Junior College Teacher Preparation," *Junior College Journal,* 19:333–346, February, 1949.

Maul, Ray C. "Can We Get Enough Good Teachers?" *Junior College Journal,* 34:3–7, December, 1963.

Medsker, Leland L. *The Junior College: Progress and Prospect.* New York: McGraw-Hill Book Co., 1960.

Moore, Everett L. "Merit Pay: Bane or Blessing?" *Junior College Journal,* 35:32–37, October, 1965.

President's Commission on Higher Education. *Higher Education for American Democracy.* Vol. IV, "Staffing Higher Education." New York: Harper and Row, 1948.

President's Committee on Education Beyond the High School. *Second Report to the President.* Washington: Government Printing Office, 1957.

Salaries Paid and Salary Practices in Universities, Colleges and Junior Colleges, 1963–64. Research Report 1964-R3. Washington: Research Division, National Education Association, February, 1964.

Teacher Supply and Demand in Universities, Colleges and Junior Colleges, 1963–64 and 1964–65. Research Report 1965-R4. Washington: Research Division, National Education Association, April, 1965.

Tillery, Dale. "Academic Rank: Promise or Peril?" *Junior College Journal,* 33:6–9, February, 1963.

Woellner, R. C. and M. Aurilla Wood. *Requirements for Certification of Teachers and Administrators for Elementary Schools, Secondary Schools, and Junior Colleges.* Thirtieth Edition, 1965–1966. Chicago: The University of Chicago Press, 1965.

11

Characteristics of Students

The community junior college cannot be understood completely without a clear, factual, and unbiased understanding of its students. Unless a college defines quite clearly the groups in its community whose educational needs it plans to serve, it can hardly escape offering a partial or an inappropriate education. The instructors need such realistic awareness so that they may adapt their methods to the facts of student abilities and purposes. Patrons and students of the junior college can profit from accurate information in attempting to square their expectations for the college with its actual tasks. Writers on educational subjects especially need this understanding in order that their recommendations for the development of higher education may be appropriate and workable.

Chapter 11 presents information on several characteristics of community junior college students, drawing on the studies that are available, whether they cover large random samplings of students or are based only on studies of one or two institutions. Data will be presented on the averages and ranges of academic aptitude of full-time students in junior colleges and on other qualities such as age, sex, educational plans, socioeconomic status, employment, marital status, and persistence in college. Facts about adult students will be presented in less quantitative terms, based on the observations of adult educators rather than on careful statistical comparison. The total consideration of student characteristics, then, will serve to reinforce and to sharpen the concept that the community junior college has several purposes, each of which merits respect, acceptance, and support.

146

A. *Academic Aptitude in the Community Junior College*

The characteristic of junior college students which has been studied most thoroughly is academic aptitude. This is an important factor which can be readily measured and which allows comparisons to be made of junior college students with students in other educational institutions. Yet the comparisons are in some ways inappropriate; a description of the tests of college aptitude and an understanding of the concept of aptitudes will demonstrate the partiality of this kind of comparison.

Several batteries of college aptitude tests have been developed, validated, and used by colleges to screen for admission the students with high likelihood of success or to aid in counseling and advising students after admission. Among the most widely used recent aptitude batteries are the School and College Ability Tests (SCAT), published by the Cooperative Test Division of the Educational Testing Service. Since fluency in the use of words and skill in the use of mathematics are closely related to success in baccalaureate degree programs, the SCAT series contains four subtests, Sentence Understanding, Numerical Computation, Word Meanings, and Numerical Problem Solving. Three sets of converted scores are reported, Verbal, Quantitative, and Total. Publisher's norms for interpreting scores are based on students from more than 100 colleges and junior colleges carefully chosen to be representative of the geographic areas of the nation.

Such tests are a necessary and appropriate counseling tool. They do indicate the chances of success of any given student in a baccalaureate program. This is their purpose, and they are reasonably adequate. Two flaws become apparent, however, when such test results are used to compare community junior college students with those in other institutions. One flaw inheres in the stereotype of the "median" or average student. It is legitimate to say that the median score of one group is higher (or lower) than the median score of another. The unwary reader may form the impression that all members of the former group are more apt for college than any members of the second group. This conclusion is almost always unsupported by the data. Again, it is easy to assume that these limited tests of "college aptitude" are tests of "intelligence." Yet psychologists are becoming increasingly aware that intelligence is not a unitary trait; rather, in any individual, "intelligence" is the result of a unique combination of aptitudes. Not all these combinations are predominantly either numerical or verbal; there are other significant and identifiable aptitudes that contribute to success in many activities, even though their contribution to traditional university learning may be comparatively slight (98). The universities and liberal arts colleges are comparatively uninterested in these other kinds of intelligence; their sphere of learning is the abstract and theoretical, expressed in verbal and numerical symbols. The community junior college shares this interest, so important to the "transfer" part of its curriculum, but it is interested also in other more practical aptitudes that may exist somewhat independently of verbal and numerical aptitudes. College aptitude tests do not measure all the human aptitudes important to the work of the community junior college.

In the light of these comments, Seashore's summary conclusions may be clearly understood. Because his study is in essential agreement with other studies of the same problem, his conclusions are quoted at length:

How do junior college freshmen compare with senior college freshmen? It is not surprising to find that junior college freshmen generally are not as able *in the areas measured by CQT* as the four-year or senior college freshmen. The following statements seem reasonable:

The median score for junior college freshmen is near the 25th percentile for senior college freshmen.

About 24 per cent of junior college men and 20 per cent of junior college women *are above the respective medians* for freshmen in four-year colleges.

There is considerable overlap of scores. These distributions tell us that there are many junior college students *whose scores would be considered superior in senior colleges,* and many low-scoring senior college freshmen would also rate low in junior colleges.

The difference in favor of the four-year student is slightly greater for women than for men. (*138*:75–76; italics added)

In comparing junior college students in transfer programs with those in terminal programs, Seashore notes that

As would be expected, the scores on a scholastic ability test such as the CQT are generally higher for the transfer group than for the terminal group . . . a large proportion of junior college transfer aspirants is at least as able as the upper three-fourths of senior college freshmen. The terminal students are clearly less [academically] able than the scholastically oriented groups in both junior and senior colleges. Since separate norms are available for terminal and transfer students, each junior college applicant can be evaluated in terms of these two major sub-groupings. Such evaluations are particularly valuable if admissions officers have a chance to counsel candidates prior to their entry into the college. In fact, advisors may well con-

sider the separate transfer and terminal norms more useful than the com-
posite norms for all junior college freshmen. (*138*:78–79)

Actual distributions of total scores on the SCAT test for students
in two community junior colleges are compared in Figures 2 and 3
with the distributions of national "norm" or standardizing groups of
freshmen. The norm sample includes freshmen from four-year colleges
and junior colleges; by definition, 10% of their scores fell within each
decile. In the two figures, junior college distributions may be compared
visually with the national distribution. It is readily apparent that
both junior colleges have students at the top level of ability, as
measured by SCAT scores; that the median scores for both junior
colleges are lower than the medians for the norm group; and that the
two junior colleges serve populations of differing aptitude. If an
assumption were made that 70% of all college freshmen (as represented
in the norm group) have sufficient "college aptitude" to do well in
achieving baccalaureate degrees, then as many as 63% of the students
from the junior college in Figure 2, and 43% of those in Figure 3,
have that degree of tested aptitude.

The SCAT data from the college in Figure 3 were reported
separately for transfer students and terminal students. Even though
the two categories are difficult to define, with a great deal of student
shifting from one to the other, they did represent the expressed
intentions of these students at the time of registration. The students
were very evenly divided between the two categories. Of the terminal

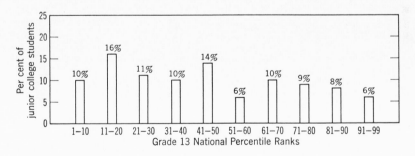

Figure 2. SCAT total test scores, 4398 junior college students, Fall, 1963, compared to National Percentile Ranks (Grade 13). If the junior college student
body included abilities identical to the national group of college freshmen used
for test standardization, 10% of the junior college group would score in each decile
group, or in each bar of the graph. The variation above or below 10% in each
decile shows how this junior college population differs from the national group
of college freshmen.

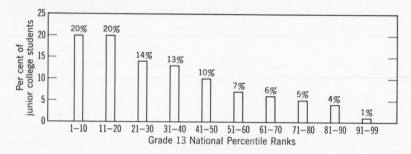

Figure 3. SCAT total test scores, 827 junior college students, Fall, 1964, compared to National Percentile Ranks.

students, 36% scored above the thirtieth percentile, and might be assumed to have sufficient aptitude for senior college success. The transfer group, as might be expected, scored higher on SCAT: 56% of them scored above the thirtieth percentile score of the norm group.

In summary, it is apparent that although average test scores of junior college freshmen are lower than average scores of liberal arts college freshmen, the range of scores in both kinds of colleges is equivalent; recommendations for further study and predictions of later academic success must be made for individual students, not for categories of students. It is further obvious, in the light of test evidence, that the various kinds of colleges in the American system of diversity are not operated for exclusively different kinds of student abilities. The selection of a college by its students is based on other differential qualities, and if the community junior college is to serve its function of democratizing higher education, it must continue to offer strong lower-division curriculums to prepare its qualified students for advanced study.

B. Other Qualities of Community Junior College Students

Sex Distribution. In American colleges generally, men students outnumber women students. In the fall of 1964, total opening enrollment of degree-credit students in all institutions included 3,051,761 men and 1,936,106 women or 62% and 38%, respectively. In the junior colleges, the degree-credit figures were 440,570 men and 272,706 women, an exactly similar ratio (122:13). When all junior college students are considered, the inclusion of terminal registrants with the degree-credit students brings the ratio more nearly to three men to one woman. Community junior colleges will vary in sex distribution of their student body in accordance with the nature of their program. Since the needs of the nation for skilled and educated citizenry cannot be met fully without recruiting greater numbers of able women into such fields as science and college teaching, it would seem that junior colleges should study their curriculums to see whether they actually offer enough programs attractive to women students.

Age Distribution. In 1935, Lide found that 87% of the students in Wright division of Chicago Junior College were under twenty years of age (*97*). At present, regular day students in community junior colleges range in age from 16 to more than 70 years. The increase in proportion of older students indicates that the community junior college is fulfilling its function of making education available to those to whom it had earlier been denied—the veteran, the housewife, the so-called "late bloomer." At Coalinga College, 10% of the students were over 30 years of age, and 17% additional were between 21 and 29 years of age. The Coalinga report remarks of these that "All would agree that more oldsters would be welcome. They have brought experience, spice, stability, and competitive push to the student body. On the first quarter Fall honor roll they captured 12 places on a roll numbering 29 students" (*163*). At the other side of the Nation, The Clinch Valley College of the University of Virginia reports a similar condition: "Especially pleasing and encouraging was the attitude of the students who enrolled. They were serious in purpose, hardworking, most interested in the venture, and very cooperative. Student as well as community pride in the college was obvious. The first year ended on a note of optimism" (*157*).

Dealing with 13,300 regular day students in 10 junior colleges, Medsker found 43% to be 19 years of age or younger; 10% were in the 20–22 age bracket, and 47% were over 23. His 16% over age 30 compares with 10% over age 30 at the Coalinga College (*109:43*). As with other qualities, age distributions also will vary from one junior college to another, but in all, there will be found an encouraging number of men and women in their twenties and thirties, seeking through education to find the key to new opportunities and to enriched personal living.

Marital Status. There was a time—not so many years ago—when marriage was cause for the expulsion from college of even a football hero. The postwar influx of veterans and the number of middle-aged students in college have changed that ruling. It is now not unusual to find a married freshman couple attending classes or a young married man or woman earning a degree while the other spouse works.

Medsker found that in six colleges that reported on this point, 23% of the students were married (*109*:45). The activity and social programs of a junior college where a quarter of the students are married may be quite different from those in an institution where a married student is exceptional.

Plans for College Attendance. Most students enter the junior college with the intention of transferring later to a four-year college in pursuit of a bachelor's degree. Yet it is a commonplace among community junior college counselors that only a minority of the entrants actually do transfer. The reasons for the unrealistic educational ambitions of the other students are many: there is the American dream that higher education is the right of every youth who will try hard enough. There is the selective function of the junior college which encourages the student to test himself in college work with comparatively low financial outlay. There is the paucity of vocational offerings in some junior colleges, so that the student has little choice other than a transfer program. Beyond these reasons lies the failure of community junior college workers to explain, early and often, to high-school students and to their parents, the purpose and nature of occupational education in the junior college. Lacking such information, students gravitate unwittingly toward the traditional and prestige-bearing transfer program. Until effective counseling procedures are developed to enable students to choose a college objective much more intelligently than they do, a large part of the efforts of the community junior colleges will be dissipated on students with unrealistic objectives.

In 1940 Eells reported that 75% of all entering students in junior colleges did not continue beyond the junior college (*42*:60). Iffert in 1958 reported that 40% of his small sample of junior college students did not go beyond the first year in their first collegiate institution (*78*:16). (For present purposes, his finding that 97% did not continue in the same institution beyond two years is not helpful, since comparatively few junior college students should continue more than two years in that institution.) Medsker found that only 33% of 17,627 students who enrolled in 63 two-year colleges in the fall of 1952 actually transferred to another college. In reverse, 67% of Medsker's total group were actually terminal students in the sense that for them the junior college represented their last period of full-time education. Medsker points out in addition that from some public junior colleges only 10% of entering students transferred, whereas from others as many as 67% pursued further study (*109*:91).

These facts of transfer contrast markedly with the expectations of students at registration. Again, the nature of the community, the defined purpose of each community junior college, and the availability of vocational and of transfer courses of study will combine with the effects of earlier guidance to determine the proportion of entrants who expect to transfer. Medsker reported that between two-thirds and three-fourths of the entering students in community junior colleges expect to transfer. Coalinga College reported 70% of its freshmen enrolled in a transfer program (*163*), and the author found from year to year that between 45 and 55% of Orange Coast College beginning students classed themselves as transfer. The observed disproportion between the expressed hopes and the eventual achievement of junior college students poses serious questions for the faculties of these institutions. How can they help students to choose more wisely and, having chosen, to achieve more consistently?

Outside Employment of Students. "Working your way through college" is a part of American folklore. Indeed, one of the advantages of the public junior college for many young persons is that they can seek part-time work in the community where they reside and are known. Students who go to a university, on the other hand, often find that they must compete for available part-time jobs with a much greater number of needy students. Havemann and West found that, of their group of college graduates, "Only 29% never turned a hand at gainful labor until they got their degrees. The other 71% worked their way, in whole or in part. . . . It is the rule, rather than the exception, to pay at least part of the expenses through one's own labor" (*61*:15).

Nationwide data are unavailable on the outside employment of students in community junior colleges. Several reports from individual colleges indicate a trend which jibes with the findings of Havemann and West. At Orange Coast College, the author found that (with slight yearly variations) about 33% of the full-time students worked fewer than ten hours weekly during the school year. An additional third (34%) worked between ten and twenty hours weekly; 19% worked from twenty to thirty hours; and one out of seven (14%) worked more than thirty hours weekly while carrying a full college load. Coalinga College reported 41% not employed. Of those who were employed, half (or about 30% of all) worked more than fifteen hours weekly. One student was reported to work as many as fifty hours each week! (*163*).

D'Amico and Raines found that 57% of the September, 1956, entering class at Flint Junior College, Flint, Michigan, were working. Approximately 63% of the 470 male students and 47% of the 281 female students had some form of part-time employment. The median number of hours worked in Flint was 20.4. Significantly, 65% of the students who worked felt that their work did not aid their studies at all; it was simply a source of funds. Comparative values are revealed by the responses to the question, "If you did not work would you or your family be able to meet your college expenses?" Almost half of the working students felt that they would be able to attend college without working; their work, then, although the authors do not state this conclusion, serves to provide for nonessentials and to relieve somewhat the burden on other family members. D'Amico and Raines do conclude, on the basis of their findings, that "An effort should be made to discourage a student from working when he or his family can meet college expenses without his working" (33:195).

Socioeconomic Background. One of the earliest advantages claimed for the public junior college was that it would make higher education more available to able young people who could not afford to attend college away from home. Several investigators have gathered data to illustrate the degree to which this purpose is actually realized. In 1929–1930, Anderson studied the socioeconomic background of 8330 junior college students, and concluded that "The tax-supported, nontuition public junior college of California . . . has a student-body drawn predominantly from the middle to upper social classes, and from the upper brackets of occupations." In his study, Anderson allocated proprietors, professional, managerial, and commercial service workers to the "upper level of occupations," and skilled, semiskilled, and unskilled workers to the "lower level." The junior college students were derived 64% from upper levels and 24% from lower levels (agricultural and clerical workers were not included in the distribution); a sample of college and university students showed 80% and 11% from the upper and lower levels, respectively. Nevertheless, Anderson reported that the lower groups were not represented in either student body in proportion to the census distribution of workers over 45 years of age in the population at that time (3:168). His conclusion was that junior college students were drawn disproportionately from the upper socioeconomic levels.

Lide raised the question of equalization of educational opportunity in relation to the entering class of 1935 at the Wright Campus of Chicago Junior College. He found that the student body came largely from immigrant families; only about a third of the fathers and two-fifths of the mothers were born in the United States. When his data on backgrounds are grouped on a basis similar to Anderson's, they show 58% from the "upper levels" of occupations, and 38% from the "lower levels" (97:675). It would seem, then, that the public junior college in the large Midwestern city approached the ideal of "democratization of higher education," in 1935, more closely than did the California colleges studied by Anderson.

Medsker reports comparable data based on 5000 students enrolled between 1954 and 1957 in 6 of the colleges in his study. Only one-fourth of the group came from the higher level in an arbitrary high-low classification. About one-third (the largest group) came from a skilled labor background. Only a tenth came from families in the professional category. Clark found that San Jose City College, a junior college, has a clientele base virtually identical with the citywide occupational structure. Also, the student body of the junior college was almost an exact representation of social areas of the city (*21*:55–58).

The Coalinga study cited earlier presents a table entitled "What is the Socio-Economic Classification of the Primary Working Parent?" Fifty-six per cent of these parents were in the unskilled, semiskilled, and skilled groups; an intermediate category of skilled white-collar, subprofessional, minor supervisory, and business workers accounted for 31%; and 11% of the parents were in professional, managerial, and executive occupations (*163*). Recent evidence, then, seems to indicate that the public junior college does in fact attract able young people from less favored socioeconomic groups, presumably also increasing the total pool of trained and educated talent in American society.

Dropout and Withdrawal. Although many community junior colleges are concerned about the high proportion of their entering students who withdraw without completing their objective, comparatively few investigations are reported dealing with the reasons for dropouts or with steps by which the rate may be reduced. Data from recent issues of the *Junior College Directory* illustrate the magnitude of the dropout problem: [1]

Full-time freshmen		Full-time sophomores		Per cent
Fall 1961	239,188	Fall 1962	122,534	51.5
Fall 1962	259,033	Fall 1963	131,144	50.6

It is known that some of these students transfer to other colleges at the end of one or two semesters, yet it is also known that as many as 10% drop out between fall registration and Christmas vacation.

[1] Data taken from totals in Table II, "Summary by States—All Junior Colleges," *Junior College Directory* for 1963, 1964, and 1965. Washington: American Association of Junior Colleges, annually.

Orange Coast College kept careful records of withdrawing students from its opening in 1948. In its first resurvey of educational and occupational needs, a report on withdrawing students was included as a part of the evaluation of the program of the college. Some of the conclusions, which seem to have pertinence for many community junior colleges, were stated as follows:

A. Age seems to be a significant factor in this analysis. While 14 per cent of the school population were over 25 years of age, 27 per cent of the dropouts were above that age. . . .

C. 75 per cent of the total number of dropouts were made up of first- and second-semester students.

D. For every 100 full-time students who enter Orange Coast College for the first time in September, the best estimate will be that 39 will drop out before the school year ends, 15 will not return for the third semester, 11 will drop out during the second year, and 35 will graduate.

E. One-third of the dropouts seem to be due to some extent to a failure of the college, while the balance seem to be justifiable. A more careful analysis should be made in an effort to learn the real reason for each withdrawal. This would necessitate tracing and obtaining an exit interview with those individuals who fail to complete a formal withdrawal. The largest group of withdrawals here classified as "unjustified" includes those who are dropped because they no longer attend classes. The college may not have failed with all of these. Follow-ups might determine that these dropouts occur for "justifiable" reasons—financial need, permanent jobs, or the like. . . .

F. Academic ability scores seem to be of no value in predicting dropouts. . . .

H. The counseling service does not have the time nor opportunity to act with one-third of the dropouts, which occur in the first ten weeks of the Fall semester. (38:128–129)

Other studies indicate that these conclusions are not unusual. In addition to scholastic discouragement and failure, withdrawals occur because of ill health, financial need, family moving away, finding employment, too much outside work, illness at home, lack of transportation, marriage, and need to work more to keep up car payments. In addition, Amori suggests that emotional maladjustment was a major contributing cause for withdrawal from junior college, in spite of the "face-saving" reasons offered by students. Traditionally, he states, attempts to reduce dropout rates have centered on addition of terminal courses and survey courses, when clinical counseling would be a more appropriate measure (2).

Attitudes of Students. The view of Amori may be countered by the conclusions reached by Tibbitts in a study reported in 1931. The conclusions may still be valid. On the basis of four attitude tests given to students in one junior college, he wrote

It may be fairly safely concluded that these small but probably typical groups of junior college students live more for immediate than future pleasure, that they value health and cleanliness as a personality trait, that they are in a measure altruistic, that an even temperament or disposition is their objective, that they are scientifically-minded in that they emphasize accuracy in small matters, that they favor the individual with self-confidence and evidently strive for that attainment, that they do not respect authority which is not well-grounded; [they believe] that alertness of mind is essential to a strong personality, that leadership is a very desirable trait, that social fitness is very desirable, and that fine looks are not essential to personality. (*154*:149)

C. The Part-Time Student

As the junior college developed in the midst of existing educational institutions and practices, it adopted terms only partially appropriate for its functions. So it was with "adult students." In an evening high school, the clientele of classes for adults is quite distinct from that of the regularly organized high-school classes. In the public junior college, however, when as many as half of the regular students may be over 21 years of age, careful definition is needed to clarify the scope of an "adult program." In general, it may be said that "extended-day" or "adult" classes are those offered primarily for students who attend only part time and whose full-time occupation is something other than college study. Hardly any other element of the program is common to all who are enrolled. In any community junior college, there will be found adult students with college degrees and others who have not graduated from high school. Some classes will be offered during the daytime, others in the evening. Some will parallel the regular college offerings and allow credit toward degrees, and others will be offered without credit on a flexible time schedule.

Because of this variety of purposes, it is difficult to present a meaningful summary of median characteristics of the adult student in the junior college. There are housewives interested in homemaking, child care, general culture, or preparation for employment. There are workers from every walk of life interested in courses to improve their skill in their present work, to prepare them for advancement or change of employment, to afford them avocational experiences, or to expand their general education. There are young adults who have not graduated from high school and others who hope through part-time study to earn a college diploma. Finally, there are retired persons, seeking through education to develop new interests and new companions for their less active years. In the public junior colleges, part-time enrollment is 52% of the total enrollment (*118*:Table III), although the hours attended by adults are only a fraction of the attendance of regularly enrolled full-time students. The absolute numbers of adult students in junior colleges may be expected to grow rapidly as more junior colleges are established and as the adult programs in more and more communities are turned over to the local junior college for unified administration.

It has been said that the community junior college exists "to provide post-high-school education for all the children of all the people and for all of the people too." Information available on the ranges of aptitude, of purposes, of ages, of socioeconomic backgrounds, and of educational objectives seems to indicate that they are beginning to achieve this all-inclusive aim. Many more studies of student characteristics are needed to complete the qualitative description of the clientele of the community junior colleges.

Selected References

Clark, Burton. *The Open-Door College.* New York: McGraw-Hill Book Co., 1960.

Dressel, Paul L. "Educational Demands Arising from Individual Needs and Purposes." Chapter III in *The Public Junior College.* Nelson B. Henry (editor). Fifty-fifth Yearbook of the National Society for the Study of Education. Chicago: The University of Chicago Press, 1956.

Goette, Mary H. and Howard L. Roy. "A Ten-Year Survey of Scholastic Aptitude of Junior College Students," *Junior College Journal,* 21:3–8, September, 1950.

Iffert, Robert E. *Retention and Withdrawal of College Students.* U.S. Office of Education Bulletin 1958, No. 1. Washington: Government Printing Office, 1958.

Junior College Directory. Washington: American Association of Junior Colleges, Annually.

Knoell, Dorothy M. "Focus on the Transfer Program," *Junior College Journal,* 35:5–9, May, 1965.

—— and Leland Medsker. *From Junior to Senior College: A National Study of the Transfer Student.* Washington: American Council on Education, 1966.

Lubick, Emil E. "Vocational Objectives of Entering College Students," *Junior College Journal,* 25:319–326, April, 1955.

Medsker, Leland L. *The Junior College: Progress and Prospect.* New York: McGraw-Hill Book Co., 1960. Chapter 6, "The Junior College Student."

Wise, W. Max. *They Come for the Best of Reasons—College Students Today.* Washington: American Council on Education, 1958.

III

The Community Junior College in Operation

12

Developing the Curriculum

"Students accept the kind of public school instruction that is about." Thus, in 1930, did Victoria McAlmon express her conclusion, as a junior college registrar, that young people would enroll for inappropriate courses if suitable offerings were not available to them (*105*:95). This tendency to glorify the value of "going to college—any college" may explain a large part of the dropout rate mentioned in the previous chapter. In addition, it emphasizes the necessity for the community junior college to make certain that appropriate instruction "is about." New educational purposes arising from the development of technology and the increasing need of the American people for higher education combine to require the community junior college to devote constant attention to the development of its curriculum. In this work, special techniques are required. The procedures described in textbooks on elementary or high-school curriculums are partially inappropriate for planning the increasingly specialized offering in the junior college. Similarly, relying solely on the traditional determinants of the liberal arts curriculum will cause the community junior college to overlook a major part of its special responsibilities.

Two aspects of curriculum development in the community junior college merit attention. One is the definition of the breadth of the total offering. Through what techniques can an administrator reach a sound decision on the program to be offered in his college? The second aspect is the depth and quality of the curriculum. After an adequate scope of the curriculum has been agreed upon through administrative studies and decisions, instructional changes must be effectuated in the classrooms by the instructors. The first aspect, it might be said, looks to external influences on the scope of the curriculum, whereas the second is concerned with those procedures within the college that assure that purposes are achieved. Chapter 12, then, will consider techniques of curriculum development within each of these two categories.

A. Determining the Scope of the Curriculum

College-Parallel Courses. Planning the college-parallel offerings of the community junior college is not a simple task. Both in the early days of a new junior college and throughout each year of its existence, a competent faculty member should be assigned the responsibility and the time to keep informed of university requirements. The fundamental principle of junior college transfer curriculums is that they enable the student to know and fulfill the requirements of the college he plans to attend next, so that he may be accepted there as a student in advanced standing and proceed to his objective without loss of time.

Several obstacles impede the full realization of these objectives. Since colleges and universities and the schools and departments which they include are constantly studying and changing their own requirements, much effort is required to keep the junior colleges fully informed. But no community junior college sends transfer students to only one university—it is not at all uncommon for graduates of a junior college to be enrolled at as many as thirty or even fifty upper-division institutions in a given year. Each of these institutions, of course, has a pattern of lower-division requirements that differs slightly from all the others. The junior college student himself may further complicate the picture. Some lack the prerequisite courses from high school and must complete them before their lower-division work proceeds; some will drop a single difficult course from a carefully planned freshman program, thus causing a delay in the completion of their transfer requirements; others will change their vocational objective or their choice of an upper-division college with an accompanying loss of time.

It is apparent that the junior college cannot duplicate every one of the lower-division offerings of even one large university, let alone of forty or fifty. The first step in establishing the transferable offerings is to analyze the requirements, for each major field of study, of each of the senior colleges to which a sizable number of students will be likely to transfer. A chart showing the exact lower-division requirements in social sciences of several nearby institutions in the fields of liberal arts, preteaching, premedicine, engineering, and other popular fields of study may well reveal a very considerable similarity among the institutions. Such a chart might indicate that the minimum program in social sciences for transfer purposes would need to include history of Western civilization, United States history, American government, and introductory psychology. In addition, one college might require specifically a course in economics, while another stipulates simply three (or six) semester hours in any of the social sciences. The single course in economics, then, could be made to satisfy both sets of requirements. Beyond the bare minimum initial offering, a list of priorities might be established naming additional courses to be introduced to satisfy the same requirements and also the divergent interests of students, as growth of enrollment and of faculty permit. In social sciences, this list might include, in order, such subjects as political science, philosophy, sociology, geography, and anthropology. The administrator will strive to reduce the variety of courses while meeting the demonstrated transfer needs of his students. Quality of instruction and faculty load are improved and scheduling of students is made easier, if two sections of one elective subject are offered in preference to one section each of two elective subjects. When growth permits the assignment of several instructors in the social sciences, of course, a greater variety of offerings becomes both feasible and educationally desirable.

The analysis suggested for the broad field of social sciences should be completed also for each of the other lower-division areas, such as English, foreign languages, mathematics, physical sciences, biological sciences, art, music, and home economics. It is not unlikely, in a new and small junior college, that it will seem impossible to offer a specialized course required in a specific major field at a single university, since only one or two students a year at most will want to enroll in it. An example might be Latin for Pharmacists. Students with this objective must be advised either how they may fulfill the requirement after they have transferred or to enroll immediately at the School of Pharmacy (or other school, as the case may be).

The completion of these analyses for a new junior college will enable the administrative staff to decide upon the number and the qualifications of the initial faculty members. A little later, the same information can be used by counselors to advise students on the proper choice of subjects to prepare them for transfer to their chosen institution and to their chosen degree major field.

The list of offerings of college-parallel subjects should never be considered static and complete. Constant effort is needed to keep abreast of the changes in requirements of the several schools of the colleges and universities to which students transfer. The continuous development of the scope of subjects in this area of the curriculum is based on yearly review of the latest catalogs. In addition, it will be useful to send the interpretation reached by the junior college counselor, on the basis of this review, to the respective university admissions officers for checking and for suggestions about new or pending developments. A frequent report of transfer students is that they were not advised to fulfill one or another requirement of their senior college. It is the responsibility of the curriculum officer of the junior college to see that such courses are available, so that the guidance worker may include them in the student's class schedule.

It is not impossible, as junior colleges increase in number, in enrollment, and in educational quality and self-confidence, that the problems of curriculum for transfer may be simplified. At present, graduate schools of universities ordinarily admit students holding acceptable baccalaureate degrees from accredited colleges or universities and allow them to enroll in all courses for which they have completed the stated prerequisites. Junior colleges also, as they earn full accreditation, will eventually achieve the right to define the nature of their lower-division general education, so that their recommended graduates may enter the upper division of colleges and universities without restriction, and with the right to continue their study in any field for which they have completed the stated prerequisites. Senior colleges will recognize that high achievement, in any demanding course of study, is better preparation for further study than average achievement in rigidly prescribed general subjects. Under these conditions, each junior college will be encouraged to develop a single general education program of high quality, supplemented by as much academic specialization as its own students need to prepare for their future study. Preparation for transfer will be evaluated in regard to its equivalence to that provided by the receiving college, rather than for its "parallelism." Fiscal economy, educational quality, the scarcity of teachers, and the best interests of transferring students all reinforce the desirability of such a development.

Occupational Curriculums. Other techniques are needed, to develop the nontransfer elements of the junior college curriculum. The entire process of curriculum development for occupational education is summarized in the first chapter of a junior college survey:

The Study is conceived to be an on-going program which essentially can never be fully completed. Involved at any stage are at least three phases which may be described as (1) research, (2) development of plans, and (3) implementation.

This Report sets forth the initial findings of Phase 1. Answers to the following four questions were sought:

a. What are the occupations for which training should be provided in the public schools of Contra Costa County, and what evidence is there that this need exists?

b. What levels of skills and competencies are used in these occupations and what evidence is there that training in these skills and competencies is necessary for successful placement and advancement in the occupation?

c. What are the present educational practices in preparing for these occupations?

d. At what grade in the educational system in Contra Costa County should various levels of these competencies be developed, and what evidence is there that this is the most appropriate grade for their development?

It will be clear to the reader that not all of the aforementioned questions are answered, even in part, for each of the occupational areas with which the Study is concerned. This is a report of progress upon which all concerned can commence to build programs of occupational education for the youth and adults of Contra Costa County.

Phase 2 of the Study, *Development of Plans,* will require immediate attention to problems such as the following:

a. Which of the occupational curricula for which need is disclosed in the Study are feasible or defensible projects?

b. What shall be the criteria of inaugurating occupational education programs for those curricula deemed feasible or defensible?

c. What special facilities and personnel will be required to inaugurate such programs?

d. What will be the costs for each program?

e. What will be the time schedule?

f. How can the curricula best be organized—e.g.,

1. Resident day programs
2. Evening or adult classes
3. Cooperative programs
4. Apprentice programs

g. How can occupational education programs best be coordinated with offerings of other schools, particularly junior and senior high schools?

h. How may an effective guidance program involving the junior and senior high schools and the Contra Costa Junior College system be developed?

Phase 3 will be concerned with *Implementation* of the plans developed in Phase 2, including such items as

a. Recommendations for new occupational curricula, additions to or modifications of existing curricula, and perhaps discontinuance of outmoded or unnecessary curricula.

b. Recommendations regarding
   1. Personnel
   2. Facilities, equipment, buildings, land, etc.
   3. Costs

c. Provision for continuing study of occupational growth and development of the area served by the Contra Costa County secondary schools to the end that they may always be in tune with community needs and desires to the greatest degree possible and feasible. (*120:2–4*)

The three phases described in this quotation are essential parts of any junior college survey of its community. Such careful study of educational needs not only provides factual assurance to the governing board, the administration, and the faculty that their program of occupational education is soundly conceived; it has additional value in that the study involves large numbers of citizens from all walks of life. They become informed about the nature and purposes of their community junior college and adopt toward it an attitude of personal involvement that helps the college to accomplish its objectives of realistic education and later placement of its graduates.

When information gained from the educational-occupational survey indicates that a given series of occupational courses is desirable, the next step is the organization of *lay advisory committees*. Peterson and Thornton have described the process by which the educational implications of a survey were interpreted to a representative general advisory committee of more than 100 lay citizens. The members of this general advisory committee were then interviewed individually to secure nominations for membership on the several special advisory committees for each training area. The special advisory committees so formed meet at least twice yearly; the general advisory committee, concerned with all aspects of the college operation, meets annually to hear reports on problems and progress during the preceding year and a forecast of plans for the coming period (*125*).

Although it is purely advisory, having no legal authority or responsibility, the general advisory committee can serve the following functions:

1. To assist the college administration in interpreting developments in the economy and the consequent educational needs of the community.

2. To develop community support and understanding of the educational program of the college.

3. To advise the college board and administration, in the annual meeting and individually thereafter, on problems of college policy submitted to them.

4. To help in interpreting the junior college to the many groups from which the general advisory committee's membership is drawn.

Special advisory committees have more limited functions, since they are formed to give advice in relation to a single course of study or to a closely related group of such courses. When data from the general survey indicate the possible need of an occupational course, the first step in its development is the appointment of an advisory committee. Several representatives of employer groups and several workers in the occupation will form the major membership of the committee. After the organization meeting, the chairman will usually be drawn from the lay membership. In addition, at least one responsible officer of the college and if possible one or more instructors from related occupational fields should be appointed to the committee; they will be able to carry on further investigations essential to the committee's work and to interpret educational policies and practices to the lay members.

Each advisory committee assumes a number of functions. After verifying that a need exists for employees with junior college training, it will consider the overall scope of the course of training to be offered, including specific occupational classes, related instruction, and general education. When these decisions have been reached the committee can turn its attention to needed classroom space, equipment, and supplies; it is very likely that members of the committee will be able to assist the college in acquiring some of these. The next concern will be the development of a description of desirable qualifications for the instructor, followed by assistance in screening of applicants. After he is employed, the new instructor will use the committee as a resource in developing his course outlines; he will ask them to contribute to instruction as guest lecturers or to suggest opportunities for field trips. After establishment of the course, the advisory committee will continue to meet at least twice a year to consider problems as they arise, such as placement opportunities for students, criteria for selection of students, policies on student performance of useful production, interpretation of the program to unions, to employers, and to the community at large, evaluation of the program, new technical developments that require changes in the course requirements, development of cooperative work experience for students, and the selection of additional instructional equipment. In all its deliberations, the lay committee serves in an advisory capacity only; the agenda for each meeting should be presented in a way to stress the nature of the committee's function. Ultimate decisions rest with the college board of trustees and its responsible employees. In nearly all cases, however, the recommendations of a lay advisory committee will prove to be so soundly and so sincerely developed that the college officers will desire to follow them. That, in effect, is the purpose of the advisory committee.

Some curricular needs may not be discovered either through the survey of transfer courses, the community occupational survey, or the meetings of advisory committees. It is true especially in the area of adult part-time study that the first impetus for the development of a course may come from a group of persons interested in enrolling or from the personnel officers of a number of local industries who see a need that has developed since the last survey. In various community junior college areas, requests for adult courses may include such offerings as industrial supervision, animal husbandry, advanced mathematics, electronic technology, philosophy for the aging, physical education, or gems and mineralogy. College credit may be a minor consideration; the petitioners most often are interested in a single course, even of very short duration, rather than in a complete program of studies. The problem of the community junior college in relation to program development in these areas is to achieve a proper balance. On the one hand, the college desires to be truly and flexibly responsive to every legitimate educational need of its community; on the other, it is conscious of a need to maintain its educational integrity by insisting on a high quality of instruction. An additional advisory committee of public-spirited citizens, not restricted to any single trade, profession, or special interest, can be of service to the college administrator in elaborating the general policy to be applied in deciding upon such requests in the field of adult education.

Another important source of information on which to base the further development of the curriculum is the *follow-up study of former students*. Questionnaires and interviews with former students who are enrolled in upper-division curriculums can provide many insights into their estimate of the quality of their preparation. Their comments about instruction, counseling, student government, the activity program, or subjects offered may indicate aspects of the curriculum that need attention. Together with the grade achievement of transfer students, these comments are very useful indicators of the overall quality of the college-parallel program of the community junior college. Although it is easy to overemphasize the validity of these opinions, which can be no better than the experience and judgment of the undergraduates who hold them, they are still a necessary and useful part of the complete evaluation of the curriculum.

The graduate of an occupational course and his employer are additional sources of insight into the effectiveness of the curriculum. Are graduates employed in the fields for which they have been trained? What difficulties do they face for which the junior college could have prepared them in finding, keeping, and advancing on their jobs? Do employers feel that junior college graduates are better trained, more mature, more effective, than workers obtained from other sources? What opinion have they formed of graduates' attitudes toward work? Are their shortcomings, when reported, due to their experience at the junior college, or to influences beyond the control of the college? Do they arise from the deficiencies in the occupational courses, or in the general education program? Students who drop out before completion of a course should be able to provide some penetrating suggestions for curriculum improvement. Their value in this respect is lessened, of course, by the greater difficulty of finding them after a lapse of time, by their reluctance to answer questions if the answer does not do them credit, and by the possibility that their negative attitudes at the time of leaving college still persist.

Statewide Influences. Not all external influences on the curriculum of the community junior college are local ones. State agencies exert both regulatory and advisory pressure. In some states, legislation may require the teaching of specific courses (such as physical education) or the organization of certain services (such as education for adults). The state department of education may exert leadership through organization of statewide conferences on specific topics such as counseling, or improvement of instruction, or general education. Cooperation by several agencies is another avenue of curriculum development. The "California Study of General Education in the Junior College" (*81*) was sponsored by the California Junior College Association, The California State Department of Education, The School of Education of the University of California at Los Angeles, and the American Council on Education. The State Steering Committee on Vocational Education in the Junior College was established jointly by the State Department of Education, the Association of Adult School Administrators, and the Junior College Association. Similarly, state universities and other state agencies in each of the states that authorize public junior colleges exert some measure of influence upon their curriculums.

Nationally, the American Association of Junior Colleges is an important stimulating force upon the junior college curriculum through the *Junior College Journal,* the *Research Bulletins* of the Association, and the Commission on Curriculum. The United States Office of Education employs a Specialist in Community and Junior Colleges to gather and disseminate information about these colleges and to provide consultative service to the states in relation to the establishment and the development of the junior college curriculum.

It is apparent, then, that the total process of defining the scope of the community junior college curriculum depends upon information and stimulation from many sources. In the process of this development the community junior college receives requests for service from the community, studies the programs of other junior colleges, colleges, and universities, keeps abreast of the emphasis and proposals throughout its state and the nation, and actively searches for ways to fulfill its responsibility to provide for the post-high-school educational needs of its community.

B. Maintaining the Quality of Instruction

The external influences described in the previous section help the administrator to decide which courses should be offered in each community junior college. These decisions are only the first necessary steps in establishing an effective educational program. Many further decisions about class schedules, about methods and materials for the various courses, and about selection of students and evaluation of instruction will influence the extent and the quality of the curriculum to which the students have access. A course in humanities, for example, may be approved after considerable study, and included in the junior college catalog. Yet it may fail entirely in its intended influence on students because teachers are unavailable or poorly trained or uninterested in it, because adequate classrooms or instructional supplies are not made available, because guidance workers fail to call it to the attention of students, or even because it is scheduled at an unattractive or conflicting time. Provisions that have been found effective in assuring the high quality of the curriculum include the appointment of a curriculum officer, often named the Dean of Instruction, the establishment of a college-wide curriculum committee, a continuous program of research and evaluation of curriculum, and the encouragement of faculty members to prize and to aspire to competent and enthusiastic instruction.

Dean of Instruction. It is the responsibility of the Dean of Instruction to promote continuous review of the offerings of the college to the end that the quality of the faculty, the organization of the courses, and the auxiliary services of the college may all combine to provide excellent educational opportunity for all classes of students. His duties in relation to the instructors will include a forecast of needed additions and replacements each year, development of their assignments for each semester, elaboration of plans for the induction of new teachers and for continuous in-service training of the entire faculty. One of his most important functions is the supervision of instruction. Through classroom visitation he gains a concrete acquaintance with the nature of the curriculum and refreshes his awareness of the daily problems of instructors; he is enabled to provide realistic help to them in improving their techniques of presentation, as well as in considering revisions of the course purposes or materials. In meetings with the staff of the several departments or divisions of the college, he is enabled to interpret to them such matters as university regulations or the meaning of college policies; at the same time, he keeps himself informed of the instructional problems which are engaging the attention of the faculty.

The Dean of Instruction is typically responsible also for the preparation of the junior college catalog, especially for the sections that present suggested programs of study for various objectives of students and for the descriptions of each course offered. The schedule of classes expresses all curricular research and philosophy as it joins the converging forces of instructors, students, time, buildings, equipment, and units of credit into a single educative process. Most of the decisions involved in the schedule, and not a little of the detailed cross checking, rest with the Dean of Instruction. As a basis for his decisions, he will need a continuous flow of information on matters such as past course enrollments, projected enrollments, trends in student demand, comparative student-contact hours of instructors, rates of withdrawal from classes, room capacity, faculty preferences, and classes that are likely to conflict.

Curriculum Committee. The Dean of Instruction will exert most of his efforts for the continuous development of the quality of the curriculum through the curriculum committee, of which he is typically the chairman. This committee is charged with the responsibility of considering all proposals for major changes in the curriculum of the college, from whatever source; the changes that it approves are recommended to the president and to the board of trustees for official action. In addition to its work as a review board for curricular proposals from all sources, the curriculum committee ordinarily assumes leadership in the development of plans for improvement in the college offerings and initiates and supervises needed studies of the instructional functioning of the institution. Its membership will include the Dean of Instruction as chairman; other administrative officers who are concerned with instructional matters, such as those in charge of summer session, adult education, vocational education, and other specialized offerings; representatives from the library staff and from counseling and guidance; the deans or chairmen of the instructional divisions of the college and several representatives of the teaching faculty. Suggestions have been made that the curriculum committee should also include lay persons and members of the student body. Such representation is probably unnecessary if the functions of the curriculum committee are limited, as suggested, to instructional problems and if the pattern of general and specialized lay advisory committees is utilized to advantage. In addition, an effective curriculum committee will meet with comparative frequency; participation should be a part of the assigned load of the members. Lay persons should not be expected to contribute so much time to this professional function.

Within a given year, a curriculum committee might well achieve a series of projects such as the following:

1. *Routine review of the entire curriculum:* Each division of the junior college reports at a scheduled meeting, presenting its enrollment trends and its problems of schedule or equipment or student recruitment or instructional effectiveness together with recommendations for additions or deletions of courses.

2. *Curriculum studies:* (a) The committee considers and acts on results of a vocational survey, proposing a course in laboratory technician training. (b) Considers a proposal from an interested instructor for the inauguration of a course in children's literature for prospective elementary teachers.

3. *Policy investigations:* (a) After noting wide variation in proportion of "A" and "C" grades given by instructors and by divisions, the committee assigns a subcommittee to develop a statement of the meaning of each letter grade. Arranges for consideration, revision, and approval of the statement in order by the committee, the faculty, and the board of trustees. (b) Investigates teacher load, by departments, in other colleges, as a basis for considering a redefinition.

4. *Faculty studies:* (a) The committee sponsors a study by each division of the college, under leadership of the division chairmen, of the meaning and application of the aims of general education in its own classrooms. After this consideration, some changes may be recommended in the requirements for graduation or in the nature of specific courses offered by several of the divisions. (b) Recommends the financing and planning of a workshop during the summer in which

instructors involved will attempt to clarify their purposes and outline of materials in one or more of the required courses.

Ingles suggests several criteria to be used by a curriculum committee and the administrator in deciding whether to install a proposed new course. He suggests that evidence should be gathered for each proposed course on

1. *Need*—Does the course contribute measurably to transfer, occupational, or remedial education? Could an existing course be modified to satisfy the need?

2. *Relation to other courses*—Will the proposed course duplicate, supplement, or replace another course?

3. *Scholarship level*—Is it clearly a course appropriate for the junior college, rather than to upper division or to high school? Is the unit value in harmony with that of similar offerings? (79).

The administration, after receiving the proposal from the curriculum committee, will consider the problems of the need for a lay advisory committee, the need for added staff, the duplication unnecessarily of offerings in nearby institutions, the present and future cost of the course in relation to other desirable expenditures, and the long-range prospects of student enrollment.

In view of its responsibilities and its functions, the curriculum committee in the community junior college exerts a decisive influence not only on the scope and the quality of the class offerings; it is equally effective in safeguarding the conditions that encourage excellent teaching and in interpreting the faculty to the administration and vice versa. It helps to create the enthusiasm and morale among the instructors that arise from the recognition by the entire college that its purposes are achieved only when they are achieved in the classroom.

Research. Constant reference has been made in the pages of this chapter to the need for continuous research as a basis for curricular decisions. Such fact gathering is never completed. The questioning faculty is an improving faculty, if it discovers answers. For this reason the collection and interpretation of all kinds of information are essential elements of a program of curriculum development. Many useful facts are easily and conveniently available, if only someone has the time to gather and tabulate them, and the interest to search for their meaning. The list that follows is not intended to be exhaustive. It merely suggests some of the kinds of information that must be kept up to date and made available to teachers, deans, counselors, curriculum committees, and junior college administrators as essential tools in their daily tasks.

Many kinds of knowledge about the community of the public junior college are needed. The college offering is affected by population growth or decline, economic stability, breadth of industrial, commercial, or agricultural employment, socioeconomic composition of the community, other colleges in the area, income, and assessed valuation trends, to name only a few of the factors. The students require careful analysis also. How many are coming through the lower schools? What are the characteristics of those who enroll at the junior college? What trends are discernible in age, health, marital status, aptitude, and educational plans? How long do they persist in attendance and how well do they do in their studies? What of the success of the graduate in his next endeavor, whether work or study? Administratively, how do annual unit costs compare with those of comparable junior colleges? What legislation affects the college, in the state or nation? Are the student-faculty ratios and the teaching load within acceptable limits? What evidence is available about the quality of instruction, through observation, faculty opinion, student reaction, available tests of achievement, later study, and other sources? The community junior college that gathers such data as a basis for its educational planning will be a busy institution; by the same token, it will almost certainly be one of high instructional quality.

Selected References

Fields, Ralph R. "The Program Defined and Implemented." Chapter 9 in *The Public Junior College*. Nelson B. Henry (editor). Fifty-fifth Yearbook of the National Society for the Study of Education. Chicago: University of Chicago Press, 1956.

Harris, Norman C. *Technical Education in the Junior College: New Programs for New Jobs*. Washington: American Association of Junior Colleges, 1964.

Ingles, E. T. "Criteria for Adding New Courses to the Junior College Curriculum," *California Journal of Secondary Education*, 32:218–221, April, 1957.

Johnson, B. Lamar. "California Junior College Curriculum Development," *California Journal of Secondary Education*, 31:134–138, March, 1956.

———. *General Education in Action*. Washington: American Council on Education, 1952.

Peterson, Basil H. "A Self-Appraisal of Educational and Occupational Needs of the Coastal Area of Orange County," *Junior College Journal*, 25:385–391, March, 1955.

——— and James W. Thornton, Jr. "Building a Functional Program for a Junior College," *Junior College Journal*, 19:119–124, November, 1948.

Weide, D. L. "Relationship of Junior College Terminal Courses to Local Industry," *Junior College Journal*, 20:460–467, April, 1950.

13

The Curriculum:
Occupational Education

Today there is a vast array of occupations for which at least two years of college study are necessary. These occupations are often referred to as middle-manpower jobs, the semiprofessional and technical positions which comprise the major category of employment in business, industry, and the professions. These jobs are an outgrowth of the technological revolution in which automation has combined with mechanization to replace the unskilled and even the skilled worker in many instances in factories, in offices, on farms, and in hospitals and laboratories.

It is ironic that, while there is wide-spread unemployment today, there is a growing shortage of people to fill the new and more sophisticated jobs in American business and industry. Almost all work today requires education and training of the individual as a thinking, problem-solving person, rather than as an automaton engaged in repetitive tasks which require only manual effort. The market for the unskilled and even the semi-skilled is shrinking rapidly (116).

For more than forty years, writers about the junior college have advocated the establishment of courses to prepare students for immediate employment. This concept of one of the functions of the junior college has been recognized officially by several of the states in their laws authorizing the establishment of public junior colleges. Since its first issue in 1930, the *Junior College Journal* has carried articles and editorials about occupational studies. A great majority of the junior colleges in America offer one or more courses designed to prepare students for immediate entry into employment.

175

Nevertheless, the idea of junior college education for occupational life has not yet achieved full acceptance in American educational or social thought. A good many administrators of public junior colleges remain unconvinced of the propriety of collegiate occupational programs and limit their offerings to two or three courses. The lay citizen, even in communities with extensive junior college occupational offerings, is only partially aware of the nature of and the need for these courses. Workers in other segments of the educational system are likely to share the lack of information and the misconceptions of the layman. Students also, as they come to the junior college to enroll, are often unaware of the nature of occupational offerings. As a result,

Less than a quarter of all junior college students are enrolled in organized occupational curricula. In 1960, the most recent year for which comprehensive figures are available, 170,831 students were enrolled in such curricula in two-year colleges. . . . Of these, 59,004 were in engineering-related curricula, and 111,827 in nonengineering-related curricula. 1960 graduates from the former category numbered 10,190, and from the latter 22,958 (*158*:88).

Further confusion is added to the definition of occupational courses in junior colleges by the lack of agreement, even among institutions that have established such courses, on the kinds of occupations for which junior colleges should prepare students and on the scope and level of appropriate instruction. Chapter 13 attempts to clarify the field of community junior college occupational education. It presents a series of definitions of terms frequently used (and sometimes confused) in discussing this function. Thereafter, evidence about the nature and prevalence of occupational courses is presented, followed by a discussion of some of the current issues in the development of community junior college occupational education.

A. *Terminology of Occupational Education*

In the literature dealing with junior college preparation for employment, several terms with overlapping connotations are employed, sometimes interchangeably. A brief discussion of the background and meaning of each term will lead to a clearer understanding of the field of community junior college occupational education. Among the phrases essential to an understanding of this aspect of the curriculum are "terminal education," "vocational education," "semiprofessional education," "technical education," and "occupational education." In addition, some of these are at times used in combination, as "terminal-technical" or "vocational-technical."

Terminal Education. In 1925, Koos contrasted the "isthmian" function of the junior college with its "terminal" function (*91*). The term "isthmian," intended to indicate that the junior college serves as a bridge between high school and senior college, was never widely adopted. The word "terminal," indicating education planned for those students who did not intend to continue their attendance beyond the junior college, proved to be a more useful term. Several authors object to it because of a growing understanding of the fact that learning is lifelong, that it does not cease at the end of any period of school attendance. Another objection arose from an early tendency in some junior colleges to segregate students unnecessarily into classes of "transfer" and "terminal" students; this practice in effect created two distinct student bodies with certain unwholesome social and even educational consequences. According to one point of view, moreover, the distinction between transfer and terminal functions was invalid and unnecessary, since occupational training might result from appropriate combinations of transfer courses (*59:73*). With the growing recognition of the need for technical education, this concept of the dual-purpose course is losing its earlier degree of acceptance (*60:62*).

In spite of the objections, there is a use for a term with the implications of "terminal education in the junior college." "Terminal" may be defined as applying to community junior college courses of study planned primarily for the student who intends that the completion of the program will mark the end of his full-time enrollment in organized classes in schools. By extension, of course, the adjective may apply also to the student who enrolls in such courses. Certain corollaries of the definition should be understood. Terminal courses may be of any appropriate length, whether a semester, a year, or two years, as the majority of occupational courses. Again, a change in the objective of the student who may decide after all to continue his education does not invalidate the concept of terminal courses; a major purpose of the program of studies and the original intention of the student were both "terminal." Finally, it should be noted that terminal courses are not necessarily occupational in nature; a general course of study leading to no specific occupation may be terminal, depending on the purposes of the college in planning it and of the student in enrolling in it.

Vocational Education. "Vocational education" has come to be restricted, in much educational writing, to preparation of "less than college grade" for specific job fields in the areas of agriculture, trades and industry, distributive education, and homemaking. Such preparation has been federally subsidized since 1917 and has been developed mostly in the high schools. Some junior colleges have offered vocational education programs which qualified for federal aid under this series of acts; recently, however, there is a tendency to develop junior college courses of study that prepare for families of occupations and to give up the specific training programs required under earlier federal legislation.

The limits of the concept of vocational education may be established by means of a series of sentences taken from an official bulletin:

To the learner, vocational education is learning how to work. . . . To the educator, vocational education is teaching others how to work. It is a systematic program for discovering the knowledge, skills, and attitudes people must have for successful participation in a specific area of work, for organizing these inter-related elements into graded courses and experiences, and for integrating these courses and experiences within the total educational program. . . . Vocational education is always specific. It must prepare the individual to *understand,* and to be able to *do* the specific activities found to be necessary in accomplishing a given task. . . . It must be set in a laboratory equipped with the actual tools and materials which are used in the occupation and operated in such a way as to parallel the activities on a real job. (*159:1–3*)

In the limited and usual sense, then, vocational education implies a series of courses preparing for a specific occupation in the fields of agriculture, trades and industry, distributive occupations, or homemaking. When offered in a community junior college, it forms only a part of the total program of studies of the student; its major emphasis is on practice rather than on theory, and it is legally considered to be of "less than college grade." The concept is a more limited one than either "terminal" or "special" education.

In the "Vocational Education Act of 1963," the entire traditional concept of federally supported vocational education was revised. Support for specific occupational fields was withdrawn, and funds were made available at any appropriate level of education, so that all persons might have access to training or retraining in any occupation. Vocational education, under this Act, emphasizes the citizen who needs training, rather than the industry that needs workers.

Semiprofessional Education. The term "semiprofessional education" was coined to dignify junior college occupational courses; it has come to be used in a more restricted sense to indicate the preparation of aides for professional workers. Such helpers are deemed to need more than high-school training but not a bachelor's degree. They include engineering technicians, laboratory technicians, dental assistants, and other workers in manufacturing, in business, and in service occupations who must combine a measurable understanding of the field with a considerable skill in technique. In effect, it is possible to consider "semiprofessional" to be an inclusive euphemism to indicate the desirable difference between the vocational education offered in the secondary schools and the broader and deeper courses of study to be developed by the community junior colleges. The term has been applied at one time or other to nearly all the occupational fields for which junior college programs have been developed, even though their relationship to a profession might be extremely tenuous.

Technical Education is a specialized category of junior college two-year education; it prepares for jobs in which some manipulative skill is required but in which technical knowledge is emphasized. In general, "technical education" implies preparation for occupations within scientific and engineering fields where the worker will make use of instruments rather than tools and mental effort rather than muscular exertion. With the advent of the electronic age, the demand is increasing for technicians in all fields—business, national defense, construction, manufacturing, medicine, service, and design, to name but a few. The preparation of technicians is an appropriate undertaking for junior colleges, since these workers require more maturity and depth of scientific knowledge than the high school graduate has achieved, although the scope of their operation and education is likely to be narrower than that of the graduate engineer or scientist under whose direction they will work.

A publication of the Office of Education lists six examples of day programs in "Vocational-Technical Education"; all but the third description apply to courses appropriate for community junior colleges:

1. Curriculums with broad technical content in specific industrial fields, designed to prepare persons for engineering technician occupations; usually two years in length, on the post-high school level; commonly known as educational programs of the technical institute type.

2. Curriculums designed to prepare persons for technical specialist occupations, usually confined to one area within an industry; commonly six months to two years in length, on the post-high school level; scope of content narrower than that of technical institute type curriculums.

3. Vocational-technical curriculums in technical high schools, designed to prepare youth for positions similar to those of engineering technicians but on a somewhat lower level.

4. Curriculums which combine technical content with sales content, cost content, and the like; frequently two years in length, on the post-high school level.

5. Vocational-technical curriculums which lie outside the fields of engineering, such as biological laboratory technology, or medical assistant technology; usually two years in length, on the post-high school level.

6. Short intensive programs designed to prepare persons for specific vocational-technical occupations of comparatively low level (44:9).

Occupational Education. Each of the terms just defined is inadequate as a single designation for all the courses of study offered in community junior colleges for the purpose of preparing students to enter an occupation at the end of the course and to succeed and advance in it. The term "occupational education" is sufficiently broad to include areas such as nursing education or secretarial training together with technical and trade training; at the same time, it has not been pre-empted by specialized segments of the entire field of training or employment. "Occupational education" is used in this chapter to denote all organized junior college programs of study, of whatever length, that combine appropriate proportions of technical, manipulative, general, and elective courses to prepare the student for employment upon the successful completion of the course.

The practice of occupational education in community junior colleges may be demonstrated by the course of study suggested in one catalog for the mechanical technology curriculum. The two-year sequence is intended to prepare personnel for work in drafting and design, material control and testing, manufacturing processes, production control and efficiency, and maintenance. Entrance requirements include high-school graduation and satisfactory preparation in English, algebra, geometry, and drafting. Other community junior colleges might organize such a program in different fashion, perhaps as suggested by Harris (60:65–66). The curriculum outline on page 181 shows the combination of general and specialized courses considered effective in a large community junior college in an industrial city.

B. Kinds of Occupational Courses

American Junior Colleges (Sixth Edition) (56) presents information on the curriculum of each of 655 accredited public and private junior colleges. The information in Table 9 on occupational courses is derived from a summary in Appendix IV of that work.

It is apparent that *secretarial and clerical* courses, with 297 op-

Curriculum in Mechanical Technology

Name and Number of Course		Semester Hours of Credit
General Courses		14
Human Relations 291	Industrial Orientation	2
Political Science 132	Introduction to American Government	4
English 105–106	English Composition	6
Physical Education:	Two Semesters Required	2
Physical Science and Mathematics Group		17
Math. 161–162–261	Mathematics and Measurement	9
Physics 262–263–265–266	Mechanics; Heat, Light, and Sound; Fluid Power	8
Drafting and Design Group		12
Engineering Drawing 141–142	Engineering Drawing	6
Engineering Drawing 241	Product Drawing	3
Engineering Drawing 242	Tool Drawing	3
Electrical Group		3
Electricity 101	Circuitry	3
Materials and Processes Group		16
Materials and Processes 121	Industrial Materials	3
Materials and Processes 122	Metals and Alloys	2
Materials and Processes 123	Casting and Forming	3
Materials and Processes 124	Welding	3
Materials and Processes 221	Machining	3
Materials and Processes 225	Gaging and Inspection	2
	Total Hours	62

portunities, are the most frequent occupational offerings in junior colleges. The total business field, with an additional 431 curriculums, is also the most frequently taught broad field. The total of 728 curriculums compares with a similar tally of 595 four years earlier. Since the general category of "business" accounts for more than one-fourth of all employment in the United States, even smaller junior colleges can enroll enough students to justify the offering of business training and find suitable employment for them when they complete the course. For this reason, business courses are the usual first occupational offering of junior colleges.

Engineering Technology was not listed as a separate category in the 1960 edition of *American Junior Colleges,* although some 279 of the curriculums listed might be broadly defined as technically based. The recognition of the need for technicians is demonstrated by the emergence in a four-year period of 403 curriculums specifically labeled as engineering technologies. The electrical and electronic emphasis is most frequent, with 109 colleges offering work, followed by a total of 82 curriculums in general engineering and engineering technology, and 66 in mechanical technology.

Table 9. Number of Accredited Junior Colleges Offering Named Occupational Courses of Study, 1962–1963 [a]

Course of Study		Number of Colleges
Total Business Courses		728
Secretarial and Clerical	297	
General Business	106	
Accounting	106	
Administration and Management	86	
Sales and Retailing	96	
Data Processing	37	
Total Engineering Technology		403
General Engineering	37	
Engineering Technology	45	
Aero and Aero-Space Technology	7	
Air Conditioning Technology	19	
Architecture and Civil		
Engineering Technology	45	
Chemical Technology	30	
Electrical and Electronic		
Technology	109	
Industrial Technology	31	
Mechanical Technology	66	
Metallurgical Technology	14	
Total Trades and Industry		347
General Trades and Industry	34	
Aviation	19	
Construction	47	
Electricity and Electronics	73	
Metal and Machine	65	
Mechanical	78	
Industrial Arts	31	

(Continued)

[a] **Source:** Appendix IV, "Curricula Offered by Junior Colleges, Fall Term 1962," *American Junior Colleges* (Sixth Edition).

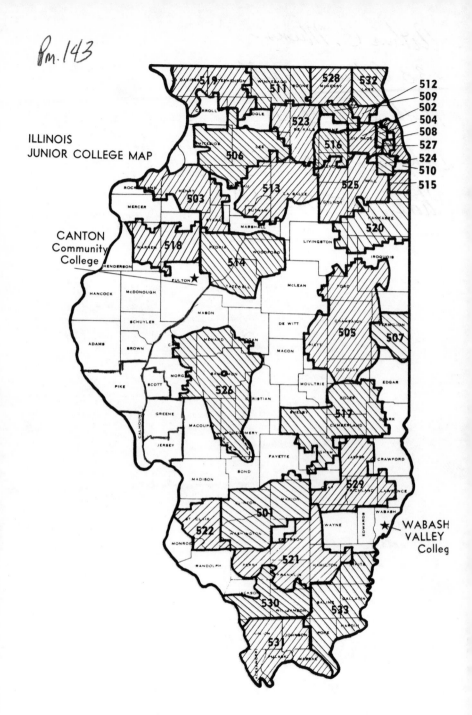

Pm. 143

ILLINOIS
JUNIOR COLLEGE MAP

CANTON
Community
College

WABASH
VALLEY
Colleg

512
509
502
504
508
527
524
510
515

Dr. Arthur C. Muns
133 Adams Hall
Northern Ill. Univ.
DeKalb, Illinois 60115
Phone 815-753-1781

Table 9 (*Continued*)

Course of Study	Number of Colleges
Nursing	148
Drafting	100
Medical Secretarial	79
Art	76
Home Economics	63
Agriculture	52
Medical Technology	47
Music	40
Police Science	39
Architectural Drafting	32
Dental Assisting	28
Physical Education and Recreation	25
Food and Hotel Technology	23
Printing	19
Speech and Drama	19
Teaching	18
Dental Hygiene	18
Journalism	18
Clothing Technology	16
Therapy	13
Forestry	9
Dental Technology	8
Miscellaneous Curriculums [b]	186

[b] In 197 colleges, 186 miscellaneous courses were offered under 61 different occupational titles. Specialized courses in barbering, child study, cosmetology, gunsmithing, petroleum technology, real estate, and watch repair were included among those available in one or more of the junior colleges listed.

On the other hand, *trade and industrial* courses in junior colleges seem to be declining in frequency, unless the change is merely one of title rather than of essential nature of the offerings. Since the basic data were reported differently by the colleges for the two editions of *American Junior Colleges,* it is difficult to be certain, but there seems to be a definite trend away from the manipulative training concept of vocational education, and toward the scientific and mathematical emphasis of technical education. Each of the subcategories of trade and industrial education (except metal work, which held constant at 65 colleges) shows a decrease in the number of offerings over the four-year period between 1958 and 1962.

Technical assistance in the *health fields* is an important curriculum area in junior colleges. Curriculums in nursing (148), medical secretarial (79), medical technology (47), dental assisting (28), dental hygiene (18), therapy (13), and dental technology (8), total 341 offerings in these semiprofessional areas in the 655 junior colleges reporting.

In the *service area*, police science appears for the first time in the tabulation in *American Junior Colleges* (Sixth Edition), with 39 offerings. Teaching as a terminal curriculum in the junior college drops from a total of 76 colleges in the 1960 edition to 18 in the Sixth Edition; food and hotel technology, another new listing, is offered in 23 colleges. Agriculture, in recognition of its increasing emphasis on advanced scientific training and its decreasing importance as an employment field, has declined from 86 two-year courses in 1958 to only 52 in 1962.

Taken all together, the 655 public and private accredited junior colleges offer 2554 terminal occupational courses of study, a mean of about four offerings per college. The listing justifies the conclusion that junior colleges have fully accepted the responsibility for occupational education. In addition, it points up the fact that each college defines its own responsibility for these courses in the light of the demands of its constituency and its own philosophy of junior college education. A few colleges offer occupational courses only of a technical nature, whereas others concentrate almost entirely on business or business and trade courses. The statistical picture presented in Table 9 may be somewhat more extensive than the reality, since some junior colleges may at times list in their catalogs courses for which very few students enroll, or which are not offered at all in a given year.

Reference to three junior college catalogs will illustrate the diversity of practice in occupational education. The three colleges are located in different areas of the nation; all three enroll between 2000 and 3000 full-time freshman and sophomore students. Each of the three cities is a prosperous industrial community. Yet the differences in their occupational courses are greater than the similarity of college size and situation would lead one to expect. One college offers 555 semester units of technical nontransfer courses in a dozen two-year degree curriculums, including business (56 units), cosmetology (44), machine technology (43), nursing (39), and electricity and electronics with a total of 178 units. In addition, this same college offers 28-unit pre-employment trade curriculums in eleven fields, including carpentry, sheet metal, plumbing, and refrigeration. Related training courses for apprentices, offered only to full-time apprentices who are part-time students, account for 228 semester units available in twenty-three trades. Extension courses for vocational advancement of employed workers are offered in ten trades for a total of 98 units. The total terminal course offerings in this college amount to 1185 units; and the part-time annual enrollment is more than three times as large as its full-time freshman and sophomore enrollment.

The second college, situated in a similar city in another area of the nation, enrolls only slightly more part-time students than full-time. It offers technical work for full-time students in thirteen occupations, including five business specialties. Its two-year curriculums need a total of 307 semester units, including electricity (28), business fields (119), nursing (40), and 20 units of technical sciences and mathematics courses required in several occupational courses of study. Extension work for part-time students is offered in ten occupational fields, and amounts to a total of 119 units, or 426 units in all. The third college has half as many part-time students as full-time freshmen and sophomores. It offers a total of 201 semester units of terminal work, in eight occupational fields. Among these are business (56), electrical technology (47), nursing (24), and dental hygiene (18).

The three colleges exemplify three stages of occupational education in the junior college. The first, with its all-inclusive coverage of full-time technical and vocational education, apprenticeship related training, and extension courses for vocational advancement, represents the fullest possible development of this aspect of junior college curriculum. There is some evidence that nationally the trend is away from such complete coverage, and that trade and apprenticeship courses may be decreasing in the junior colleges in favor of technical education. On the other hand, if junior colleges generally accept the role of "area vocational school" authorized in the Vocational Education Act of 1963, this community junior college may become the model for future development of other colleges.

The second college takes a middle position. It offers both pre-employment and extension work, but limits its courses to the technical and business areas. It has a balanced appeal to the full-time and the part-time student. It can defend each of its offerings as of junior-college level, and is probably representative of the modal position of community junior colleges of this size. The third college seems much more conservative in its approach to occupational education, and may well be just at the beginning of its development of this aspect of the curriculum. It makes no separate and explicit provision for the part-time employed student, and limits its offerings to courses that have been tested in other colleges in other communities.

Frequency of Occupational Courses. From the same Appendix IV in *American Junior Colleges* (Sixth Edition), another insight may be gained into the scope and frequency of occupational education in accredited junior colleges. The appendix names each of the colleges and indicates by an asterisk each of the listed terminal courses offered in that college. It is possible, therefore, to gain an approximation of the median frequency of these terminal offerings in junior colleges. The "miscellaneous" category introduces a slight inaccuracy into the calculation of the median, since some of the junior colleges offer several "miscellaneous" courses of study. A tally of the number of terminal programs offered by each accredited junior college provides the information summarized in Table 10. It is of interest to note that

Table 10.   Frequency of Terminal Offerings in 655 Accredited Junior Colleges, 1962–1963 [a]

Number of Terminal Offerings	Number of Colleges	Per Cent of 655 Colleges	Cumulative Percentage
0	181	27.7	27.7
1	80	12.1	39.8
2	64	9.8	49.6
3	60	9.2	58.8
4	51	7.8	66.6
5	40	6.1	72.7
6	35	5.3	79.0
7	19	2.9	80.9
8	21	3.2	84.1
9	17	2.6	86.7
10	10	1.5	88.2
11–15	51	7.8	96.0
16–20	15	2.3	98.3
21–25	7	1.1	99.4
26–31	4	0.6	100.0
Total	655	100.0	—

[a] Source: Appendix IV, "Curricula Offered by Junior Colleges, Fall Term 1962," *American Junior Colleges* (Sixth Edition) (*56*).

181 of these 655 junior colleges offer no terminal courses. The median listing is three terminal courses; no college offers more than 31 of them.

C. Current Issues in Community Junior College Occupational Education

Expansion of Junior College Occupational Education. Junior college administrators and theorists are in substantial agreement that occupational education is one of the functions of community junior colleges. All of them tend to accept also the principle that each junior college should offer courses that are appropriate to its own constituency and its own community. A majority of junior college administrators, especially in public junior colleges, agree further that business education is a fully acceptable kind of junior college occupational education. At this point, any appearance of unanimity ceases. Some junior colleges resist the encroachments of "vocationalism" upon the college curriculum, while others search aggressively for new opportunities to serve their communities through the establishment of needed occupational courses.

The employment crisis of the sixties is based on the increasingly cognitive nature of a great amount of employment. Human strength and docility are no longer prime qualities in the employment market. The unemployed are largely the uneducated, the unprepared; yet the newspapers are filled with advertisements for workers with skills suited to automated production. White-collar jobs outnumber blue-collar jobs in the labor force, and their share of the total force increases yearly. In spite of these trends, more than half of all junior colleges offer fewer than three curriculums emphasizing any occupational skills; among the courses offered, the business rather than the technical competences predominate.

The issue may be simply stated: either the community junior colleges will accept in practice the responsibility for middle-level technical education, or some other institution will be established to carry out this essential educational task.

Articulation with Other Institutions. In developing its occupational programs and in defining its role in occupational education within any region, the community junior college must work closely with other educational institutions. It seems to be true that the public high school will play a diminishing role in specific vocational education as the age of first employment rises and the technical requirements for many jobs are increased. During the transitional period, however, the junior college staff must work closely with the high-school authorities, in the interests both of fiscal economy and of educational efficiency.

Several of the states that are developing or extending their system of public junior colleges have previously established separate trade, vocational, or technical schools. In most instances, these schools have concentrated on the direct preparation of their students for immediate employment in a given occupation, without concern for more than a bare minimum of education in nonvocational subject matter. Junior college occupational education includes a balance of special and general education and may be presumed to have greater value both for the student and for society. It may well be that in the long run the vocational schools and the junior colleges will be amalgamated in all states as they have been in North Carolina and Hawaii; until such unification of effort is possible, however, junior colleges face continuing problems in the coordination of their occupational offerings with the existing, although limited, opportunities already available in the community.

A third area of articulation concerns the relation of junior college occupational courses to advanced standing requirements in four-year colleges and universities. Students sometimes hesitate to enroll in terminal occupational courses because they fear that credit will be denied for such study if later they decide to seek a bachelor's degree. The question of appropriate credit in bachelor's degree programs for such courses has long been a source of concern to junior college counselors and to university registrars. In general, it may be stated (1) that no single rule can possibly apply to the acceptance of credit for all occupational courses from all junior colleges in fulfilling requirements at all four-year colleges and universities in every major field; (2) that the quality of a student's junior college achievement is a more reliable predictor of his success in upper-division study than is the specific pattern of lower-division courses he has completed; (3) that necessary prerequisites to specific advanced courses cannot be dispensed with, no matter how high the level of a student's marks in other junior college courses; and (4) that each junior college and each senior college will need to analyze the applicability of specific occupational courses to specific degree programs to determine whether the courses that were established for one (terminal) purpose may or may not be accepted in certain cases as meeting another (transfer) purpose.

Balance of Elements in Occupational Programs. Because of the briefness of the junior college period and the multiplicity of its functions, curriculum makers are constantly faced with a choice among educational values. The enthusiastic occupational instructor often feels that he could engage the entire two years of the student's full-time study without preparing him adequately for employment. A contrary pressure is exerted by the generalists on the faculty, who realize how far from ready their students are to bear the responsibilities of life in present-day civilization. The suggested pattern of studies set forth in any organized program is a compromise between these two forces, complicated further by the possibility of legal requirements of courses that must be taught to all students or completed by all graduates.

Several rule-of-thumb suggestions have been made for the resolution of this conflict. Eells has suggested that an occupational program

A Global Course Organization in Building Trades

		Units of Credit	
Number and Name of Course		Semester I	Semester II
The First-Year Program			
English 51A–51B	Language Skills	3	3
American Problems 10A–10B	History and Government	3	3
Orientation 1	Educational and Vocational Planning	1	
Industrial Drawing 30A	Fundamentals		3
Building Construction 58A–58B	Vocational Course	8	8
Physical Education		½	½
	Semester total	15½	17½
The Second-Year Program			
Psychology 51	Applied Psychology	3	
Speech 51	Business Speech		3
Health Education 1	Physical and Mental Health	2	
Physical Education 31A	First Aid		1
Electives		2	3
Industrial Mathematics 53	Fundamentals	3	
Architectural Drawing 30A	Working Drawings		3
Industrial Science 63A–63B	Physical Sciences	3	3
Building Construction 64A–64B	Vocational Course	4	4
Physical Education		½	½
	Semester total	17½	17½

should include 40% specialized study and 40% general courses. He recommended that 20% of the total study for graduation be reserved for elective courses so that the student might pursue any field in which he had a personal need or a worthy interest. Several of the examples of curriculum patterns described by Harris (60:63–76) require from 72 to 76 semester units of study. Of these, about 20 are assigned to general education subjects—about 25%, with limited opportunity for free elective courses. A more traditional curriculum pattern of 62–64 semester hours would permit most students to complete their degree and occupational requirements in four semesters of full-time study. Of this, about half, or 30 semester hours, should be assigned to specific technical courses; about one-third, or 20 semester hours, to required general education; and the remaining one-sixth, or 10 semester hours, for elective courses. The important consideration is to assure a reasonable balance of breadth and specialization in each occupational program, so that it may constitute for each student a harmonious collegiate experience.

Program Development. The organization of instruction in occupational areas varies between junior colleges and also between several occupational fields in the same junior college. Little research is available to help determine which pattern of organization is more effective in training for any given employment. In trade training, a "global" organization is frequently found. Under this plan, one instructor is in charge of all the lecture and laboratory work in the occupational course for a comparatively long period of time; periods of three or four hours scheduled on three or five days a week are usual. This plan has the advantage of flexibility, in that lecture and laboratory work may be combined in any proportions; laboratory periods are of economical length, so that only a minor fraction of the time need be used in changing clothes, issuing tools, and cleaning up. Field trips can be arranged within the time schedule for the class, without the need for excusing students from other teachers' classes. Disadvantages of the global pattern may include the difficulty of finding a single instructor who is able to teach all aspects of the course, the fact that the laboratory or shop is not used with greatest economy, since it will be vacant whenever the instructor is lecturing, and the inability to care for the student who does not desire the entire occupational course, but only a single aspect of it.

The alternate plan, a series of separate courses in various aspects of the occupation, is more usual in business, home economics, and agriculture. This plan allows for specialization of teaching; it also permits a single class section to be used as a portion of the course of

A Specialized Course Organization in Automotive Technology

Number and Name of Course		Units of Credit	
		Semester I	Semester II
The First-Year Program			
English 1–2	Composition	3	3
Political Science 5	Survey of American Government	3	
Physics A	Introductory Physics	3	
Psychology 5	Personality Development		2
Shop Practice 1	Basic Machine Tools		2
Automotive Training 1	The Automotive Industry	2	
Automotive Training 2	Construction of the Automobile	4	
Automotive Training 3	Elementary Electricity	2	
Automotive Training 4	Internal Combustion Engines		4
Automotive Training 5	Starting and Lighting Systems		4
	Semester total	17	15
The Second-Year Program			
Speech 3	Elementary Speech	2	
Business Mathematics 1	Business Arithmetic	2	
Business Administration 1	Business Organization		3
Accounting A	Practical Accounting		4
Retailing 1	Fundamentals of Retailing		4
Automotive Training 6	Generating and Battery Systems	4	
Automotive Training 7	Fuel Systems and Carburetion	4	
Automotive Training 8	Ignition Systems	3	
Automotive Training 9	Diagnostic Laboratory		4
	Semester total	15	15

study of students in varying major fields. It separates laboratory time from lecture time and so may make possible a greater utilization of specialized equipment. It suffers a disadvantage in that conflicts in schedule with general education courses are more frequent; however, some students will not enroll in all the courses essential for complete occupational preparation; their related training may be taught by instructors with only a minimum acquaintance with the specialized occupational field (when technical mathematics, for example, is taught by a mathematics teacher who does not know electronics); and the single courses may be elected by students whose objectives are not occupational. In a community junior college of medium size, moreover, it may well be that a single instructor is required to teach the entire series of separate courses, so that no advantage of specialization is gained over the global course organization.

The detailed courses of study from two community junior colleges demonstrate the difference between the global and the specialized course organizations. The global organization is represented by a major-field program entitled Building Trades, with concentration in Pre-Trade Carpentry. This program includes sixty-eight units, of which twenty-four (35%) are in the major course and an additional six units (9%) are in drafting. General courses account for a total of thirty-three units (48%), if Industrial Science and Mathematics and Business Speech may be considered a part of the general rather than occupational studies. Electives are limited to five units (7%) of the total of sixty-eight. The vocational course requires fifteen hours of classtime weekly in the first year, and ten hours weekly in the second year.

A course for Automotive Technicians at another community college demonstrates the use of a variety of courses of lesser unit value to achieve a similar intensity of occupational training.

In this program, the major course accounts for thirty-one units (50%) of the total recommended program in addition to the two units in shop practice (3%). A series of vocationally related courses in the business field requires thirteen units (21%) of the student's total credit and sixteen units (26%) are allocated to general education. In this suggested program no time is provided for free election of courses. Both programs provide for intensive study of occupational topics and related knowledge and both provide a good opportunity for general education. The elective opportunity, however, is limited in the one program and nonexistent in the other.

Specialization of Training. The desirable *degree of specialization* of the offering is another problem in program development. It is not difficult to determine the content and the equipment of a course that trains carpenters, or body and fender workers, or television repairmen; but the realities of technological change suggest that broader training may be advisable to prepare graduates adequately for their futures. For this reason, community junior colleges have attempted to develop courses which prepare for families of occupations, such as mechanical technology, electronic technology, or civil engineering technology.

Not only does such training prepare the graduate to progress to a position of responsibility in his work; its scope and variety make it more suitable to the junior college than the more limited trade training that may properly be found in vocational schools or in high schools.

Cooperative work experience is a further opportunity in the development of occupational programs. In cooperative education, students preparing for occupations spend part of their time in classes on the college campus, both in general education and in occupational courses. In addition, a part of their junior college course is devoted to work in the occupation for which they are preparing. The junior college staff arranges for the student's placement, supervises his work, and grants limited credit for successful completion of the assignment. In some plans, the students work as much as half-time and receive learners' rates of pay; in others their work is limited to fewer than ten hours weekly, and they receive no pay. Under either plan, the important outcomes from the standpoint of the community junior college are the first-hand acquaintance the student gains with the requirements of employment and the added understanding he brings to his class work.

Cooperation with Labor and Management. Occupational courses are soundly established only as a result of thorough and continuing study of the employment opportunities and the training needs of the industry. This information is available most readily from those who are currently working in the field, either as workers or managers. Advisory committees including representatives of both interests are essential to the development and maintenance of any occupational course. Such a committee can keep the community junior college abreast of trends in the occupation. It can help with placement of students and graduates, with choice and procurement of equipment, and with interpretation of the training program to workers and to employers. No occupational course should be established without the advice and encouragement of a broadly representative local advisory committee.

Retention of Students. In a period of low employment opportunity, the junior college is more concerned with finding work for its graduates than it is with keeping them in school until completion of the program. In a time of high employment, however, the timing of student employment may be a perplexing problem. The community junior college, with the cooperation of its advisory committee, plans an occupational program which it considers to be well-rounded and unified. The student who completes the program will have received training enabling him to obtain and to progress on a job; if he leaves before completion, he leaves with only partial training. Employers and students, however, sometimes fail to take this long-term attitude. The employer is certain that the half-trained bookkeeper, technician, draftsman, or secretary is superior to any of the untrained persons otherwise available to him. The student feels, justifiably, that he came to the community junior college to prepare to get a job which is now offered to him; it is difficult to convince him that an additional year of schooling would increase either his earning power or his preparation for living. The advisory committee may take a stand in this area by discouraging employers from hiring students prior to their graduation, but for the most part the decision to work or to study will be reached by the student in the light of the values that have become apparent to him.

Selection of Students. One of the most pressing issues in occupational education continues to be that of helping students to choose the course for which they are best fitted. Some degree of error is unavoidable; some students must be permitted to attempt curriculums in which their success seems unlikely. A good deal of the disproportion between ambition and achievement, however, derives from inadequacies of the junior colleges. In part, there is a failure to provide a suitable diversity of nontransfer courses. One or two terminal business courses (and half of the junior colleges offer no more) will not meet the needs of all nontransfer students. A second inadequacy lies in the failure to inform students and their parents, early in their high-school careers, of the availability and of the purposes of junior college occupational education. A good many students would choose their programs realistically, if only they had appropriate information. Lack of effective personal guidance is another contributor to failure and dropout. Students who are helped to see the relationship between their patterns of interests and abilities and the requirements of available occupations and of educational programs are enabled to choose wisely. Without such information, their choices must be blind and almost haphazard. It is becoming increasingly important to provide for some students a semester or more of preparatory studies so that they may have the educational background to succeed in the chosen technical course (60:83–86).

The Recruitment and Training of Occupational Instructors. Studies of certification standards for junior college teachers stress a combination of academic training equal to a master's degree or beyond, plus a meaningful period of work experience in a field related to the major subject (69:217–224). For teachers in occupational fields, the preparation requirements are even more stringent than those for teachers of traditional subjects. These teachers, in business, in technologies, or in trade subjects, need thorough academic knowledge of their specialty and adequate training in the methods and materials of teaching. Beyond this, they need actual vocational experience of sufficient scope to enable them to prepare their students realistically for the conditions and responsibilities of employment. They need to have achieved sufficient standing in their occupational field to work with members of the advisory committee on a basis of equality and mutual respect. Since such experience connotes considerable maturity, salary schedules must recognize this kind of experience and preparation as well as academic degrees and experience in teaching. Further, since such mature persons can rarely devote a year or more to full-time teacher-training programs, it is often necessary to enable them to complete the requirements for certification while they are teaching.

It seems probable that a major deterrent to the development of occupational education in junior colleges has been the scarcity of qualified instructors in these subjects. Until plans can be elaborated for the effective recruitment and training of instructors, the offerings will continue to be scanty and only partially suited to the educational needs of junior college students. In the words of Jarvie,

The inadequacies reported in the current preservice preparation of junior-college instructors do not, however, represent new findings or observations. . . . And yet, little is being done today to improve the preservice preparation of junior-college instructors. It also seems likely that the current situation will deteriorate before it improves. With the forthcoming expansion of enrollment, a shortage of teachers can be anticipated. Under these conditions, the quality of teacher preparation is all too likely to decline rather than to improve. (69:223)

His remarks apply with additional force to the preparation of teachers for occupational courses.

Selected References

Brooking, Walter J. "Accreditation of Vocational-Technical College Courses," *Junior College Journal,* 20:130–133, November, 1949.

Eells, Walter Crosby. *Present Status of Junior College Terminal Education.* Washington: American Association of Junior Colleges, 1941.

———. *Why Junior College Terminal Education?* Washington: American Association of Junior Colleges, 1941.

Emerson, Lynn A. *Vocational-Technical Education for American Industry.* Office of Education Circular No. 530. Washington: Government Printing Office, 1958.

Gleazer, Edmund J., Jr. (editor). *American Junior Colleges* (Sixth Edition), 1963. Washington: American Council on Education, 1963.

Harris, Norman C. *Technical Education in the Junior College: New Programs for New Jobs.* Washington: American Association of Junior Colleges, 1964.

Henry, Nelson B. (editor). *The Public Junior College,* Fifty-fifth Yearbook of the National Society for the Study of Education, Part I. Chicago: The University of Chicago Press, 1956, Chapters VI and XI.

Johnson, B. Lamar. *General Education in Action.* Washington: American Council on Education, 1952, Chapter XI.

Kintzer, Frederick C. "Education of Semi-Professionals Is on the Move," *Junior College Journal,* 35:19–23, May, 1965.

Medsker, Leland L. *The Junior College: Progress and Prospect.* New York: McGraw-Hill Book Co., 1960.

National Advisory Committee on the Junior College. *A National Resource for Occupational Education.* Washington: American Association of Junior Colleges, 1964.

Snyder, William H. "The Real Function of the Junior College," *Junior College Journal,* 1:74–80, November, 1930.

Torpey, William G. "National Concern for Engineering Technicians," *Junior College Journal,* 34:12–15, December, 1963.

Venn, Grant. *Man, Education, and Work.* Washington: American Council on Education, 1964.

Ward, Phebe. *Terminal Education in the Junior College.* New York: Harper and Row, 1947.

14

The Curriculum: General Education

Each student's program of studies is made up of three elements: preparation for occupational specialization, elective courses, and general education courses. Occupational specialization courses appear in many forms, but they include all the subjects required of any individual student as a part of his total preparation, immediate or remote, for his life's work. In this sense, calculus for the pre-engineering freshman and zoology for the premedical freshman are just as truly occupational education as technical electronics or stenography for the technician or the secretary.

The elective section of a given student's college education may include any course listed in the college catalog. After the graduation requirements of the college and the specific requirements for occupational specialization have been met, a student may complete his education by free choice from any of the courses for which he has met the prerequisites. For others, the same course may be a part of specialization; for him, it is an elective, chosen to satisfy an individual interest. The only distinction, in this case, arises from the student's purpose in enrolling in the course. "Shakespeare" serves a different function for the English major than it does for the future architect who happens to enjoy drama. Many courses, as in sociology, psychology, history, art, music, philosophy, trades, or sciences, have an inherent interest for students who have no intention ever to use them vocationally. By enriching the personality, such courses may in fact improve the student's working effectiveness, but that is not his reason for enrolling in them.

Some writers include this category of elective courses under the heading of general education. Such a confusion of purpose then leads to suggestions that "Anthropology (or astronomy, or ceramics) is a good general education course." More enthusiastic advocates see general education as inhering in all aspects of the curriculum (*81*:40–46). Yet other writers object that if the program is collegewide in its scope, the responsibility for it becomes so diffuse that no precise provision will be made. Chapter 14 examines the concept and definition of general education, presents some of the patterns of general education courses discovered in junior college curriculums, and describes courses in several fields which might contribute to the achievement of the goals of general education.

A. Definition of General Education

General education is but one element of a complete education; nearly all students will need to add to it courses which prepare them for their occupations and courses which satisfy specialized interests of a nonvocational nature. General education refers to programs of education specifically designed to prepare young people for the responsibilities that they share in common as citizens of a free society and for wholesome and creative participation in a wide range of life activities. It is that part of education which prepares the student to assume

his roles as an individual, as a member of a family, and as a citizen. While it may contribute to his choice of occupation and to his success as a worker, vocational skills are not its main objective. It is called "general" because its purposes are conceived to be common to all men; it is that part of the total collegiate offering which is concerned with men's likenesses rather than with their divergent interests. It intends to assist the student to feel intellectually and psychologically at home in a world which makes new economic, social, civic, physiological, spiritual, and intellectual demands upon him. (*153*:2)

Several phrases in the definition deserve elaboration. General education programs, it states, are "specifically designed." This concept is not shared by all students of general education; college lower-division programs often attempt to provide for general education by recommending a sampling of established introductory courses from several areas—English, science, social sciences, humanities. The sampling plan has the advantage of fiscal economy, since a single course may be made to serve several purposes. In most subjects, however, the introductory course is planned principally for those students who will study further in the field; the purposes of the nonmajor students are likely to be subordinated or completely ignored by the instructor, himself a specialist in the field. The establishment of a separate pattern of general education courses is justifiable on the grounds of (1) economy of the student's time, (2) the impossibility of a student's enrolling in all the needed introductory courses, (3) the student's need for a coherent and unified interpretation of modern scholarship, rather than for an introduction to five or six unrelated aspects of it, and (4) efficiency in organizing instruction to achieve general education purposes directly rather than as by-products of specialized courses.

The key phrase in the definition, that which distinguishes general education from vocational and elective education, is "preparation for the responsibilities which they share in common." In previous chapters, attention has been called to the range of student differences in the public junior colleges and to the need for many varieties of educational opportunity to accommodate these differences. At the same time, common citizenship and common humanity beget common educational needs that may be overlooked under the pressure of our increasing specialization and the sheer volume of modern knowledge. The multiplication of courses in every department of our colleges makes necessary the conscious exertion of a countering centripetal force; too rigid a concentration in any field may deprive the student of the opportunity to acquire understanding which he needs in his roles as citizen, parent, and person.

The specific meanings of the phrase "wholesome and creative participation in a wide range of life activities" have been enumerated by Johnson as a series of goals of general education:

The general education program aims to help each student increase his competence in

1. Exercising the privileges and responsibilities of democratic citizenship.

2. Developing a set of sound spiritual and moral values by which he guides his life.

3. Expressing his thoughts clearly in speaking and writing and in reading and listening with understanding.

4. Using the basic mathematical and mechanical skills necessary in everyday life.

5. Using methods of critical thinking for the solution of problems and for the discrimination among values.

6. Understanding his cultural heritage so that he may gain a perspective of his time and place in the world.

7. Understanding his interaction with his biological and physical environment so that he may better adjust to and improve that environment.

8. Maintaining good mental and physical health for himself, his family, and his community.

9. Developing a balanced personal and social adjustment.

10. Sharing in the development of a satisfactory home and family life.

11. Achieving a satisfactory vocational adjustment.

12. Taking part in some form of satisfying creative activity and in appreciating the creative activities of others. (*81*:21–22)

Such objectives are not new in American higher education; the novelty consists in their clear and explicit recognition and in the realization that students do not achieve them accidentally as a result of exposure to a random selection from the hundreds of available courses. Certainly no college will attempt to establish twelve courses, each to contribute to one of these goals. It is equally certain, however, that introductory courses in single disciplines are not the most direct means to effect the changes contemplated in the final six goals.

It is unfortunate when a community junior college commits itself to goals which it makes no provision for achieving. If the definition and the ideal of general education are valid, they are valid for all students. The college then must ensure that each student, and certainly each graduate, makes some progress in "improving his competence" in these areas. This obligation can be discharged in part through the establishment of a limited number of specially designed courses required for graduation. Because students differ in their competence, some provision for exemption or for advanced opportunity is necessary to serve those who already surpass the minimum standards. Organizing an attractive series of general courses, however, will not complete the task; especially in the community junior college, there simply is not time for the student to achieve these goals completely and finally in individual courses. Every instructor should become aware of these goals and be committed to them, so that every course in every department contributes as it can to general education; conscious planning is essential. "The effective program of general education includes *both* a college-wide emphasis on general education outcomes *and* provision of courses which are addressed primarily to particular objectives" (*81*:53).

B. Practices in General Education

To some extent, the philosophy of general education which a community junior college adopts in practice may be deduced from a study of its graduation requirements. It is true that such requirements are sometimes decided by agencies outside of the college; they may be copied after university curriculums or they may be prescribed by state law or regulation. Furthermore, if the college administration believes in a policy of individual election of general education courses, graduation requirements are unlikely to reveal the fact.

In an effort to sample the offerings in the several areas of the curriculum, the catalogs of thirty public junior colleges were analyzed. These colleges represented one-twelfth of the public junior college membership of the American Association of Junior Colleges. Enrollments ranged from more than 10,000 full-time students to fewer than 200. Public junior colleges in every region of the Association were included in the sample. Two cautions are necessary in considering data of this nature. Not every course described in a catalog is offered every year, and the catalog gives no indication of the proportion of students who actually enroll in a course. If a course is required, though, it may be assumed that a large proportion of the entering students and all those who graduate will complete it.

Of the colleges sampled, thirteen had specific course requirements for general education, and fifteen had a broad distributional requirement, with stated numbers of credits to be chosen from a list of courses in each of two, three, or four broad fields. Two of the colleges listed no subjects that were required of all graduates, but in one of these every program described in the catalog included one of several courses in English Composition—the only element common to all programs. Practice in general education, in this sample of colleges, seems evenly divided. Half hope to accomplish this purpose by requiring the student to become acquainted with some course in each of the major areas of learning, while the other half (with one exception) require specific courses in English and social sciences, often in physical education and in health and hygiene, and sometimes in humanities or sciences.

In 1945 Reynolds found evidence which led him to doubt that junior colleges had well-defined policies governing their provisions for the general-education needs of their students. He concluded that the area of general education in most local public junior colleges had received little or no attention. Johnson reached a similar conclusion in the California Study of General Education in the Junior College, when he reported that "As one examines the graduation requirements of California junior colleges with the goals of general education in mind, he is impressed (1) by diversity of practice, (2) by the spotty and limited recognition given some of the general education objectives, and (3) by the apparent failure as yet to make any provision for some of the others" (*81*:49). In the sample surveyed, there is evidence that attention has been paid to the need for general education; while Johnson's observations seem to apply nationally as well as to California, more colleges are now making provision for general education than at the time of the two earlier studies.

Nine of the thirty junior college catalogs included a statement about general education as one of the purposes of junior college students. The longest statement listed the goals of general education presented by Johnson (*81*:21). One catalog contained the following listing of objectives:

The College's Intellectual, Social, and Personal Objectives
for the Student

A. To broaden perspectives by his successful acquisition of basic knowledge in the humanities, social sciences, and sciences.

B. To introduce him to a systematic approach to additional disciplines and skills depending on his educational goals, the requirements of a particular program or those of the college to which he plans to transfer, and consonant with standards set by the faculty.

C. To guide him in the methods of acquiring knowledge so he may draw upon them for solving future problems, since learning is a life-long process.

D. To enable him to understand his own potentialities, limitations, motivations, and to make responsible decisions on the basis of that knowledge.

E. To develop intellectual honesty, and intellectual curiosity.

F. To develop the ability to communicate, to read, to write, to speak, and to think with clarity and precision.

G. To foster respect for the dignity of fellow-man, recognizing man's unique capacities and potential contributions toward common intellectual, social, and personal goals.

H. To develop a cooperative attitude, a sense of fairness, and a personal meaningful relationship to the total college environment.

I. To encourage him to become an active, well-informed citizen of the community, state, nation, and the world; aware of the significant social, economic, political, and moral issues of our times.

Communication. With one exception, all the public junior colleges in the sample group require for graduation some study of English. A one-year course is the usual prescription, with eighteen of the thirty colleges listing this as their requirement. Eleven colleges require either one or two additional semesters of English, and one adds a requirement of a course in speech, for a total of 15 semester hours.

The second year in each junior college emphasizes literature more than basic composition. The universality of the requirement indicates that in the area of communication, at least, all public junior colleges attempt to increase their students' competence in expressing their thoughts. In composition, especially, the major purpose of the freshman course has always been that of general education rather than of introduction to further study. Although English faculties often question the efficacy of their efforts, at least the opportunity for general education in this area is available.

The effective emphasis on "increasing competence" in communication is demonstrated also in the prevalence of remedial or developmental opportunities. Twenty of the thirty colleges offer some work in clinics, laboratories, or specialized classes to enable students to correct deficient skills in reading. These courses usually carry a minimum credit toward the associate degree but not toward transfer to a four-year college. The so-called "subfreshman" course in the mechanics of writing is offered in 27 of these public junior colleges, and is usually required on the basis of a pretest of writing ability. The catalog statements, unfortunately, do not indicate how many students need or avail themselves of these opportunities to achieve minimum skills in communication.

An example of the nature of offerings in communication skills is the description of English 1, a two-semester course carrying six units of credit, in one of the catalogs in the sample group of thirty.

Freshman English, required of all students in the academic division, provides instruction in (1) the four communication skills—listening, reading, speaking, and writing; (2) the use of the library; (3) spelling. Speeded reading is taught as a part of the regular English course. Laboratory period: As part of the course, each student is assigned to one-hour laboratory period per week. As soon as he shows marked progress in the fundamentals of grammar, diction, sentence structure and the principles of composition, he may be excused from laboratory at the discretion of the instructor.

Social Science. Twenty-seven of the thirty colleges require some study in the field of social sciences for graduation. Usually this requirement is either in American history or in a combination of American history and government. The credit value of the requirement ranges from no credit for passing a test of knowledge of American government in one junior college, through ten units from a list of social sciences at another, to a maximum graduation requirement of twelve units in social sciences. Only two colleges listed a course for students with deficient background in social science. Although the social science requirement certainly is established in hope that it may

increase students' competence in democratic citizenship, critical thinking, and understanding of the cultural heritage, the courses which
satisfy the requirement are usually organized as chronological treat-
ments of United States history.

In this sample, only nine examples were found of courses in
social sciences which seemed to be specifically organized for the
purposes of general education. Only one is required of all graduates.
One of them is described in the catalog as carrying six semester
units of credit for the year's study:

A factual and interpretive study of man, his culture and his institutions.
A brief survey of contemporary political, economic, and social situations
and problems, with their relationships to historical periods. A year sequence
furnishing the background for all social sciences and laying a basis for
understanding contemporary socio-economic problems. Challenges the analytical and critical faculties of students in preparation for more detailed
studies, such as courses in economics, political science, and sociology.

Physical Education. Physical education is required for graduation
in twenty-seven of the thirty colleges, sometimes as a result of a
prescription in state law. The requirement usually includes two hours
of participation weekly, either for one year or for four semesters. In
four of the colleges the required participation earned no credit toward
graduation whereas in seven it afforded a total of four units of credit.
The pattern of two hours weekly for one-half unit of credit is the
most frequent one. The scope of the offerings in physical education
also varies greatly.

Some catalog descriptions indicate that the course consists mostly
of calisthenics, supplemented by team play in two or three sports;
others list as many as forty kinds of physical education opportunities.
The more extensive programs include classes for men, for women, and
for mixed groups, and they supplement the usual intercollegiate team
sports with activities of value in after-college life such as golf, badminton, and bowling. Only three of the colleges make mention of
opportunities for special physical education for the convalescent, for
the handicapped, or for other students with special needs such as
posture improvement or weight reduction. The extent of variability of
the offering indicates that although some public junior colleges are
seriously attempting to improve their students' competence in maintaining good health and balanced personal adjustment, others have not
yet developed any courses specifically directed toward the attainment
of these goals.

An idea of the scope of physical education programs in a single public junior college may be gained from the description of the opportunities in the required course:

All undergraduate students taking nine units of work who are under 21 years of age are required to attend physical educational activities a minimum of two hours a week. A physical examination record must be on file with the department.

The department offers varied activity courses planned to meet the interests and needs of all students. Each student should have a varied program including one semester from each of four of the following groups. All physical education majors should register for two physical education courses each semester.

Aquatics.

Beginning swimming (co-ed). Basic skills of floating, elementary back stroke, American crawl, and methods of entering the water.

Intermediate swimming (co-ed). Covers four basic strokes: crawl, back, side, and breast. Prerequisite: ability to swim free style the length of the pool.

Team Activity.

Volleyball, basketball, softball, baseball, touch football, and football.

Rhythmic Activity.

Modern dance.

Social, folk, and square dance (co-ed). Basic dance steps and rhythms. Recommended for elementary school and physical education majors.

Individual Activity.

Tennis, badminton, fencing, cross country, golf, track.

Body mechanics, women. Individual analysis of posture.

Exercises prescribed for improvement, correction, and prevention of postural defects. Instruction and practice in doing everyday movements with maximum efficiency.

Archery (co-ed). Beginning and intermediate skills in target archery.

Gymnastics. Trampoline, tumbling, weight fitness.

Game Activities. Games commonly included in elementary programs.

Instruction in personal and community hygiene is less usual than instruction in physical education. Fifteen of the thirty junior colleges include a one-semester course in hygiene, usually for two units, in their graduation requirements. Six additional colleges require a course in biological science, which may include health education topics.

Other Requirements. Orientation, psychology, human relations, or personal adjustment courses are required for graduation in twelve of the thirty colleges; the one-unit orientation course accounts for nine of these. Additional requirements include twelve requirements in humanities, and twenty-one in science, math, or a combination of these.

In so far as graduation requirements indicate the effective commitment of public junior colleges to the concept of a common minimum of general education for all students, it is possible to conclude that the colleges agree only on the skills of communication as elements in that minimum. There is substantial agreement on courses that are intended to prepare students to assume the duties of citizenship and on physical education courses. Beyond that, more than half of these colleges have attempted through prescription to ensure that their graduates have been exposed to a well-rounded and carefully planned curriculum in general education, although only nine of them include a specific catalog statement on the nature or objectives of general education.

C. Courses Planned for General Education

Nearly all the public junior colleges require for graduation one or more courses which they consider to be part of the background essential for all their students. In addition several of the colleges have made tentative and scattered attempts to devise appropriate courses. The courses so designed are rarely required for graduation; in student programs, they often take second place to the more "practical" and conventional courses in occupational training or in traditional disciplines. A brief discussion of some of the general education courses described in the thirty catalogs studied will indicate the nature and the extent of the effort being made at present to provide directly for these goals.

Preparation for Marriage. Twenty of the thirty colleges list a course in "Marriage and Family Life," "Marriage Problems," or "Family Relations"; none of the twenty requires the course for graduation. The courses are developed in recognition of the increasing difficulty of establishing and preserving wholesome and stable families in an affluent, mobile, self-indulgent society. In general, they combine subject matter from the fields of sociology, psychology, biology, and home economics in an attempt to help students prepare to make rational choices of mates and to achieve attitudes and insights that will contribute to satisfactory home and family life. They are offered in the departments of sociology, home making, or psychology. It is not possible to determine what proportion of the students in these colleges actually enroll in these courses, nor what effect the courses have on improving students' later behavior as homemakers. They are examples, however, of direct attempts to achieve through classroom instruction several of the goals of general education.

One of the junior colleges in the sample group offers two separate courses in the area of preparation for marriage, both in the home economics department. The first is a one-unit *"Preparation for Marriage.* Open to men and women. This lecture course presents some of the facts—physical, emotional, and social—essential for the development of a mature attitude toward a wholesome, satisfying marriage." The three-unit course is *"Marriage and Family Life.* Open to men and women. This course deals with family relationships and the effect these have on the development of each individual. It helps the student to understand the problems involved in courtship, marriage and home-making."

Applied Psychology. Fourteen colleges offer no-prerequisite courses in the field of psychology, other than the university-parallel "Introduction to Psychology." These courses are planned to help the student increase his competence in maintaining good mental health for himself, his family, and his community, and in developing a balanced personal and social adjustment. Presumably they also contribute to the ability of critical thinking, as well as to several others of the goals of general education. The titles adopted for courses of this nature include: Psychology of Adjustment, Personality Development, Applied Psychology, and Human Relations. None of the colleges requires a course in psychology for graduation, although several have a requirement in Orientation, taught in the Psychology Department.

The nature of the human relations course is outlined in one of the catalogs surveyed.

A study of the individual and his adjustment to contemporary society. Topics include the following: the dynamics of the adjustment process; the influence of personal, social, and cultural factors on the development of the individual and his adjustive patterns of behavior; the problems that the individual faces in adjusting to family, school, peers, and job. Emphasis is placed on the development and maintenance of a healthy personality. Techniques of readjustment, such as counseling and psychotherapy, are studied.

Sciences. For some reason, the survey course in physical sciences, designed for the nonscientist, is offered more frequently than a survey in biological sciences. Twenty colleges of the sample of thirty offer an introduction to physical sciences, with credit ranging from three to six units. Laboratory experience is required in about half of these surveys. In biological sciences, only eight of these colleges offer a course that is ostensibly different from the standard one-year transfer course in general biology. Credit value in this course also varies from three units in one semester to six units in a year-course.

In one college, a coordinated year sequence is described as

Natural Science 88. A general study of the nature and behavior of matter, machines, electricity, sound, and light. Attention is given to the relation of the earth to other parts of the solar system, seasons, weather, etc. Particular attention is given to developing the ability to read and understand the materials in this field and to express this understanding both orally and in writing. *Natural Science 89.* A study of organisms and their relation to each other and to their physical environment. Emphasis is placed on the ability to read and understand material in this field and to express such orally and in writing.

Other General Courses. Courses specifically designed to contribute to other accepted goals of general education appear infrequently, and are rarely a part of a coordinated collegewide plan for a comprehensive general education. There are ten examples of introductory courses in the social sciences, with titles such as Man's Cultural Heritage, Introduction to Social Sciences, or Man and Society. Only four of the colleges offer courses in Consumer Economics or Personal Economics. In the integrated humanities field, six interdisciplinary courses are offered, three for a full year and three for a single semester.

It is possible that the preceding paragraphs present an overly pessimistic picture of the present status of general education in the junior colleges. The analysis of offerings and the comments about them were based on the two assumptions that general education courses should be specifically designed to achieve general education goals and that education for common responsibilities should be required of all students. It is certain that some courses which bear traditional subject titles are organized and taught primarily for general education. It is equally true that counselors in some junior colleges encourage students to broaden their education by the election of courses that will increase their general competence. Nevertheless, the fact remains that fewer than half of the colleges enforce any requirements beyond English, history, and physical education, and fewer than half organize any pattern of courses specifically for general education. The evidence is conclusive that the public junior colleges have not yet, in practice, accepted general education as one of their primary purposes.

D. A Suggested Program

Many conditions contribute to the failure of public junior colleges to develop comprehensive patterns of required general education courses. Not the least of these is the sheer complexity of the undertaking; the leadership, the money, the time, and the faculty members simply have not been available for planning on the necessary scale. The autonomy of the public junior colleges makes it necessary for each one to work either independently or imitatively in developing its curriculum, and few of these colleges have the resources to initiate thorough studies independently.

Transfer requirements of universities are another restricting force. The investment required to prepare students for future study in engineering, sciences, business administration, education, social sciences, and the other hundreds of university specializations leaves little opportunity for the development of courses which deviate from accepted practices. These same requirements, moreover, so fill up the time of the students that it is difficult to obtain adequate enrollments of qualified students in experimental courses, even when they are provided.

The limitation of time affects the general education of the students in occupational courses as well. The advisory committees and the instructors who plan vocational training are convinced that their subjects are important and that they require a major part of the students' time and effort. They are likely to conclude that the financially unremunerative goals of general education can be ignored, or at least deferred, in planning programs of study. The students also may accept this judgment in their eagerness to achieve vocational competence so that they may begin to earn.

A further difficulty inheres in the uncertainty regarding the nature of the educational process itself. Is it possible to teach directly so as to achieve the intangible and attitudinal goals of general education? Or is the educator limited to teaching facts and skills in the hope that, from these, time and experience will bring about appropriate wisdom, attitudes, and practices? These doubts are reinforced by the inertia of faculty members, who find security in teaching as they were taught and a sense of immortality in preparing acolytes to follow in their footsteps and perpetuate the cult of their discipline. The net result of these difficulties has been to paralyze initiative and to discourage experimentation in general education, so that no public junior college exhibits a coherent, comprehensive, well-planned and carefully evaluated curriculum to lead all its students toward the twelve goals of general education. The following suggestions are offered as a framework on which such a complete curriculum might be constructed. Several preliminary comments must be kept in mind as the proposals are evaluated.

In the first place, the community junior college cannot devote the major portion of its program to general education. Some four-year colleges require their students to complete a general program equivalent to as much as three-fourths of their entire lower-division credits; because of its functions in pretransfer and in occupational education, the community junior college will find that it cannot require more than twenty or twenty-one units of specific general education courses. Again, at present it is difficult for the junior college to secure university acceptance of experimentally developed courses. Careful preliminary planning of the course, perhaps in consultation with university officers, will help in gaining favorable evaluation, as will assignment of the ablest instructors available to the courses. Even so, for some time it may still be necessary to provide alternative courses by which students preparing for certain transfer specialties may meet the requirements. An easy evasion of university domination is to require newly developed courses only of the nontransfer students, but the experience of several colleges indicates that such a limitation on enrollment creates psychological barriers to the development of a course that can be taught enthusiastically and studied eagerly.

The problem of university domination of the community junior college curriculum has been mentioned before; it is one of the pervasive influences that must be recognized in any consideration of the curriculum. At times, this domination is advanced as an excuse for inactivity by the junior colleges; at other times it proves to be a truly frustrating and unnecessary deterrent to soundly conceived experimentation. The solution lies partly in acceptance by the community junior colleges of full responsibility for the preparation of their graduates, with the implied guarantee that the transferring student has achieved an education equivalent to although not identical with that of the four-year-college junior. The other part of the solution lies in the recognition by senior institutions that community junior college faculties have the ability, the resources, the desire, and the obligation to develop curriculums for all their students. When these conditions are achieved, the community junior colleges will begin to develop acceptable general education offerings such as those here proposed.

Course titles present an added difficulty in devising a suggested program. Traditional titles such as History of the United States or Freshman Composition are both misleading and restricting when applied to broader courses that draw materials from several disciplines. The alternative practice is to devise titles that concentrate attention on the purposes of the courses rather than on their content, such as Preparation for Marriage. These titles may be so explicit or so unusual that considerable effort must be devoted to explaining and defending both the titles and the courses. The difficulty arises from attempting to compress great precision of meaning and a concise summary of content into a three-or-four-word title. A name should be adopted that affords a convenient and simple reference to the course, without confining the expectations of students and others too rigidly to a single discipline. American Civilization might be a better title for one course than Social Science I or History of the United States. For another, Communication might be a more acceptable title than either the traditional Composition and Rhetoric or the somewhat pretentious Elementary Linguistics.

The final caution has to do with content. The elimination of material is just as important as the selection of content, in developing a course for general education. General education became necessary because the bulk of knowledge grew until no human, no college freshman, could hope to encompass any major part of it. Barzun has summarized the point of view as follows:

That same abundance of information has turned into a barrier between one man and the next. They are mutually incommunicado, because each believes that his subject and his language cannot and should not be understood by the other. . . . Of true knowledge at any time, a good part is merely convenient, necessary indeed to the worker, but not to the understanding of his subject: one can judge a building without knowing where to buy the bricks; one can understand a violin sonata without knowing how to score for the instrument. . . . With a cautious confidence and sufficient intellectual training, it is possible to master the literature of a subject and gain a proper understanding of it: specifically, an understanding of the accepted truths, the disputed problems, the rival schools, and the methods now in favor. This will not enable one to add to what is known, but it will give possession of *all that the discipline has to offer the world.*[1]

This concept is by no means an advocacy of superficiality. No useful purpose is served by teaching generalities. The haste, compression, and triviality that have sometimes characterized courses for the "nonmajor" student are useless, even harmful. General education demands the most careful selection of topics to be considered, coupled with thoroughness, depth, scholarship, rigor, and intellectual discipline in the study of these topics. It is not necessary to teach everything known in order to teach thoroughly.

---

[1] Quoted by permission from Jacques Barzun, *The House of Intellect,* pp. 11–12. New York: Harper and Row, 1959. Copyright 1959 by Jacques Barzun. Italics in original.

In order to achieve a course of this quality, a faculty will need to steel itself to achieve some fundamental rethinking of educational practice. The first analytical task is the definition of purposes. These will be stated not as material to be covered but as changes expected in the students. In order to increase their competence in the desired activity, what attitudes must be developed? What skills achieved? What knowledge mastered? Through what educational avenues may these outcomes be reached? The answer to these questions may evoke a dozen possible answers. One analyst will suggest that his introductory course as now organized does just what has been described. Other suggestions will include an approach through biography, a laboratory experience, concentration on a single problem of contemporary America, a sampling of interesting units from several disciplines, or a thorough study of a current problem as it appeared in an earlier society. The planning group may realize that the goals may be approached in any of several ways, and that it must select the course organization that seems most adaptable to available instructors, facilities, and students.

Detailed planning will follow upon choice of basic approach. Here again selection of material is crucial. The temptation is to cram too much into a single course, so that a great many topics are mentioned, not mastered. Instead, conscious effort should be exerted to provide for depth of understanding in a few areas rather than breadth and superficiality over the entire field. This is why a planning committee is necessary to bring to light contributions from various specialties; at the same time, a single instructor, training himself to succeed in all phases of the new course, is likely to be more effective than a corps of instructors, each presenting a single aspect of it.

Can a series of such courses be organized to require no more than one-third of a junior college student's time and to contribute significantly to the increase of each student's competence in the twelve goals of general education? It should be possible to construct a series of four courses, comprising twenty-one semester units and affording all students opportunity to improve their preparation "for the responsibilities they share in common as citizens in a free society, and for wholesome and creative participation in a wide range of life activities." The following suggestions are presented as a demonstration of the feasibility of this approach and in the hope that one or more public junior college faculties may undertake to refine the analysis and to develop an experimental program. Such experimentation might help to determine whether or not it is possible to organize instruction with emphasis on the purposes of the learners, rather than on the complete and logical organization of single disciplines.

Certain of the objectives quoted at the beginning of the chapter are closely related to each other and can be achieved at the same time and in a single course. It is possible to imagine four manageable courses which in combination would contribute directly to the student's attainment of every one of the twelve goals. Additional study in elective and in vocational courses would extend each student's competence in one or several of the goals, whereas the suggested basic offering in general education would attempt to make sure that no student ignored completely any one of the goals. The four courses proposed may be summarized thus:

Course A   Communications   6 units; Primary goals 3,5,12, secondary, 2,9.
Course B
   American Civilization   6 units; Primary goals 1,5,6, secondary, 2,11.
Course C
   The Physical World   6 units; Primary goals 4,5,7,8, secondary, 11.
Course D   Human Behavior   3 units; Primary goals 8,9,10, secondary, 11.

Course A, Communications, would combine the purposes of helping each student increase his competence in expressing his thoughts, thinking critically, working creatively, and appreciating the creative activities of others; indirectly, the activities of the course should lead to a clarification of his values, and to a more balanced personal and social adjustment. The *content* of the course would consist of consideration of excellent examples of communication in all mediums. Subject matter could be drawn from written materials in any field and from music, painting, sculpture, and dramatics. Such content can be adapted to any level of previous student achievement by selection of examples; the purpose is to help each student increase his competence. The experience of considering the communicative effort of other men will provide the students with rich incentives for writing and speaking. Some of the difficulty in freshman composition has come from the student's lack of desire to compose because he has nothing to say. In a course such as this, his reactions and his attempts to clarify his critical thinking will provide ample stimulation to write and to discuss. For the teacher, English as a deadening service course in mechanics, concentrating on uninspiring sentence errors and inspired misspellings, will be replaced by the exciting experience of watching young minds increase in appreciation, in critical thinking, in desire to express their thoughts clearly.

Course B, American Civilization, would explain and prepare for participation in American civilization by concentrating on helping the student increase his competence in citizenship, in critical thinking, and in understanding his cultural heritage. The development of spiritual and moral values and of satisfactory vocational insights would be a concomitant but indirect outcome of the methods and the materials of study. A chronological study of history might not be the most effective approach to these goals. Rather, the analysis of a selected few aspects of present American society might prove both more stimulating to the students and more effective in contributing to the desired goals. It seems likely that such an approach in depth might both increase understanding and help to encourage thoughtful involvement in civic affairs.

Course C, The Physical World, or perhaps Sciences and Mathematics, will be difficult to plan and to teach. A decision to devote, for example, six weeks to chemistry, six to physics, and six each to botany, zoology, community hygiene, and mathematics would destroy the entire concept of the course. The materials must be selected, in this general education course, for their contribution toward "helping each student increase his competence" in using basic mathematical and mechanical skills, in critical thinking, in understanding his interaction with his environment, and in maintaining good health for himself and for others. From these studies, some indirect contribution to vocational choice and adjustment may also arise. The purpose of this course is not to train scientists—it is to achieve the goals stated. For these comparatively modest goals, it is possible that content might be drawn almost exclusively from one discipline; on the other hand, principles from several sciences might be brought together to help the student increase his understanding. The goals that are accepted for this, as for other courses, may be attained by means of quite different organizations of experiences. The important consideration is to plan for the achievement of goals and not for the coverage of all the content of a scientific discipline (52:Ch. X). A study of biography might provide a stimulating vehicle for learning in this field. The work of men such as Galileo, Francis Bacon, Lavoisier, Pasteur, Newton, the Curies, Albert Einstein, and Charles Darwin could yield many insights into the skills and understandings which are sought here.

Course D, Human Behavior, is restricted to one semester and to three units because of time limitation rather than because of the lesser importance of the topic. A junior college which began the experimental development of its general education along the lines suggested here might soon find it necessary to rearrange the allocation of goals to specific blocks of content, and to increase or diminish the relative credit values. It will be possible to make some contribution, within one semester, to student competence in maintaining mental health, developing balanced adjustment, and sharing in developing satisfactory family life; if these abilities are improved, vocational adjustment will also improve. In a course directed toward the achievement of these goals, content would be drawn as needed from psychology, biology, sociology, home economics, philosophy, and perhaps from other disciplines. Once more it is essential to state that this sampling would not be done through a series of brief superficial presentations of each separate subject. In this course, presenting each topic is not the primary goal; the personal and intellectual growth of the student is the objective. Content may be chosen by asking at every point "Will this material assist students to gain the insights which will enable them to improve their practices in human relations?" It goes without saying that the instructors in such a course must add to a thorough knowledge of psychology a broad acquaintance with other fields, and in addition, they must be themselves fully mature and balanced personalities.

In colleges and junior colleges throughout America, examples may be found of courses similar in organization and purpose to each of the courses suggested here. None of the public junior colleges in the sample of thirty offered all the courses, and none of them required all students to complete a program of courses leading to the attainment of all the goals of general education. Yet these goals are too important to be subordinated to other objectives. The junior colleges must begin to adopt them and to institute patterns of instruction specifically designed in accord with them, or continue to fail in one of their primary functions. Courageous experimentation in general education is one way in which the junior colleges may prepare for their constantly increasing responsibility in American higher education.

Selected References

Bell, Reginald. "A General Education Program Based on Student Needs," *School and Society,* 70:39–40, July 16, 1949.

French, Sidney J. (editor). *Accent on Teaching.* New York: Harper and Row, 1954.

Henry, Nelson B. (editor). *General Education.* The Fifty-first Yearbook of the National Society for the Study of Education, Part I. Chicago: The University of Chicago Press, 1952.

Johnson, B. Lamar. *General Education in Action.* Washington: American Council on Education, 1952.

Rice, James G. (editor). *General Education: Current Ideas and Concerns.* Washington: Association for Higher Education, 1964.

Thomas, Russell. *The Search for a Common Learning: General Education, 1800–1960.* New York: McGraw-Hill Book Co., 1962.

Thornton, James W., Jr. "General Education." Chapter VII in *The Public Junior College.* Nelson B. Henry (editor). The Fifty-fifth Yearbook of the National Society for the Study of Education, Part I. Chicago: The University of Chicago Press, 1956.

———. *General Education: Establishing the Program* (pamphlet). Washington: Association for Higher Education, 1958.

15

The Curriculum:
Education for Transfer

In devising the pattern of course offerings that will prepare a large percentage of its students for further college study, the community junior college must reconcile several conflicting forces. Students who hope to earn bachelor's degrees in every conceivable field of study have a right to expect that their junior college will provide the lower-division courses that are required as preparation for later specialization. Each college and university that accepts transfer students expects the junior college to offer freshman and sophomore courses which are fully parallel, in content and in standard, to its own offering. Graduates of any junior college will apply for admission to many senior colleges, each of which has its own highly individualized concept of the content of lower-division preparation. The junior college, on the other hand, must use its human and fiscal resources economically, limiting the number and variety of its offerings. It must reserve some part of its teaching personnel and financial assets to meet the needs of its students who do not plan to transfer. It realizes that many of its students with transfer ambitions will not transfer after all, and so it tries to develop courses that are not solely preparatory, but which have an inherent value as well.

In their reactions to all these forces, community junior colleges seem to have been influenced most by the lower-division requirements of nearby universities and by fiscal limitations. Previous chapters have demonstrated that junior colleges are financed, organized, and administered according to a number of regional patterns. In their transfer

217

curriculums, however, they show much greater uniformity. In the various lower-division disciplines, public junior colleges all over the nation provide a very similar minimum offering, organized and titled in conformity with the practice of the nearby public university and comprising in essence the same traditional subject matter. Private colleges, even private junior colleges, have exercised imagination and ingenuity in curricular experimentation; they have blended scholarship in subject matter with awareness of student needs to produce exciting new courses in communications, in sciences, in mathematical theory, in social sciences, and in the humanities. The public junior colleges, as evidenced by the sample of thirty catalogs, have developed few courses of an experimental nature in the academic fields.

It is possible that the currently increasing demand for higher education may encourage public junior colleges to be more active in defining anew the nature of lower-division preparation for further study. Suggestions are increasing in frequency that transfer students from junior colleges should be accepted only after they have completed the full two-year junior college course. If such a practice comes to be adopted throughout the nation, qualitative standards for transfer will follow. At present, receiving colleges are likely to scrutinize the transcript of the entering junior college transfer in search of a one-to-one conformity of courses completed at the junior college with those required of their own freshmen and sophomores. Courses for which the university offers no parallel may not be accepted for full credit; on the other hand, if the transfer student has neglected to complete a specific course required in the freshman or sophomore pattern of the receiving institution, he is refused junior standing until the course is "made up." This additive or quantitative approach to education for further study denies the junior colleges the right to develop, in mature and responsible fashion, courses which might well constitute superior intellectual fare for all their students. It causes frequent criticism and ill-feeling among the universities, the junior colleges, and the transferring student. Furthermore, it hinders the development by the junior colleges of courses appropriate for their terminal students, since they must concentrate too much of their attention on copying the offerings of several departments of several colleges and universities.

The community junior colleges will very soon be faced with the responsibility of exerting leadership in the development of lower-division preparatory curriculums. University leaders continue to be critical of the quality and nature of these programs, within their own institutions as well as in junior colleges (*148*). The community junior colleges have from their beginning resented the excessive domination of their curriculum by outside agencies—the universities. If present trends continue, it seems inevitable that the greatest part of freshman and sophomore study will be completed in junior colleges. All these trends combine to encourage university and junior college leaders in each region to agree on statements of the purposes of this segment of education and to define standards of equivalence of training. With such understanding of purposes and standards, the junior colleges can accept the responsibility of developing curriculums that will be fully satisfactory to them as well as to the receiving colleges and universities.

In the future, agreements must be negotiated to allow students to transfer with full junior standing, with status equivalent in every way to "native" students of the college, and to engage in any studies for which they have met prerequisites, if they have earned the associate degree in an accredited junior college with satisfactory grade standing and if they have demonstrated, through courses or through examinations, aptitude for the field in which they intend to major. Such a pattern of admission would not only assure the senior college and university of the seriousness of purpose and the ability of its transfer students; it would also free the junior college to concentrate on a high quality of achievement in all its offerings, even though the exact course outlines of some university courses were not closely "paralleled" anywhere in the curriculum.

Such freedom in curricular experimentation is rare at present. Chapter 15 presents brief descriptions of the usual offerings in each major area of the lower-division curriculum in public junior colleges. Conclusions on the extent of the offering are based on the same survey of thirty public junior college catalogs described in Chapter 14. In the present analysis, the courses are those that serve as preparation for further study in a senior institution; it may be assumed that the courses are in fact offered every year in most of the colleges represented and that the students for whom the courses are required are enrolled in them.

A. Courses in English, Speech, and Journalism

The freshman composition course is one constant feature of almost every college in America; in almost every college it is one of the requirements for graduation. Countless hours have been spent in efforts to improve it, to reorganize it, to work out ways to make it more effective in changing the communicative habits of students. Many emphases are found, from the study of formal grammar to the use of materials from philosophy or social sciences as a basis for more literate discussion and writing. In colleges of all types a provision is found for admission of the entrant to the freshman English class only after he has passed a screening examination or written a qualifying essay; those who fail to qualify usually are required to complete noncredit courses until they can demonstrate the minimum competence for entry into the required freshman course. Other colleges enroll all students in a single first course and require supplementary work in clinics or in remedial sections for those students who need extra help in correcting faulty habits of expression. The public junior colleges follow the four-year institutions both in the uniformity of their requirement and in the variety of their approaches to course organization.

Of the thirty public junior colleges studied, six offer fewer than twenty semester units of transferable credit in English. The minimum listing provides for freshmen a two-semester course in composition, often including some speech training and an introduction to literature, and for sophomores a two-semester course in English literature. This basic offering is exceeded in varying degrees, depending somewhat on the size of the college. Twelve of the colleges offer between twenty-one and twenty-six transfer credits in English; these colleges usually add elective courses in advanced or creative writing and some study of European or specialized literature to the two-semester courses in composition and literature. The largest colleges offer more than fifty semester units of transferable study in English, expanding their offering by specialized composition courses for prospective engineers or teachers, or by additional courses in creative writing or literature. Although exceptions are found, English courses are usually organized to afford three units of credit per semester and to meet three hours weekly.

Remedial courses in communication are not provided in all the public junior colleges. Four of the thirty studied list no work preparatory to freshman English and no clinics for the development of skill in reading or in writing. On the other hand, the colleges that do offer such courses exhibit a wide range of specialization. Four of them list only one course, without credit. Six colleges offer English for Foreign Born, and sixteen have special developmental courses in spelling, grammar, speech, or reading. Assignment to such courses is based on demonstrated lack of competence. In some colleges students whose first papers in the regular English course indicate that they need additional help are required to undertake remedial work as a supplement to their regular course. In others, tests of composition, mechanical skills, vocabulary, or reading ability are used as bases for assigning students either to regular or to subfreshman classes. Pooley concluded that:

The problem of the less competent student seems best met by the creation of clinics. Several communications programs have developed excellent clinics in the fundamental skills to help the floundering student pull himself up to class level. Clinics are created for writing skills, speaking skills, and reading skills. Usually the student needing the help of the clinic is referred to it by his section teacher. In some cases he attends the clinic in lieu of class attendance; in other cases the clinic is additional. Teaching in the clinic is individualized. The typical clinic consists of a room with space for one or several instructors; it is equipped with books, materials, and apparatus of help in the particular skill. The student is tested, given a goal to work for, and provided with materials for his own self advancement. He practices the skills he needs, tests himself, and continues until he feels ready to be tested by the director of the clinic. When he has raised himself to reasonable competence in the skill for which he was referred he leaves the clinic, but may return for special help whenever he needs it. (52:119)

In many public junior colleges, some instruction in speech is a part of the basic required course in English. In addition, all the colleges in the analyzed sample offer separate courses in public speaking; the number of courses tends to increase with the enrollment of the college, although it conforms closely to the lower-division speech program of the state universities. The first course is likely to be for one semester, entitled Public Speaking. Other public junior colleges extend this course to a full year and provide additional experiences in debate, verse-speaking choirs, oral reading (for prospective teachers), and voice and diction. Speech correction is offered for credit in a very few instances. One large college lists forty units of transferable work in speech; several of the courses are specifically planned to meet the needs of future elementary-school teachers. In two-thirds of the college catalogs analyzed, the total transferable offering in speech ranges between six and fifteen units; again, the three-hour, three-unit credit pattern is almost universal.

Journalism also is frequently associated with the English department. The courses serve as an introduction to the place of the press in American life; at the same time they afford practice in newswriting and enable the college to issue a student newspaper at regular intervals. Ten of the colleges studied offer no work in journalism; the others range from a single three-unit course to as many as thirty-seven units. A common practice is to offer a freshman two-semester course as Introduction to Journalism and to follow that by a second year in Newswriting or Editorial Techniques. Junior colleges expand their journalism departments by specialized courses in column writing, advertising, or news photography. Since similar courses are often included in the upper-division programs of the university department of journalism, these specializations are of doubtful preparatory credit value to the transferring major in journalism; they do offer an opportunity for students to gain valuable experience by working independently under the guidance of an instructor in publishing the junior college newspaper.

B. Foreign Languages

Several objectives are offered to justify the inclusion of foreign languages in the curriculum. It is claimed that foreign language study helps one to understand and to use his native tongue better and that the study of a foreign tongue leads to appreciation of the culture of other peoples and so to international harmony and cooperation. Further, knowledge of a foreign language is urged on economic grounds; more extensive involvement in trade, in military defense, and in economic development of other countries requires more workers who can speak other tongues than English. It has been argued that the effort itself of learning a foreign language has a salutary effect on the mind and the character of the student. Certainly some students will derive real enjoyment from the mastery of another tongue and from the ability to read and to converse in it, quite apart from economic or disciplinary rewards.

But the methods of instruction in foreign language have not always contributed directly to the attainment of such objectives. The parsing of sentences and memorization of paradigms seems to add little to cultural appreciation, and the labored, halting, senseless translations turned in by many students certainly are not calculated to improve their use of English. Even the economic value of the study of foreign languages may be largely illusory, unless the language is studied to the point of fluent and correct usage. Criticisms of this nature have led in recent years to marked changes in the materials and the methods of foreign language instruction. Classes are more frequently conducted in the language studied; films, meaningful reading materials, and instructional recordings are used to encourage students to listen, speak, read, and write the new language as a means of communication rather than to dissect it as an exercise in philology. Under such realistic approaches, there is encouraging evidence that usable skills can be attained by many students within the customary two-year period of study of foreign languages.

The community junior college is keeping pace with these developments in foreign language instruction. It receives from the secondary schools students at all levels of achievement in languages; some have had no instruction, others may have had four years of excellent high-school work in a single language. The junior college, in the same way as the four-year college, must assess each student's proficiency, compare that with the student's goal and with the requirements of his chosen four-year college and his major field, and then assign him to the next level of instruction. Because of this intermediate function, the patterns of foreign language instruction in public junior colleges in all parts of the country are remarkably similar. In any language that is taught, the junior college will usually offer four semesters of work; the first semester is a beginning course, and the fourth stresses reading and conversation.

The languages most usually taught, as revealed by the analysis of thirty public junior college catalogs, are French, Spanish, and German. French and Spanish were taught in all thirty colleges, and twenty-six colleges taught German. In addition, Russian appeared in eighteen, Italian in ten, and Latin, Hebrew, and Greek in three each. One large college in the sample offered thirteen languages—Spanish, French, German, Russian, Portugese, Arabic, Hebrew, Italian, Latin, Chinese, Greek, Japanese, and Hindu.

The semester-credit value of the basic language courses varies from three to five units; for this reason, the four-semester offering may vary in total credit value from twelve to twenty units. In a few programs, especially in the less popular languages, only two semesters of work are offered; most of the colleges offer additional courses beyond the four-semester pattern, in such areas as Conversational French, Scientific German, or Spanish Literature. Most public junior colleges offer foreign languages primarily for transfer purposes, and the organization of their courses is patterned very closely after that of the college or university to which most of their students go. There is a growing trend, however, toward emphasis on conversational courses in foreign languages, in tongues other than the traditional French, German, and Spanish.

C. Social Sciences

Junior college courses in the social sciences share two major objectives with their counterpart courses in the four-year colleges. They are expected to contribute to the development of responsible and intelligent citizenship on the part of the student; at the same time, they must be planned so as to provide a foundation for further study to the small proportion of each class who will later specialize in any one of the social disciplines. The added responsibility to provide civic education for those students who do not plan to transfer may complicate the social science curriculum for the junior colleges, especially the smaller ones. The evidence indicates that the public junior colleges offer a considerable variety of social science courses, and that the basic offering is nearly the same in all of them.

In developing the transfer curriculum in social sciences, the first effort is to provide two-semester courses that parallel the university offerings; subjects are introduced that meet lower-division requirements for a sufficient number of the students. As numbers of students and faculty increase, expansion within the social science areas takes two paths. The introductory courses in other social disciplines are added, and more specialized courses are introduced in the original subjects.

Every one of the thirty colleges studied offers two-semester courses in American history and in political science; all of them also offer at least a semester each of introductory psychology and sociology. Economics is available in twenty-nine of the thirty, usually in a two-semester sequence. Expansion of the curriculum within these five fields begins with the addition of European history or Western civilization in almost every college. A course entitled either mental hygiene or psychology of adjustment is the usual second offering in psychology. In political science, however, the second offering is not usually an additional opportunity for the student majoring in the field; rather it is a substitute course for students who need a course of limited scope to meet a state or a college requirement for graduation. In economics and sociology, nearly all the colleges offer either one or two two-semester sequences. Those that offer second courses plan them primarily for specific occupational needs, such as for business students or teachers, and not as an additional year of advanced study.

Table 11 summarizes the offerings in all of the social sciences in the thirty colleges whose catalogs were analyzed. In general, a similar pattern of an introductory two-semester course, with the addition of additional specialization when conditions justify it, is indicated also in geography, philosophy, and anthropology. Education courses are taught extensively only in those states in which the public junior colleges participate in the training of teachers. In states where a bachelor's degree is a requirement for a teaching certificate, public junior colleges ordinarily offer no courses in education or only a single introductory course. Eleven colleges offer an integrated course in social sciences, carrying usually six semester hours of credit.

Table 11. Number of Public Junior Colleges Offering Instruction in Stated Social Sciences and Extent of Offering in a Sample of Thirty Public Junior Colleges

Units Offered					Subject Fields					
	Hist.	Psych.	Pol. Sci.	Econ.	Sociol.	Geog.	Educ.	Philos.	Anthro.	Integrated Soc. Sci.
31 or more	5	1					1			
25–30	1	3	1			1		1		
19–24	9	6	1	1	1	2	1			
13–18	7	5	7	4	6	1	1	3	1	1
7–12	8	12	10	17	14	4	2	11	4	1
1–6		3	11	7	9	18	15	6	14	9
Total colleges	30	30	30	29	30	26	20	21	19	11
Total units	639	458	316	299	300	207	156	216	120	81
Mean units [a]	21.3	15.3	10.5	10.3	10.0	8.2	7.8	10.3	6.3	7.4

[a] "Mean units" lists the arithmetic mean of units available in the subject in the public junior colleges of the sample which offer it.

D. Sciences and Mathematics

Biological Sciences form a part of the required lower-division education in several professional fields. Some study in the area is required by many four-year colleges as part of the lower-division work of all liberal arts students, native or transfer, and some students in each year are likely to plan to specialize in one of these sciences, either as teachers or as researchers. The multiple nature of this student need obligates the public junior colleges to provide an extensive range of courses in the field. In the sample of thirty public junior college catalogs, courses are listed in the fields of zoology, botany, biology, anatomy and physiology, bacteriology, microbiology, and paleontology. In addition, there are six examples of generalized survey courses in biological or life sciences in colleges which offered biology also. The smallest of the sample colleges provides courses only in three fields of biological science; zoology appears in every catalog and biology and anatomy-physiology in all but three. In any biological science, expansion of the offering beyond the introductory course is provided to meet the needs of specific occupational groups, such as nurses, laboratory technicians, or agriculture majors; introductory courses of two different varieties are not found, as they were in social sciences. Rather, increasingly specialized courses or additional subject fields seem to be added in most of these colleges to care for specialized training needs.

A reader familiar with course-credit patterns in the life sciences will discern that the most frequent offerings in each area consist of only one or two semesters of work, with laboratory. In Table 12, the category "1–6 units" includes semester courses of four or five units as well as two-semester lecture courses, organized in the familiar pattern of three weekly meetings. In the "7–12 unit" group will be found the two-semester courses with laboratories, yielding credit value of four or five units each semester. The distribution of course titles and the extent of the offering indicates that these junior colleges offer ample opportunity for their students to prepare for further study in biological sciences.

Physical Sciences in the public junior colleges are addressed principally to the education of engineers. A sequence of four unduplicating courses in chemistry is offered in every junior college in the sample group. In physics, a three-semester sequence is common; only one of the thirty colleges offers less than that amount of work. In both sciences, catalog evidence indicates that the engineering requirements

Table 12. Number of Public Junior Colleges Offering Instruction in Stated Biological Sciences and Extent of Offering in a Sample of Thirty Public Junior Colleges

Units Offered	Zool.	Bot-any	Biol-ogy	Anat. Phy.	Bac-teriol.	Micro-biol.	Pale-ont.	Sur-vey
			Science					
19–24	3		3	1		1		
13–18	3	2	4	2		1		
7–12	16	11	13	13	1	1		1
1–6	8	12	7	11	7	19	4	5
Total colleges	30	25	27	27	8	22	4	6
Total units	299	187	297	223	40	119	17	31
Mean units	10.0	7.5	11.0	8.3	5.0	5.4	4.3	5.2

in the universities control the basic course offering, as well as the organization and sequence of topics. Junior colleges that offer work in chemistry and physics in addition to the minimum requirements for engineers do not ordinarily offer specialized advanced work. Instead, they offer other sequences of introductory study, often of shorter duration, which enable them to separate the engineering students from the general students and those preparing for other professions.

Twenty-one of these colleges offer geology, primarily as an additional elective course for the engineer. At times it also serves as a general physical science course for those transfer students who lack the mathematics to undertake a sequence of courses in chemistry or in physics, but who are required to complete some study in physical sciences. Except in petroleum-producing regions, not more than a single two-semester course combining physical and historical geology is offered. Introductory courses in astronomy and in meteorology are offered in a scattering of colleges. Even the colleges with planetariums offer limited transfer courses in astronomy. The distribution of courses is shown in Table 13.

A survey course in the physical sciences is listed three times as often as a survey of life sciences. This excess may exist merely in name, since the course titled General Biology or Introduction to Biology and offered in twenty-seven colleges may be in reality the same as a survey of life sciences. Half of the colleges studied, at any rate, list a Physical Sciences course; it is most frequently organized as a two-semester course.

Table 13. Number of Public Junior Colleges Offering Instruction in Stated Physical Sciences and Extent of Offering in a Sample of Thirty Public Junior Colleges

Units Offered			Sciences			
	Chem.	Physics	Geology	Phys. Sci.	Astronomy	Meteor- ology
37 and over	6	1				
31–36	7	6	1			
25–30	10	11	2			
19–24	4	7	1			
13–18	3	3	3			
7–12		2	11	7	1	
1–6			3	13	12	7
Total colleges	30	30	21	20	13	7
Total units	925	753	265	125	60	21
Mean units	30.8	25.1	12.6	6.3	4.6	3.0

The total of units offered in chemistry and physics in the public junior colleges is greater than that in any other subject area, except in the fine arts. The nature of the courses offered indicates that the preparation of transfer students who have a professional need for these sciences—future engineers, physicians, and scientists—is being accomplished adequately. In addition, some provision of courses in physical science is becoming available to other students. For the most part, nonmajors in biological sciences must compete with the future specialists in extensive courses in zoology or biology, or else avoid science altogether.

Mathematics courses in junior colleges also include all the courses in mathematics usually found in the lower-division curriculum of the scientific or the engineering student. The mean credit value of all courses in mathematics, in these thirty colleges, was 50.2 semester units. All but two offered a course in college algebra, and all of them offered analytic geometry and calculus for credit ranging from ten to eighteen units. In addition, several colleges offered a choice of patterns of analytic geometry and calculus either for honors courses or to permit more rapid completion and enrichment of the standard topics. These duplicating offerings were not included in the tally of the basic credit hours in calculus.

Twenty-six of the colleges offered the usual high school courses in intermediate algebra and plane trigonometry; of these, eighteen also offered beginning algebra and geometry courses, to permit students to complete the minimum requirements in mathematics for the baccalaureate degree. Thirteen of the colleges surveyed offer a nontechnical course in mathematics for general education, with titles such as "Mathematics for General Education," "Structural Approach to Mathematics," "Contemporary" or "Modern Mathematics." This course is described in one catalog as follows: "Introduction to logic, the number system, set theory, functions and probability. This course is not remedial or fundamental in nature. A term paper is required. Recommended for pre-law students."

In discharging their responsibility to the "late-blooming" student, and to the technical student who has neglected mathematics in his high school course, fourteen of the colleges offer a refresher course in arithmetic under titles such as "Basic Mathematics" or "Fundamental Concepts in Mathematics." In some of the colleges, this course is a required prerequisite to other mathematics courses for students who fail to qualify on an entrance test in mathematics. It rarely carries credit toward the Associate in Arts degree, and never for transfer purposes.

In sciences and mathematics the evidence shows that the junior colleges provide a broad opportunity for the student to specialize in scientific study. In every college except the very smallest ones, transfer students can complete lower-division preparation for later study in engineering, in sciences, and in mathematics at the university, so that they need lose no time after transfer in making up subjects required of university freshmen or sophomores. Opportunities for the non-specialist, especially in biological sciences, appear to be somewhat inadequate. There seems to have been little effort to discover whether other selections of material and of course organization are appropriate for these students. At any rate, there are few courses listed that are designed for them.

E. Engineering

In addition to the science and mathematics courses required in the lower division of the engineering curriculum, public junior colleges also commonly offer a limited number of units in the department of engineering itself. Of the thirty colleges in the sample group analyzed for this chapter, all but one offered some engineering subjects. The mean credit value of engineering subjects in these twenty-nine colleges was twenty semester units, with a range from four to fifty-four units.

In all twenty-nine colleges, engineering drawing is offered, with as many as four semesters of study made available. In addition, some of the colleges list also a high-school-level introductory course, for those students who have had no previous drafting course. Surveying and a course in properties of materials are taught in more than half of the colleges, as part of the professional education of the civil engineer. The larger junior colleges then enrich their engineering offering by one or more introductory courses such as statics, mechanics, dynamics, and shop practices. The expansion of the curriculum beyond the universal offering in drafting is determined primarily, and properly, by study of the lower-division offering of the school of engineering to which most of the junior college graduates transfer.

F. Fine Arts

Music. Study of the catalogs of thirty public junior colleges demonstrates that junior colleges afford a wide variety of opportunities for group and individual study of vocal and instrumental music, supplemented by several courses in the theory of music. In one college, which enrolls approximately 1500 full-time students, the transferable units available in music total 190, with seven music instructors. In this case, as in others with less extensive listings, it is evident that individual opportunity for practice under supervision was made available to students. It is probable also that students would not enroll for every one of the individual instruments listed in every semester. Listing the courses in the catalog indicates merely that students are encouraged to extend their musical ability while they are in junior college and that instructors stand ready to instruct, supervise, and examine any interested musical student. Table 14 shows offerings in the fine arts.

This emphasis on music indicates also that a large proportion of the students in every public junior college are able to participate in some musical activity. There are courses suited to all qualities of musical talent; the credit earned is transferable, even though non-transfer students also enroll. Music appreciation and chorus classes are open to all students without prerequisites of vocal training or instruction. For the student whose interest in music is more serious, courses in sight reading, harmony, and counterpoint supplement group practice in glee clubs and a cappella choir or in orchestra and band. In the colleges that have the personnel and facilities, this group instruction is supplemented by opportunity for individual vocal or instrumental study.

Table 14. Number of Public Junior Colleges Offering Instruction in Stated Fine Arts Subjects, and Extent of Offering in Sample of Thirty Public Junior Colleges

Units Offered	Subjects						
	Music	Art	Home Econ.	Drama	Human-ities	Arch.	Phot.
91 and over	5						
61–90	3	5		1			
31–60	14	9	1	2		1	
25–30	6	6	4	1		2	
19–24	1	3	3	1		1	
13–18		3	10	7	2		4
7–12	1	3	1	5	2	1	3
1–6		1	2	7	2	4	6
Total colleges	30	30	21	24	6	9	13
Total units	1612	1065	398	392	56	146	118
Mean units	53.7	36.5	19.0	16.3	9.3	16.2	9.1

Art and Photography. All the public junior colleges in the sample offer some work in art. An introductory course in art appreciation is the most frequent offering, with design, color, and drawing as the usual basic offerings in applied work. Beyond these fundamental subjects, the junior colleges adapt their programs to the previous high-school study of their students, the artistic interest of the community, and the expectations of the universities. Some colleges content themselves with a minimum of choice in specialized art study; others seem to exert every effort to enable students to gain thorough background in many techniques. Such subjects as craft work, lapidary work, water color, oil painting, portrait painting, advertising art, and ceramics appear in one or more catalogs. In some junior colleges only one semester of work is offered in one or two fields; yet there are junior colleges in which a student may pursue a four-semester course, meeting from six to twelve hours weekly, in painting or ceramics or advertising art. Such courses ordinarily are presented as part of the transfer offering of the junior college, even though few transfer students would be able to spare time, because of other requirements, for more than one or two of the specialized courses. In the colleges with the most extended listing of courses in art, it is likely that a good many nontransfer students enroll in some of the more advanced courses.

Photography is included in the art offering in several of the colleges, ordinarily as a two-semester course combining study of cameras and films with opportunity to expose, develop, and print pictures as a part of the laboratory work. It is not unusual for these classes to accept assignments to provide some photographs of campus activities for the college newspaper or annual. Although the courses in photography are presented as transferable rather than as occupational preparation, it is doubtful that any student can present as part of his preparation for the bachelor's degree all of the eighteen units in photography listed in one public junior college catalog.

Home Economics courses are offered in twenty-one of the public junior colleges in the sample group of thirty. The fundamental curriculum for transfer purposes includes one two-semester course in foods and nutrition and a second in clothing. Additional courses include home management, child development, family budgeting and purchasing, home planning and decoration, and specialized courses required in the prenursing or preteaching curriculums. In several junior colleges, these are offered as dual-purpose courses, appealing both to the young woman who plans to earn a degree in home economics and to the one who is looking toward early marriage. Other colleges find it desirable to separate the two sets of student objectives and to organize additional courses with appealing titles for the nonprofessional students. In these colleges, the home economics department may list such titles as Clothing for Secretaries and Family Meal Planning among its course offerings. The opportunity exists for junior college women to prepare themselves for these important aspects of their lives; but the testimony of instructors indicates that only a minority of the students enroll in the courses.

Drama is a frequent offering of the public junior colleges; twenty-four of the institutions in the sample group offer some experience in the field. As in the other arts, the offering includes study of the theory and the literature of dramatics, supplemented by application in stage craft and in acting, through a series of formal and informal theatrical presentations. Introduction to Theater is a two-semester course which may be taught in a usual classroom or in one with only a minimum stage. It concentrates on reading and analyzing plays and discussing techniques of acting and playwriting. If an auditorium is available, production of plays may be undertaken either as a noncredit activity or as a series of organized classes for credit. As the curriculum is expanded toward the eighty-five-unit maximum offering found in these colleges, additional specialization is introduced in lighting, stage design, costuming, and makeup.

Humanities courses, under that departmental title, are offered in only six of the thirty public junior colleges studied. In general, the influences noted in the discussion of other subject areas operate here. If the universities in the state offer and require integrated courses in humanities, the junior colleges will offer similar courses. If the universities require credit in separate subject fields, the public junior colleges will be unlikely to develop strong and popular courses in humanities. For like reasons, even the junior colleges that do list a department of humanities sometimes include in it courses such as World Literature, Great Books, or Religious Concepts rather than experimentally established courses such as The Arts at Pennsylvania State College for Women, described as "a two-year sequence, required of all students, integrating material from literature, drama, music, painting, sculpture, architecture, and the dance" (52:77). At present some activity is discernible in this area from a study of the college catalogs, but it is still seemingly hesitant and tentative.

Architecture is offered as a transferable subject in nine of the thirty public junior colleges studied. Because of its severe limitations as a field of employment, not even all the larger universities have schools of architecture. It is unlikely that the smaller community junior colleges will enroll enough architectural aspirants to justify an extended preparatory specialization in the field. In most junior colleges, the pre-architectural student will be advised to choose the required mathematics, physics, drafting, and art courses from the available curriculum and then to transfer to a university school of architecture for the more specialized work. Two of the public junior colleges in the sample that offer architectural courses are in large cities close to university schools to which their students may transfer.

G. Business Administration

Lower-division courses in the field of business administration are offered in every one of the thirty public junior colleges surveyed. Not all of the courses could be completed for transfer purposes by any one student, since one college lists 45 units of transfer business courses, and 14 have more than 24 units of courses. In these cases, specialized courses are offered for the needs of students with a variety of business administration objectives; undoubtedly the courses are taken by terminal and special students to prepare for work in the local community, as well as by those planning to earn degrees in business administration.

Principles of Economics, discussed under social sciences, is a course usually required of lower-division students in business. In addition, as many as four semesters of work in accounting may be offered as preparation for enrollment at some Schools of Business. A limited amount of work in typing and shorthand may be applied toward a business bachelor's degree, especially by students planning to be business teachers. Junior colleges sometimes consider the first year's work in each of these subjects as transferable and all work beyond one year as primarily occupational preparation. Other courses included in one or more of the catalog listings in business administration are Business Law and Introduction to Business, with Mathematics of Investment or Elementary Statistics offered in the mathematics departments of several colleges. The average number of transferable units in business offered in the thirty-college sample was 24.9, sufficient to indicate that in business administration, also, the junior college student can complete the usual lower-division requirements for further study.

H. Evaluation of the Curriculum for Transfer Students

Preparation of students for further study at the four-year college or university was the first responsibility of the junior college. It is still the function on which the junior colleges expend most of their effort and in which most of their students express interest. Evidence presented in previous sections of the chapter indicates that public junior colleges offer the courses required to provide adequate lower-division preparation. In the larger colleges the curriculum develops to a point at which preparation may be completed for almost every university area of specialization. It is possible that this multiplication of courses may in itself become a source of weakness and unnecessary expense.

Although its comment is addressed to all undergraduate colleges, the President's Committee on Education Beyond the High School offers advice that is particularly appropriate for curriculum makers in the community junior colleges:

The proliferation of narrow course offerings is worthy of note. In part, this simply reflects man's desire to categorize his ever-growing specialized knowledge. But, just as it is surely unwise for all institutions to attempt to offer detailed courses in all areas of knowledge, it seems equally unwise for any institution to conduct numerous small classes on peripheral or narrowly specialized subject matter, particularly at the undergraduate level. The result may be to dissipate teaching resources without necessarily strengthening the student's education. The Committee strongly suspects that the majority of colleges and universities could improve the quality of education offered by reducing substantially the number of courses offered and using the resources thus released, including faculty and student energies, to improve the rest. (*139*:32–33)

Some indications of such overdevelopment of courses were noted in some of the fields of science, in business, in photography, and in music. Some of the excessive specialization, when it exists, arises from a desire to match similarly specialized university requirements in the same subject areas. In other instances it is evident that the public junior colleges have elaborated transfer courses far beyond the lower-division needs of their students and beyond the limits of acceptability at the upper-division colleges. Although it must acknowledge responsibility for some of the shortcomings in junior college curriculums, the university is not the sole culprit. Exaggerated faculty enthusiasm causes a part of the uneconomical excess.

In an opposing vein, it seems probable that in some areas not enough courses have been developed. In their concentration upon preparing some of their students for professional specialization, the public junior colleges have tended to overlook the fact that other students need a layman's introduction to certain disciplines outside of their individual areas of concentration. The lack of conceptually rich and intellectually demanding nonprofessional courses in sciences, social sciences, and mathematics was mentioned as a case in point. In extenuation, community junior colleges may well point out that frequently they cannot afford to duplicate certain offerings. They feel that it is better to offer the specialized course, in that case, and to require too much of the nonspecialized student, than to serve the needs of the nonmajor student and so slight the education of the future professional.

If such a dilemma is in truth presented, the junior colleges have chosen the proper alternative. Yet it is possible that in some cases university domination is an excuse rather than an adequate cause for junior college conservatism. As a new and vigorous segment of American higher education, the community junior college should demonstrate ingenuity and energy in seeking solutions to curricular problems. With the extension of educational opportunity, new purposes of students have emerged that require new approaches to the organization of instruction. The community junior college too often has been complacently imitative, when it should have been diligently seeking better ways to educate its transfer students. Before many years, community junior colleges will enroll the major share of lower-division students; now is the time for them to prepare for the responsibilities that will accompany this role.

Finally, since the introduction of the concept of occupational education as a function of the community junior college, there has been a constant awareness that the provision of extensive transfer courses frequently interferes with the development of occupational education. The prestige of the transfer curriculum, in the minds of faculty as well as students, combines with the limitation of resources to constrict the breadth of offering. The community junior college that favors either aspect of its program at the expense of the other makes a serious error. The community that supports the college needs a well-developed college-transfer program of highest quality; it also needs, for a majority of those who enroll at the college, a vocational program of excellent quality. The two are equally respectable, equally important, equally possible. The question is not so much one of priority as it is of the means for harmonious and concomitant development.

Selected References

Baskin, Samuel. *Higher Education: Some Newer Developments.* New York: McGraw-Hill Book Co., 1965.

Bird, Grace V. "Preparation for Advanced Study." Chapter V in *The Public Junior College,* Nelson B. Henry (editor). Fifty-fifth Yearbook of the National Society for the Study of Education, Part I. Chicago: The University of Chicago Press, 1956.

French, Sidney J. (editor). *Accent on Teaching.* New York: Harper and Row, 1954.

Gleazer, Edmund J., Jr. (editor). *American Junior Colleges, 1960.* Washington: American Council on Education, 1960. Appendix IV.

Holmes, Charles H. "The Transfer Student in the College of Liberal Arts," *Junior College Journal,* 31:456–461, April, 1961.

Johnson, B. Lamar. *General Education In Action.* Washington: American Council on Education, 1952.

Knoell, Dorothy M. and Leland L. Medsker. *From Junior to Senior College: A National Study of the Transfer Student.* Washington: American Council on Education, 1966.

Stickler, W. Hugh (editor). *Experimental Colleges.* Tallahassee: Florida State University, 1964.

16

The Curriculum:
Continuing Education

In addition to the regularly organized day-time curriculum of transfer courses, general education, and occupational education, community colleges typically schedule extensive programs designed to satisfy the growing demand for continuing education. Citizens who are not full-time students desire to work toward a degree, to improve their occupational skills, to prepare for a new occupation, or simply to extend their understanding and knowledge. Community colleges accept the responsibility for providing opportunity for this continuing education.

The term "adult education," formerly used to describe this function of the community college, has become less appropriate as both the nature of the part-time student and the scope of the offerings change. Only eight of the thirty colleges in the sample studied for these chapters refer explicitly to adult education in their catalogs. All of the others recognize the responsibility, but discuss it under such headings as extension, evening programs, or continuing education. There are cogent reasons for this change of terminology.

At one time, it was possible to define adult education as consisting of courses offered to persons over 21 years of age who were employed full time, who attended classes only during evening hours, who were not interested in degree credit, and who probably needed the classes for Americanization or employment. At that time, these qualifications effectively distinguished the adult student from the regular day student. At present, none of the distinctions is fully accurate.

Nevertheless, community colleges are giving increased attention to providing evening courses identical to those given in the day, carrying the same requirements and credits, and leading to the same objectives. In the words of one catalog,

... evening classes provide the adult community with freshman-sophomore level college-credit classes and non-credit activities. The courses in large part do not duplicate courses offered by other agencies in the community. They are designed to serve employed adults and others seeking enrichment of their lives and occupational values, who need or prefer evening hours for classes. Evening classes are an integral part of the college curriculum, and evening credits are not distinguished on transcripts from day credits.

Chapter 16 discusses the extent of the part-time enrollment in community colleges, considers the purposes of the students and of the colleges in making the courses available, and discusses several current issues in the development of programs of continuing education.

A. *The Extent of Part-Time Study in Community Colleges*

Enrollment data in the *1966 Junior College Directory* (*118*) are presented for October, 1964. A part-time student is defined as one who is enrolled in at least one course for credit and who carries less than three-fourths (less than 12 semester hours) of a normal full-time load. There are in addition, a large number of part-time unclassified students, defined as students not counted as freshmen or sophomores, who may not have fulfilled requirements for matriculation or who are enrolled in college-level courses for which they receive no credit. It is apparent that the part-time category includes students who are fulfilling requirements toward a degree or certificate, students who take one or two courses for credit for any reason, and auditors (*118:6*).

The *1966 Junior College Directory* presents entries for 503 public and 268 independent junior colleges. Table 15 is derived from data presented in the *Directory*.

It is apparent that part-time students are enrolled in public junior colleges more often than in independent ones, and in greater numbers. In fact, the part-time students outnumber the full-time students in the public colleges. In public junior colleges, part-time students account for 53% of total enrollments; in independent junior colleges, 23% of all enrollments are part-time students. In a few of the public junior colleges, part-time enrollments are more than twice as large

Table 15. Statistics of Part-Time Enrollments in Public and Private Junior Colleges, October, 1964 [a]

	Public	Private	Total	Per Cent Public
Number of junior colleges	503	268	771	65.2
Number listing part-time students	429	178	607	70.8
Per cent listing part-time students	82.9	67.0	78.7	—
Enrollment, part-time	486,975	26,970	513,945	94.8
Enrollment, full-time	424,676	92,082	516,758	82.1

[a] Source: *1966 Junior College Directory (118)*.

as full-time enrollments; at Long Beach City College, for example, they are four times as large (19,997 as compared to 5213).

In 1948, Martorana reported a questionnaire survey based on offerings in "adult education" offerings; of 337 respondents, 144 colleges reported having adult programs. Of these, only 56% offered courses to adults which paralleled their transfer courses in the regular program (*101*). This finding contrasts markedly with the more limited sample of 30 junior college catalogs for 1964–1965, in which most colleges describe their extended day programs as fully comparable to the day-time offerings, and avoid the use of the term "adult education."

In summary, except for the most recently established public junior colleges, all but a handful offer organized programs of instruction for several categories of part-time students, and the total of part-time students outnumbers the regular full-time enrollment. There has been a distinct trend toward graded classes offered for college credit, and away from the earlier concept of offering any class desired by a sufficient number of adults.

B. Purposes of the Part-Time Student

The President's Committee on Education Beyond the High School estimated that

One of every three adults in the United States is engaged in some kind of continuing education during any single year. Rough estimates indicate that 50,000,000 persons participated in programs of adult education in 1955, a nearly fourfold increase in 30 years. Approximately 2,800,000 people were contributing some or all of their time to operating these programs. (*139:66*)

At the same time, a team of researchers reported in a study of junior college needs in Minnesota that

The area of adult education is just beginning. The forces that have caused its development this far are still much in evidence, forces such as social and technological change, current insecurity, continuous retraining because of war and economic fluctuations, and increasing leisure time. Without question, education is now a lifelong process both from a vocational and an avocational viewpoint. (*84:108*)

It is worthwhile to consider some of the ways in which these forces cause people to enroll for continuing education.

Basic Education. Many Americans leave school before high-school graduation, only to learn later that they are handicapped through life by the lack of a diploma. If opportunity for further study is made available to them, many of these persons will enroll in order to complete their secondary education. Although some junior colleges require high-school graduation as a qualification for enrollment in all classes, an increasing number of community junior colleges are enabling adults to complete studies leading to a certificate of high-school equivalency. The same desire for ever higher educational attainment accounts also for a large proportion of the college-level work offered in extended day programs. As many as one-fifth of the ablest high-school graduates are financially unable to continue study in college. The presence of a junior college part-time program of continuing education enables such students to make some progress toward a college degree, even though the road may be difficult and painfully slow.

In addition, in any community there are numbers of mature persons whose interest in learning is still vivid, even though they have no desire for additional college credits. Some of them may be largely self-educated; others will possess bachelors' or advanced degrees. Yet they are eager to pursue courses in subjects they were unable to study in college or to keep abreast of changing social and political conditions. For this class of students the junior college provides courses in great books, in philosophy and humanities, in current affairs, in geography, in interpretation of science, in foreign languages. The "level" of the study is comparatively unimportant to these students; they can at last pursue knowledge for the sake of their own education, without concern for the evaluation of credit by the instructor or by another college. Teaching in the basic areas of education is, under these conditions, one of the most stimulating and rewarding experiences an instructor can have.

Degree Objective. Statistics of community junior college part-time enrollments indicate that there has been a substantial increase in the number of employed adults who intend to earn the associate degree through part-time study. As a result of this increase, more emphasis is being placed on organized patterns of evening courses which parallel the courses required of the full-time student. This degree objective is in part a manifestation of the long-term trend toward higher average educational attainment in America. In addition, the demand of industry for more highly educated employees contributes to the increase, as does the desire of housewives to retrain themselves for office work or for teaching. The trend toward earlier marriage combines with compulsory military service to add another increment to degree-seeking part-time enrollments. Young men who marry during their military service still desire additional education upon release from active duty. Some of them can arrange to attend college full time; although others must seek full-time employment, they will avail themselves of the opportunity for part-time progress toward a degree if it is made available by the community junior college. This degree objective of part-time students is a recent and appealing reason for the further development of community junior college continuing education programs.

Occupational Training or Retraining. A consequence of expanding and developing technology has been the rapid obsolescence of vocational skills and the consequent need for refresher training or retraining for another occupation. The radio repairman is an example of this need. As television invaded the American home during the immediate postwar period, thousands of radio servicemen came to junior colleges and technical schools to learn the secrets of television repair. They had hardly become used to their new skills, when the introduction of color broadcasting sent them back to school for additional training. Almost immediately thereafter the substitution of the transistor for the vacuum tube brought another set of technical problems and another demand for trade related classes.

Part-time occupational training also provides the skills needed for entry into an occupation. Men in blind-alley jobs and housewives whose children no longer need their full-time attention frequently seek this training. Introductory courses in machine shop, electronics, bookkeeping, real estate, or drafting are examples of courses offered for men; secretarial training and practical nursing courses may attract women who feel the need to qualify for employment.

The related training required of apprentices is another example of study in occupational areas suitable for the community junior college, especially in metropolitan areas. In addition to the trade-related courses that are required in the apprenticeship plan, apprentices are encouraged to complete general education requirements also, so that at the end of their four-year indenture they may earn both journeyman rating and the Associate in Arts degree.

A final class of continuing occupational training is that which prepares a worker for promotion on the job. Frequently competent craftsmen are considered for promotion to supervisory positions in which they will need not only additional technical knowledge but greater understanding of personal relations and the techniques of leadership. When the demand in a community justifies courses of this nature, it is appropriate that they be offered at the community junior college.

Homemaking Education. Although nearly all women will spend a major portion of their lives as homemakers, comparatively few college women or high-school girls elect courses designed to prepare them for homemaking. One reason for their neglect may well be a feeling that the need is remote, that there will be plenty of time to care for it later. In addition, readiness is an essential precondition for learning. Community junior college teachers of homemaking are becoming aware that the best time to teach many of the skills and understandings is after marriage, and that in some courses both the young wife and her husband can profit from instruction. Classes in homemaking, therefore, are among the usual offerings of community junior college evening programs. Consumer economics, low-cost cookery, family entertaining, and prenatal and infant care are some of the courses which may be offered to part-time students either in day or evening classes to suit the convenience of the class members. For parents of young children, combinations of nursery school and child psychology classes are offered in a few community junior colleges; such classes as advanced sewing, upholstery, and interior decorating are very popular also with young parents, especially if they are offered at a time when one parent can baby-sit while the other is in class.

Avocational Courses. "Worthy use of leisure time" has been an accepted objective of public education at least since it was listed as one of the "Cardinal Principles" in 1918. Recent increases in the amount of leisure time combine with the monotonous and uninspiring nature of many occupations to encourage adults to seek avocational education through adult education programs. As Martorana discovered, 41% of the junior colleges with adult education offerings provided avocational and recreational courses (*101*:329). Critics of continuing education, in legislatures and in the popular press, comment scathingly on organized instruction in subjects such as "fly-tying" and "basket-weaving," as if these defined its entire scope. Nevertheless, increasing free time constitutes an important social problem. Some of this time can be filled with academic and vocational studies, but for some students, classes in avocational skills are equally valid and important (*141*:68–94). Among the recreational and avocational courses found in community junior college extended day programs are listed woodworking, mineral and lapidary work, oil painting, ceramics, weaving, craft work, and other manipulative skills. Astronomy, dramatics, music, and public speaking may be offered for the same reason. In addition, a good many of the adults who enroll in the more traditional courses choose them more for recreational values than because they seek college degrees or vocational competency.

The Geriatric Purpose. A new educational purpose has been created by developments of the past half century. Increasingly urbanized split-level living in mechanized houses has combined with earlier retirement ages and longer life expectancies to create a new and numerous class of senior citizens. To many of them, the new-coined adjective "roleless" applies with tragic exactitude. In each of our cities can be found a sizable group of retired men and widowed women who are still alert, able, reasonably healthy, but lonely and unoccupied. In the prime of life, men prize their hard-won free time; but when all of one's time is free, leisure becomes a dehumanizing burden rather than an opportunity. Society must face the increasing problem of its older members and search diligently for humane solutions. The junior college can contribute significantly to those solutions.

In the past, education has been considered essentially as a preparation for life. If this definition still delimits the scope of the schools, the aging citizen is no concern of theirs. On the other hand, if education can also be considered as a continuing part of life, it can make significant contributions both to the individual well-being of the older person and to the welfare of society. Engrossing interest in one or more courses of study and in the companionship of classmates can preserve mental vigor. It is possible also that such interest and activity can improve physical condition. Even the financial cost of continuing education for these citizens would be an economy in comparison with the custodial costs that might well be saved.

Community junior colleges are becoming aware of this emerging educational need, and some of them are experimenting with classes to meet it. Philosophy, history, current events, geography through travelogues, literature, and some hobby classes have all proved to be of interest and of value when offered primarily for classes of students over 60 years of age. Further experimentation is needed to determine the proper scope of junior college education for the aged. The need exists in every community.

C. Purposes of the Community Junior College in Continuing Education

The community junior college accepts the individualistic purposes of its part-time students as they request courses to satisfy their needs. In addition, it realizes its obligation to society to use educational resources in seeking solutions of social problems. The evening curriculum is therefore expanded to include activities that improve the life of the community. Among the social considerations that influence junior colleges to provide courses for continuing students may be listed the rapid increase of knowledge, the demands of enlightened citizenship, and the fact of social lag.

The Rapid Increase of Knowledge. Improved techniques of research joined with electronic data-processing devices have brought about geometric increases in the sheer bulk of available information in almost every field of human endeavor. New information, too, causes the obsolescence of certain procedures and creates a need to train operators in new methods. No man may dare any longer to consider his education completed. The physician, the engineer, the physicist, and the dentist, among others, return to the university periodically to learn of new drugs, new apparatus, new theories, new processes in their specialties. New knowledge on the professional level, however, must be accompanied by new understanding at the level of the layman and by new skills on the part of the technician. This lay and technical re-education is a responsibility of the community junior college.

In a society based on technology and dependent for its continued well-being on a constantly expanding technology, the rapid diffusion of knowledge is essential. Advertisers and broadcasters certainly contribute, from their partisan standpoints, to this diffusion; the community junior college can work more dispassionately and thoroughly than the mass media to help people to know and evaluate recent discoveries in all fields. In part, the college discharges this obligation by offering organized college credit courses for part-time students, paralleling in prerequisites and in coverage courses offered to full-time students. Beyond this, many approaches can contribute to the same ends. Individual lectures or lecture series, week-end workshops for specialized interests, laboratory demonstrations, forums, exhibitions, and conferences have been used by junior colleges in bringing summaries of recent research to their communities. Class sizes, in this sort of effort, may vary from seminars or laboratory groups to large auditorium audiences assembled to hear especially qualified speakers.

The Demands of Enlightened Citizenship. Citizenship education cannot be completed by the time of high-school graduation or at any other fixed point in man's life. A citizen who had come to understand thoroughly the civic problems and responsibilities of the 1930's might find himself completely unprepared for the prosperity of the 1960's. Some citizens, of course, through careful reading and civic participation, have always kept their learning abreast of their times. That has never been true of the majority of people; modern conditions make it ever more difficult to achieve adequate political and civic insights without help. The global nature of the national responsibility, the incomprehensible sums of national budgets, the rapid growth of metropolitan complexes with suburban needs for services of all sorts, the mobility of the population—all conspire to increase both the gravity of political decisions and the difficulty of making them wisely. The community junior college is equipped to contribute significantly to the quality of citizen participation in understanding and in solving local and national problems. Avoiding partisanship, it can still encourage study, fact finding, debate, and the acceptance by citizens of responsibility for informed action.

The Reduction of "Social Lag." Social lag refers to the serious gap between scientific invention and technological advance, on the one hand, and changes in political and economic institutions, on the other. This lag often causes unnecessary human misunderstanding and discomfort. A simple example pairs the effect of technology in releasing women from economic production in the home so that they now make their economic contribution in the office and the factory, with the continuing social belief that "woman's place is in the home." As a result, women are employed but feel degraded, even though their drudgery is lessened; husbands too find it difficult to adjust the attitudes of their childhood to the realities of their maturity. On a more complicated problem, Galbraith has called attention to the inconsistencies involved in adjusting the economics and politics of scarcity to the economy of abundance (54).

Community junior college evening programs can help to reduce this social lag and its effects. Serious adults welcome opportunities to explore developments in technology and to relate their effects on the quality of human life to the ideas that motivate so much of our activity. In many communities, the junior college will have on its faculty or readily available to it specialists in the social and technical disciplines. In addition, it will have lecture halls, classrooms, and laboratories. It avoids one of its most meaningful opportunities if it does not take the lead in bringing this sort of interpretation to its community.

D. Issues in Community Junior College Continuing Education

Elements of a Complete Program. Community junior college administrators are in substantial agreement that continuing education is distinguished from the regular daytime program as a matter of convenience rather than because of essential differences. The extended-day student is not clearly distinguished from the regular day student by age or educational purpose, not even by the number of units of credit he carries. The major differentiation is the fact that the part-time student considers that his primary occupation is something other than college attendance, and that he may not be interested in college credit for his study. The continuing program, then, consists of learning opportunities organized primarily for this category of students, at any hour of the day, with or without degree credit. The fact that some "regular" students may also enroll in such courses does not affect the classification of the course; it is recognized that at times part-time students, as defined, will also enroll in "regular" courses.

The issues on which administrators are in disagreement have to do with the scope and diversity of the program. Should a community junior college offer courses leading to the certificate of high-school equivalency? Should it offer short courses, noncredit courses, hobby courses, or vocational courses? To what extent should the community junior college seek to meet all educational needs of the adults of its community? Should it classify certain kinds of instruction as college work and worthy of its attention, relegating other studies to other agencies? Or should it decide that continuing education is accomplished best under a single administration, preferably that of the community junior college? Should the community junior college attempt, as some do, to offer any instruction for which there is student demand, so long as there is a reasonable body of knowledge, understanding, or skills, and an instructor available to conduct the course? Should it seek aggressively to extend its educational services to the community, or should it limit them to specified categories of college instruction? Those administrators who adopt the "community junior college" point of view lean toward the aggressive, all-inclusive, extended-service concept of the adult education program. Their communities respond to this effort by enrolling in increasing numbers, as was suggested in the section of this chapter dealing with part-time statistics.

Academic Credit. The proposed definition of the part-time student indicated that he is often uninterested in academic credit for his study. Some part-time students are working for credentials or degrees and must choose courses which carry credit, but many of the students who enroll in cultural, homemaking, vocational, or avocational courses are entirely uninterested in credit. They do not wish to be bothered with term papers or examinations; they feel competent to decide for themselves what values, and how much value, they wish to derive from the course. The question of credit is complicated in some courses by the presence of a small minority of students who need credit together with a majority who wish only to audit, for their own purposes.

The credit issue, then, revolves about two questions: Should a community junior college allow itself to offer courses that deviate from traditional and accreditable practices? To what extent does adulthood imply the ability of a person to choose values for himself rather than to accept those of tutors and scholars? Three sets of practices have developed in junior colleges in three attempts to reconcile the answers to these questions. Most junior colleges offer only credit courses in their continuing education program, paralleling subjects offered in the daytime schedule, and supplementing these courses by credit-carrying pre-employment courses and occupational extension courses not offered during the day.

A second group of junior colleges insists that any course which is worthy of being offered is worthy of credit. These colleges attempt to provide a broad and comprehensive range of classes; they maintain credit and attendance records for all students and classify all students as either freshmen or sophomores. Although this seems to be an extreme position, it does tend to add dignity and importance to the continuing education program and to those who enroll in it.

The third position is an intermediate one. Classes in any field which are equivalent to those offered in the regular program carry defined units of credit; students may enroll in these classes either for credit or as auditors. In addition, short courses and courses of limited scope or specialized interest are offered without credit toward any degree or diploma. It is probable that most of the community junior colleges that offer extensive evening programs of continuing education follow this eclectic pattern.

Source of Support for Continuing Education. Arrangements for the support of community junior college continuing education are complicated by the historical attitudes of legislators toward "adult education." At what point should free public education cease and the student be required to carry all the costs of his education? How can such a stopping point be defined? Are years of age, years of attendance, diplomas achieved, stated purposes of the student, or courses taken better bases for distinguishing the tuition-free student from the paying adult? Even in private colleges students pay only a part of the cost of their education; if fees are set so that part-time students do bear all the costs of their classes, will not many of them be unable to afford further education? Is it not likely that those least able to pay for additional education are those who are most in need of it? Inability to state consistent answers to questions like these is one reason why a few junior colleges offer minimum continuing programs, or none at all.

One pattern of support treats evening classes almost exactly the same as other community junior college classes. Requirements are established for the legal certification of teachers for adults, if that is required of other faculty members. State support, local support, and tuition policies apply equally to all classes of attendance; approval of courses by state departments of education is handled in the same fashion. Some method is worked out for equating part-time attendance, for purposes of state support, to that of full-time students, and foundation program funds are allocated on an equal basis. In states with laws of this nature, continuing education is fully accepted as one facet of the state's obligation to provide free public schooling for its citizens.

In other states, public junior colleges share in state support for post-high-school credit students, but are not given support for those in their adult classes. The junior college buildings, even though financed largely from state sources, are used by part-time students without additional charge. Costs of instructional materials, administrative costs, and teachers' salaries must be borne locally. In some of these states, local junior college boards may elect to bear the cost of these items entirely from public funds; in others, the local district and the continuing students share the costs through a nominal tuition charge. In still others, an attempt is made to collect the entire cost of evening instruction from the students or even to make a profit on the program. This last objective may be accomplished by authorizing only classes over a certain minimum size, charging fees which will cover the costs, and paying instructors a sliding scale in relation to the course enrollment.

There is, of course, no single best plan of financing continuing education for all states. Yet the financial plan does express in coldly factual terms the state's accepted philosophy of education. If individual and public needs for "lifelong learning" as expressed in this chapter are valid, each state should work to make further education easily available to as many as possible of its citizens. A major step in this effort would be to reduce, as far as is feasible, the tuition charges for such opportunities.

Flexibility in Curriculum Development. The ideal of some community junior college evening program administrators has been "to offer anything and everything of educational value for which there is sufficient and sustained demand" (112:151). The attainment of this principle requires a high degree of flexibility in schedule making and course approval. Courses will be inaugurated at any time of the year; instructors will be employed at short notice to teach courses which they may not have taught before. In fact, it is possible that some courses for which there is "sufficient and sustained demand" may not have been taught before by anyone. The issue created by this responsiveness to demand is that of academic control of the offerings of the college.

In Chapter 12, the careful process was described by which a curriculum committee examines new course proposals before including them in the curriculum. Under the principle stated above, however, demand, rather than the established procedures of committee deliberation, determines the curriculum. It is conceivable that a course that had been proposed and rejected in the regular curriculum might be accepted and established in the evening program. In other cases, courses paralleling regular courses might be offered in the evening program for credit toward the Associate in Arts degree or for transfer; but the instructor available might be one who would not have been employed as a full-time teacher of the same course. Standards of a junior college might suffer in such circumstances.

The enthusiastic extended-day administrator would counter these objections by pointing out that it is the purpose of his division to serve the community in all of its part-time educational needs. Many emerging needs of adults, he would claim, must be met energetically without undue red tape; the academic members of the curriculum committee might cause important damage to the total program of the college if they decided that responsible adult groups could not have a course or courses which they had petitioned for. Taxpaying patrons of the community college, in this view, are competent to analyze their own needs, and their requests should be complied with.

Standards. The definition and maintenance of standards of achievement are closely related to the issue of flexibility. The problem of standards is complicated by several factors. The diversity of courses, from chemistry and calculus to ceramics and current events, is one source of difficulty. The shortage of qualified instructors for work which is usually overtime and often underpaid is another. The inadequacy of library services during evening hours, together with the fatigue of the students themselves, militates against rigorous assignments and requirements. The scheduling of classes for single weekly meetings of several hours' duration rather than for a series of one-hour meetings makes it difficult for the instructor to command unflagging attention and limits the number of papers he is likely to assign. Student diversity in background and in purpose is an additional stumbling block, since a class may enroll twenty persons as auditors who want to define their own goals in the course, together with four or five degree-credit students who must accept the requirements of the instructor.

The difficulties in definition and maintenance of standards do not absolve the teacher of part-time students from serious concern with them. As more and more students seek to earn degrees through part-time study, the question of comparable standards becomes more acute. Careful planning of the offering, in-service training of the faculty, extension of laboratory and library opportunities, and a clear-cut differentiation of credit and noncredit enrollments can help to clarify the value of evening program courses. The vigorous growth of community junior college continuing education can be stemmed abruptly if it becomes apparent that the quality of the achievement is inferior and unsound.

Articulation with Other Agencies. The creation of new community junior colleges brings a need for the articulation of all their efforts with previously existing educational agencies. This need may be particularly acute in the field of continuing education. Many school districts have developed over a period of years extensive plans for adult education with administrative staff, arrangements for use of facilities, well-established offerings, sources of faculty, and a continuing clientele. The new community junior college may then be seen as a threat to the status of the previous program. Especially if it is independently organized and administered, the new college may be tempted to duplicate and extend the existing program. Alternatively, it may decide to offer in the evening only the courses it offers in the day program to regular students. Either of these decisions is likely to prove unfortunate; the one will beget enmities, unnecessary competition, and excess cost, and the other will deprive some adults of needed educational services which can be provided most appropriately only by the community junior college.

A better solution would be an attempt to harmonize the efforts of the existing and the new agencies, looking toward a time when unification of program and of administration will become possible. In these situations, neither the prestige of previous workers nor the ambitions of the newer faculty should be the controlling consideration. Organizational decisions should be sought that will result in making available to the people of the community the finest possible continuing education program, with due regard for economy to the school districts and for harmony among all workers.

The underlying conflict in each of the issues presented lies in the philosophies of those who hold the varying positions. An emphasis on the responsibility of the community college to meet any educational needs of any citizens beyond high-school age will lead to one kind of decision about continuing education, course credit, financial support, curriculum development, and interagency cooperation. Emphasis on the historical role of the college, on the other hand, and on its responsibility to preserve the integrity of the academic disciplines, will lead to other decisions. As yet, no clear-cut evidence indicates which tendency will prevail as public junior colleges gain experience in continuing education. There is little doubt, however, that the continuing education function of junior colleges will continue to increase in importance, both in numbers of institutions providing it and in numbers of students enrolled.

Selected References

Harlacher, Ervin L. "California Community Renaissance," *Junior College Journal,* 34:14–18, April, 1964.

Hillway, Tyrus. *The American Two-Year College.* New York: Harper and Row, 1958.

Kempfer, Homer. "Adult Education in the Community College," *Junior College Journal,* 21:18–25, September, 1950.

Martorana, S. V. "Problems in Adult Education in the Junior College," *Junior College Journal,* 18:115–123, November, 1947.

———. "Status of Adult Education in Junior Colleges," *Junior College Journal,* 18:322–331, February, 1948.

Morris, Charles S. " 'The People's College' at San Mateo," *Junior College Journal,* 14:148–151, December, 1943.

President's Commission on Higher Education. *Higher Education for American Democracy.* New York: Harper and Row, 1948.

President's Committee on Education Beyond the High School. *Second Report to the President.* Washington: Government Printing Office, 1957.

Reynolds, James W. *"Community Services."* Chapter 6 in *The Public Junior College.* Nelson B. Henry (editor). The Fifty-fifth Yearbook of the National Society for the Study of Education, Part I. Chicago: The University of Chicago Press, 1956.

Sheats, Paul H., Clarence D. Jayne, and Ralph B. Spence. *Adult Education: The Community Approach.* New York: The Dryden Press, 1953.

17

Student Personnel Services

The public junior college admits students of many backgrounds and ambitions to its broadly diversified instructional opportunities to prepare for various occupational and educational goals. This triple diversity convinced the early writers on the junior college that educational guidance was a necessary function of these institutions (45:Ch. 4). In recent years, the concept of personnel services, including guidance, has been clarified to the point of substantial agreement on the scope of such services and on the responsibility of the community junior college to make them available to its students.

Humphreys, as Chairman of the Committee on Student Personnel Services of the American Association of Junior Colleges, presented an outline of the areas of student personnel work (76:389–390). He listed as major categories (1) Orientation and High School Relationships, (2) Admission Procedures, (3) Guidance Services, (4) Student Life, (5) Job Placement and Follow-Up, (6) The Administration of Student Personnel Services. Aware of the analysis of deficiencies presented by Humphreys in the same article, Medsker decided to include an investigation of personnel practices in his extensive study of the two-year college (109:Ch. 6). His conclusions from his survey are summarized in two categories, Elements of Strength and Elements of Considered Weakness.

Under Elements of Strength, Medsker lists widespread acceptance of responsibility for personnel services, the establishment of "some level and type of counseling" in every junior college studied, the existence of well-developed student activity programs and good systems of academic records in most colleges. On the negative side, Medsker found a frequent lack of planning and professional direction for the program, definite inadequacies in the counseling program in many institutions, little research by junior colleges on the characteristics of their students, and limited evaluation of the personnel program.

Chapter 17 presents the elements of a student personnel program designed to provide the services outlined by Humphreys and at the same time to overcome the weaknesses suggested by Medsker. Although the author knows of no single program which includes all the practices described, each may be found in successful operation in one or another community junior college. A complete student personnel program will include the guidance service with its multitude of functions; student activities; placement and follow-up services; records, research, and evaluation; and an administrative organization to carry out the services.

A. The Guidance Service

Guidance Workers. In his study of student personnel services in 73 two-year colleges, Medsker found that student counseling was usually done by instructors and sometimes by the general administrators or deans of the college (109:147). In only sixteen of the seventy-three colleges studied was most of the counseling performed by counselors who had been trained in student personnel work. The instructors who do counseling are ordinarily neither trained nor qualified to do more than assist students in selecting their term schedule of classes. Problems of choice of vocational objective, improvement of study skills, and growth in personal adjustment are beyond the instructors' usual competence or interest. Since their full-time responsibility is in teaching, the instructor-advisers may feel that their guidance duties are an imposition. In practice, they may become for most of the students assigned to them merely schedule checkers rather than advisers or counselors.

The administrator-counselor, except in the smallest colleges, may also find it difficult to provide adequate service for his students. His experience and training may have equipped him to serve ably as a counselor, but the pressure of other duties and his frequent absences from the campus will tend to interrupt the progress of counseling and distract the administrator's attention from the student, even in the midst of an important interview. The instructors and the administrators have definite functions in guidance. The former will stand ready to assist any of their students in problems associated with success in their courses and will advise students referred to them by other workers about educational and occupational matters in which they are competent. The administrator can help by being convinced of the importance of personnel services as another aspect of instruction and by providing workers and facilities to carry on the services. In addition, trained guidance workers are required as the center of the organization for guidance. The scope of their responsibility may be presented by means of a description of a guidance program in operation.

The Purpose of Guidance. The purpose of guidance is to assist the student in reaching sound decisions in matters of vocational choice, educational planning, and personal concern. Sound decisions are based on adequate information made available to the student and so interpreted that he is willing to accept it and to act in harmony with it. One category of such information includes knowledge of educational opportunities. An effective guidance service will provide for informing prospective students and their parents about the purposes and achievements of the local junior college. Such orientation must take many forms and must be accomplished over a period of time, rather than in one concentrated effort during the spring before high-school graduation. Understanding of a comparatively new institution such as the community junior college, and especially of its broader and less traditional kinds of educational opportunity, requires constant and untiring interpretation. For this reason, there is an intimate relation between the public relations of the college and its guidance service. Effective liaison between the two operations will prove helpful to both.

Information Giving. The information-giving process upon which guidance is based starts with the interpretation of the college to the community through the press, through the speakers' bureau, and through the various publications of the college. Each of these efforts must be planned and carried out with a realization of its collateral importance in the guidance of students and their parents. Press releases, then, will concentrate not only on athletics and on the university success of graduates; they will include stories about vocational advisory committees, about placement of graduates of occupational curriculums, about all aspects of the community junior college program. Pamphlets describing the work of the college or the nature of a single curriculum will be given widespread circulation, all so that the patrons of the junior college may know of its existence and become ever more conscious of the varieties of educational opportunity it offers. The student newspaper, the annual, and the catalog will attempt to present in a manner appropriate to each the full scope of college activities, so as to clarify misconceptions and to contribute to adequate understanding of the purposes and the programs of the community junior college.

Such efforts are directed at the entire supporting community and only incidentally toward those who will become students. It is necessary to intensify and to focus the information-giving process for the prospective full-time student as the time for his enrollment approaches. At this stage, the wholehearted cooperation of the high-school administrative and teaching staffs becomes necessary. If they are convinced that the junior college officers are interested primarily in the welfare of their students and not just in "recruiting," this cooperation will be offered willingly. Early in the senior year, college counselors may be asked to explain to each section of senior English, or perhaps to an assembly of all seniors, the growing necessity for higher education in American society and the opportunities afforded by the community junior college. Questions comparing the junior college with other available forms of higher education can be answered candidly; perhaps a brief letter of information may be passed out for discussion at home. If such presentation of junior college purposes, offerings, and quality is to affect student decisions, it must occur comparatively early in the senior year—preferably before Christmas vacation.

In February or March, the community junior college can perform a service to the students, to the high schools, and to itself by arranging for the administration of a college aptitude test battery and perhaps of an achievement examination to all graduating seniors in those high schools from which most of its students come. The costs of such administration may be shared in any agreed proportion; even if the college bears the entire cost of administering and scoring the examinations, the expense is a good investment. The high-school counselors can use the results in informing students of their likelihood of success in achieving various educational objectives and of being admitted to various available colleges. Since choices of college are unstable until the students have completed enrollment, availability of scores of all students during the summer will be very convenient for junior college counselors. Some students are sure to appear for registration interviews after insisting that they planned to attend another college. Participation in the testing of high-school seniors within its enrollment area has four additional values for the junior college. It tends to ensure standardized administration of the tests in accordance with the instructions of the publishers, it provides comparable scores on the same examinations for all students from contributing high schools, it simplifies the problem of arranging a time and a place that will be convenient both for students and test administrators, and it focuses the attention of seniors once more on the need for decision about whether to attend college and which one to choose.

An organized visit by high-school seniors to the junior college campus is another valuable step in providing the information students need as a basis for decisions about college attendance. On this occasion, college administrators can tell the seniors about high points in the history of the college, about its excellent or unique features, and about other interesting and important facts. Division chairmen can present details of the work of their divisions and conduct tours of the facilities; each senior will attend only one or two of these divisional presentations. Student officers will describe the nature of the student government and opportunities for participation in athletics and activities. At the conclusion of this campus visit each senior should have sufficient information to make a considered choice between attendance at the community junior college and the other possibilities open to him, such as work or another college.

He may still be undecided about choice of vocational goal and the educational requirements for it. Individual counseling in the high school has surely contributed to his decisions; it now becomes necessary for the junior college counselors to assist in the process of selection of appropriate curriculums and individual courses. Armed with high-school achievement records, junior college catalogs, and scores from standardized tests, the counselors arrange a time when they can be available, preferably at the high schools, for comparatively brief interviews with any student who thinks that he is likely to attend the junior college. At this time a tentative first-semester program is worked out for discussion with parents and other trusted advisers, but subject to later confirmation at the summer registration appointment. The major values of this tentative individual discussion are that it affords the student an opportunity to clear up any questions he may have in mind and that it stimulates him to think in concrete terms of his possible course for the fall.

In some colleges, this pregraduation interview will serve as the only individual counseling prior to enrollment in classes on registration day; other colleges may forego it in favor of application for admission and registration interview by appointment during the summer. Junior colleges that have been able to provide for both interviews, however, feel that they have reduced the number of schedule changes during the first days of instruction and have also reduced the rate of withdrawal from college. In any case, the college will need to provide other opportunities for testing and enrollment for older students and for those from more distant high schools.

Orientation. Information-giving as a part of the counseling service continues after the initial enrollment. Nearly all junior colleges devote some time at the opening of each year to orientation of new students. Through a single "freshman day" or through a course designed in part for this purpose, the freshmen are introduced to the facilities of the campus, such as the library, cafeteria, auditorium, gymnasium, and specialized classrooms. They are encouraged to participate in the student life of the college and to make use of its services such as the testing office, the reading laboratory, and the health service. In orientation courses they ordinarily consider the improvement of their study skills, complete several examinations useful in guidance, and develop individual four-semester schedules of courses that will fulfill their several junior college objectives of occupational preparation, graduation, general education, and preparation for transfer.

Some of the community junior colleges require courses in personal adjustment or in psychology as a part of their group guidance efforts (81:Chs. 4, 5). One emerging pattern of such courses is a required introductory psychology course which contributes to general education by its emphasis on the understanding of the causes and processes of human behavior. At the same time the activity of the course serves as a preparation for more efficient personal counseling. Tests administered and discussed in the unit on individual differences serve as a basis for individual conferences on the relation between stated goals and measured personal qualities; this conference, in turn, leads to the development of detailed plans for the students' remaining semesters in the junior college (81:65, 88–89). In the same way, the unit on personal adjustment may encourage a troubled student to approach his counselor for individual help while giving him the factual information he needs if he is to profit from such help.

Individual Counseling. Students in every college exhibit a variety of needs for help in reaching decisions and in correcting conditions that interfere with their success in classwork. The trained counselor is charged with the responsibility of providing this help.

Vocational choice is fundamental to many other decisions of the student. As many as half of the high-school graduates who come to the community junior college will have made a firm and realistic vocational choice; they can plan an educational course and pursue it. The other half are not so fortunate. They have not yet managed to develop a firm self-concept or to relate it to occupational opportunities. The counselor will help these students to interpret and accept information about themselves derived from records of previous accomplishment and from tests. He will guide them to sources of information about occupations, such as the library, instructors in all departments of the community junior college, and employers in the community, in the hope that they can form firm occupational choices as a foundation for their educational planning.

After making a vocational choice, many students still lack information on educational requirements and opportunities. One of the major tasks of the community junior college counselor is assisting students to develop realistic long-term educational plans. Such plans will include specific semester schedules for the period to be spent at the community junior college; the next choice of institution, if any, will be listed, together with an estimate of additional time to be required and financial resources to be consumed in completing the plan. Students are confused by university catalogs and if left to themselves will often fail to include all the courses required as preparation for their specialty. The duration, grade requirements, and cost of programs such as engineering or medicine are often a shock to the eager freshman. Some also are unaware of physical requirements for certain types of work, such as size or color vision or dexterity. The sooner these matters are made clear to them, the better chance they will have to select and to complete an educational plan suited to their own aptitudes, interests, and potentialities.

Problems of personal adjustment are another concern of the counselor. A good deal of college failure is attributable not to low ability or to lack of funds so much as to personal difficulties. Such conflicts may involve self-concept, classmates, instructors, family members, or life in general. They may be temporary and relatively superficial, or deep seated and potentially dangerous. The counselor's task in relation to personal problems is first and foremost to recognize the nature of the difficulty. In some cases he himself can help the student work out his solution; in others he will need to convince the student, or perhaps his family, of the need for expert help. Every community junior college counselor needs, therefore, to maintain acquaintance with a wide range of community agencies to which students may be referred. Welfare organizations, employment offices, family service bureaus, psychiatrists, veterans' service offices, and religious counseling agencies are among the resources upon which a counseling service may call within the course of a month. An important qualification of a counselor is the humility which helps him to know his limitations and leads him to seek specialized help for his students when it is needed.

The community junior college will maintain also a limited health service in connection with its student personnel office. The service is much less extensive than that found in residential colleges. Its purpose in the community junior college will never be medical treatment, except in cases needing emergency first aid. The staff consists ordinarily of a full-time public health nurse, competent to advise students about minor difficulties, to present some topics to classes upon request of the instructor, to perform needed first aid, and to know when to insist that the student see his personal physician. A program of medical examinations of all students is very helpful to the counseling office, if it can be arranged; even a cursory examination by a physician may enable the staff to improve the educational opportunity of many students, either by arranging for correction of defects or by calling them to the attention of instructors.

In the words of Brumbaugh, the purpose of the entire guidance program "is to aid each student to discover his own abilities and limitations, to define his educational goals as clearly as possible, to clarify his vocational objectives and to solve his personal problems" (*14*:38). In achieving this purpose the community junior college provides consultation before college enrollment and during registration; it uses assemblies, courses, and individual conferences; it assigns instructors to parts of the task, trained counselors, psychometrists, or physicians to other parts of the task, and administrative officers to still other functions. The entire coordinated guidance effort is founded on the realization that the misdirected student wastes both his time and that of his instructors; the development of an appropriate and attainable educational goal is prerequisite to any worthwhile student achievement.

B. Student Activities

The student personnel service of the community junior college encourages the establishment of a broad variety of student activities as a part of the total educational effort of the college. Participation in self-government, in interest clubs and social activities, and in organized athletics contributes importantly to the achievement of the purposes of the college. Skills of citizenship are practiced, qualities of leadership are developed, broader interests are cultivated, worthwhile achievements are recognized, and wholesome social skills are encouraged when students participate in planning and carrying out the elements of a broad program of student activities. The educational growth of students is not the sole reward of these efforts, however.

Many of the tasks accomplished by students through their organizations must be done by someone in the college, by employees if not by students; other tasks contribute notably to the student morale and to the local fame of the college.

The balance of these two aspects of student activities, their educational value and their service, constitutes the true art of student activity supervision. Student government, clubs, and athletics miss their true point if they focus only on artificial learning situations. In contrast, if their service to the college and to the community is overemphasized, the result may be exploitation of the students and such negative learnings as political chicanery or cynical sportsmanship. Student activities must have meaning and importance for the students and for the college, but the students, the faculty, and the community must never forget to keep them in their proper relation to all the other aspects of the college's offering.

Student Government. The organized student council or the associated students is the agency through which students exercise control over their activities and learn the skills of self-government. Since the final authority and responsibility for the operation of a community junior college rest with the board of trustees, it is usually advisable to develop a charter for student government. Such a document sets forth the duties, responsibilities, and areas of concern of the student officers together with provisions for administrative veto power over some classes of action. The power of revocation of the charter should be explicitly reserved to the board of trustees of the college. The need to invoke such power should never arise, but its mention serves to make clear the nature of delegated authority. For the same reason, a dignified ceremony can be developed for transmitting the charter to the new student officers at each annual inauguration. In this way the students of each new generation are tactfully reminded both of their responsibility to the community and of the large measure of authority which is theirs to use wisely in their own interests.

Activities. Student government properly concerns itself with the fostering and control of student interests outside of the classrooms. *Service* to the college in such matters as orientation of new students, hospitality to college visitors, and some measure of control of student behavior outside of class is one suitable area of operations. *Social activities,* adapted to the interests and the desires of the students, ordinarily command the attention of student officers. In some colleges, *business enterprises* are conducted by the students. The student store, the cafeteria or coffee shop, and admission to intercollegiate athletic contests are frequently controlled by the student government and serve as sources of income for the support of other less profitable activities. *Student clubs* of all sorts—academic interest groups, denominational clubs, freshman and sophomore class associations, and hobby groups such as chess clubs and ski clubs—are chartered by the student government. This measure of control provides for the coordination of effort by all groups on occasional activities of importance to all students; it enables the student government to approve the budgets and to appropriate funds for each of its constituent activities.

Several persistent problems plague junior college administrators and student officers in student government and related activities. It is very difficult to develop continuity of student leadership when all the tasks of orientation, apprenticeship, election, and office holding must be completed within a span of two college years. Lack of time also hinders the development of any significant body of useful campus tradition. Almost before a class has become fully acculturated, it must pass on its folklore to the next class; traditions, for good or ill, have little opportunity to mature and to become ingrained parts of the personality of the students. The high rate of withdrawal from the junior college contributes to the difficulties of the activity program; even elected officers at times drop out before completing their terms. Some of the clubs, for all practical purposes, must begin anew every year, since only a handful of former members may return for the second year's activity.

Under such conditions the personality and the enthusiasm of the faculty advisers of the student government and of the several subordinate organizations are of major importance. Since they provide the only long-term continuity for activities, the advisers may begin either to dictate the details of the annual program or else to despair of any substantial achievement for their student group. In either case the faculty adviser must remind himself that the purpose of student activities is to help students learn through their own participation. The adviser is just as truly a teacher in this setting as he is in his classrooms, and the fact that teaching here may be more difficult does not mean that the learning is less worthwhile. The difficulties do point up the need for careful selection, both of the activities to be sponsored and of the advisers for them. Once selected, the advisers should continue with the same activity over a period of years, so that they may grow annually more competent in exercising the unobtrusive leadership that helps students develop into citizens.

Important educational values inhere in student activities; the college that neglected or refused to encourage such out-of-class experiences would provide only a partial education. Although it is facile to demonstrate that all students need and can profit from working in self-government and the social life of the college, it is impossible to attract nearly all students to participate. Formidable barriers obstruct the path. First of these is certainly the lack of student time. Since students in public junior colleges live off campus and at distances as great as thirty miles, they will return in the evening only for events that seem highly important. The student who has completed his classes at noon will be unlikely to remain on campus for a late afternoon meeting. A fifth of the students are married and more than half are employed; club meetings, all-college picnics, or the acceptance of responsibility in student government may seem comparatively unimportant to them. For students in a residential college, even frivolous organized activities may provide a welcome diversion from the loneliness of a dormitory room, but students in a public junior college are likely to find any optional campus event an unwelcome distraction from their busy routines of classes, employment, study, family life, and commuting.

A further deterrent often lies in the hidden or apparent costs of participation. To the student who is seeking higher education in spite of comparative poverty, the cost of a party dress, of tickets to several activities, of added gasoline or bus fares, and the loss of several hours of work may seem to prohibit unnecessary activity. These students are also likely to hold back because of a fear of rejection by other students who may have more time or money or more social experience. For such reasons, only half of public junior college students take part in student life, even under the best of circumstances (*81*:293–297).

On the other hand, some students participate so actively that their classwork suffers. Faculty advisers, in their desire to assure the success of a project by providing strong student leadership, may contribute to this exploitation. Overactivity by one student, of course, not only interferes with his own education but also deprives other able students of the opportunity for practice in leadership and for recognition. Some balance of honors is achieved through a quota limitation of activities. In most junior colleges an officer of any organization must maintain an acceptable academic standard in order to continue in office. Beyond this, some student constitutions assign varying point values to several categories of responsibility and set a limit on the total points a student may assume at one time. Under a system of this sort, the presidency of the student body might be assigned a weight of five points. Other elective offices, athletic-team membership, and editorship of the newspaper might have weights of four points each. In the same manner, chairmanship or membership on committees and in clubs would be assigned point values. No student, then, is permitted to assume obligations exceeding an established total of points, worked out on the basis of experience in the college.

Athletics. Intercollegiate athletics are a special category of student activities. Because of their inherent attraction for many junior college students as participants and as spectators and because of their appeal to the public at large, they offer unlimited opportunities to achieve the objectives of student activities. A well-balanced program of sports affords many students opportunity to develop physically and to learn the values of teamwork, the joys of wholesome competition, and American attitudes of sportsmanship. Through outstanding participation in sports, some junior college students are enabled to continue their education into the four-year college or to qualify for a career in professional athletics.

When they are administered in accordance with the educational purposes of the community junior college, intercollegiate athletics can also make important contributions to the learning and to the morale of the nonplaying students. Wholesome rivalry, sportsmanlike support of one's own team, scorn for unworthy tactics, the elation of victory or the dejection of defeat are vivid and worthy experiences for the young. Athletic teams serve also as one part of the public posture of the college, attracting attention both from possible students in neighboring schools and from the sports-minded constituents in the community. These positive values amply justify the establishment of athletic conferences through which community junior colleges of comparable size within traveling distance may compete in all the usual competitive sports. In order to provide opportunity for the valuable learning experiences to as many students as possible, each junior college and each athletic league should feel obligated to provide team competition in every sport it can afford. To football, basketball, track, and baseball should be added also, as it is possible, handball, swimming, water polo, boxing, wrestling, tennis, golf. Skiing, sailing, and ice skating are popular where conditions permit them. For women, too, the lessons of sportsmanship are important and should be encouraged by appropriate intramural competition in suitable sports.

But athletics are sources not only of positive values. Their drama —and their financial importance—too often blind the public, the coach, and even the administrator to their true purposes. Then overemphasis on gate receipts leads to exploitation of students, the purchase of able gladiators, the perversion of sportsmanship, and the philosophy of the hired athlete. Colleges and universities in America have struggled for years with indifferent success to establish gentlemen's agreements (buttressed by mutual spying) to control the abuses of competitive recruiting and extravagant aid to athletes. In spite of such efforts, values have been distorted to such an extent that it is rumored that the football coach at one state university is paid more than any other public employee, including the governor; at the same university, professors' salaries average below the national average for colleges and universities.

After an extended discussion of the advantages and dangers of intercollegiate athletics in junior college, Hillway concluded,

If one balances these real or fancied evils against the possible benefits of the athletic program, no doubt most administrators and a fairly substantial number of the faculty would be in favor of continuing athletics in some form or other. Certainly, however, more safeguards will have to be provided than are now set up to prevent the junior college athletic program from following the same route downward as the large university programs. . . . Every sign points to the conclusion that athletics on the two-year college campus will continue to increase in importance. If proper safeguards are created, and particularly if educational values and the welfare of the student are stressed, this may be regarded as a highly favorable development. Grave dangers, however, face the junior college movement at this point, and wise educational statesmanship will be required if they are to be avoided. (72:183–184)

C. Placement and Follow-Up

An active placement office is an important adjunct to the student personnel service in a community junior college. Since most of the students work while attending college, they will appreciate help in finding suitable employment. It is not too much to say that a placement office may, for some young people, be the one agency that makes existing higher education truly available to them; it can enable them to find work to earn the money they need to stay in college. In larger communities, the placement office can be of real service also to the former students and to graduates in helping them to find full-time employment in the fields for which they studied in the junior college.

While serving the student and the graduate, the placement office can realize important by-products also for the entire program of the college. The constant contact of the placement officer with all kinds of employers in the entire community serves to keep him aware of emerging needs for trained employees.

In an unobtrusive way, the placement officer interprets the college and its purposes to the community while contributing a constant flow of important information to the continuing community survey carried on by the college. Clues to new and promising fields for occupational education, as well as to those declining in importance, may frequently come to the attention of the placement officer before they are noticed by any other staff member.

The "follow-up" of graduates and former students is an important part of the self-evaluation of the community junior college. It is functionally related to placement and is often under the direction of the same officer. Of the two aspects of follow-up, junior colleges have been more concerned with former students who have gone on to upper-division study in colleges and universities. Few studies are reported of the success of vocationally trained graduates in finding employment in the area of their training and of their comparative success after placement. Both aspects are essential to a complete follow-up program.

The most usual method of estimating the success of the junior college in its transfer function is that of comparing grade-point averages achieved before and after transfer (88:2–3). Any junior college with a sizable number of transferring students will find such information about its own graduates comparatively easy to gather and of very real value in the continuing evaluation of parts of its curriculum. The registrars of nearly all receiving colleges are generous in supplying the needed facts; some state institutions make routine reports of the first semester achievements of all new students to the school or college last attended. Other senior colleges will respond to a simple questionnaire listing students who had applied for admission and asking such questions as (1) Did he qualify for admission? (2) Did he enter? (3) What advanced standing was allowed? (4) Is he now enrolled in good standing? disqualified? on probation? withdrew before completing a semester? (5) Units attempted in his first semester? (6) Grade points achieved in his first semester? (7) Grade-point average?

Such quantitative data can be gathered also, with somewhat greater difficulty, from employers of junior college terminal students. Since personnel officers in business and industry do not keep comparable "grade-averages" on all their employees, tact and knowledge of business procedures are needed in attempting this follow-up. Many times a personal interview must be substituted for a mailed questionnaire. Yet employers appreciate the interest of the college in preparing workers; the concept of quality control is one with which they are familiar, and they will cooperate enthusiastically if the reason for the interest of the college and the intended uses of the information are explained. Questions appropriate for this kind of interview might include (1) How was contact made—employer request to placement office, student initiative, other? (2) Starting wage, compared to usual beginning wage? (3) Advancement during employment? (4) Employer ratings of skills, personality, training? (5) Reasons for separation, if applicable? (6) Employer suggestions for improved training programs?

Both of these follow-up studies use information only from the "consumer"—the receiving college or the employer. The reactions of former students about the quality of their preparation are equally meaningful, although more difficult to gather. Reactions are gathered most readily from the more satisfied graduate—the student who is still enrolled in the college to which he transferred or the one who is still employed in the field of his junior college major by his first employer. Such graduates are more easily located for questioning; they are also more likely to respond to a questionnaire than the graduate or dropout who has not been successful in his later work. In spite of such trends toward bias, it will be worthwhile to get as much evaluative information as possible from former students.

The mailed questionnaire is the simplest means of gathering such information. Even a double postal card can elicit helpful answers, if care is taken to ask only the most important questions. Since responses of students in any case will be qualitative and based on judgment rather than on quantitative facts, questionnaire follow-up should be supplemented whenever possible by a sampling of interviews. It will be possible, for instance, to arrange to talk to some transfer students on the campuses of universities after they have completed one or more semesters. Their opinions on the quality of their preparation and their difficulties in adjusting to the new college and their advice to later generations of students may not be soundly conceived in every instance. Yet they will deserve the attention of junior college officials, if only so that they may decide whether or not action is needed. Employed graduates may possibly be interviewed on the same visit as their employer. Skills omitted from the training program, unnecessary requirements in the college curriculum, and general observations about their preparation might provide the basic structure for the interview, again with concentration on the help which these former students can afford to later generations of students.

In evaluating placement and follow-up in junior colleges in 1948, Meinecke reported that

The weaknesses most apparent are (1) a disproportionate emphasis on transfer in contrast to job placement and (2) the lack of carefully planned place-

ment programs within the whole guidance pattern of the college. . . .
There is immediate need in almost every junior college for study, evaluation, and systematic planning in the field of placement in order that an
increasingly effective and up-to-date program may be maintained. (*110:64*)

The functions both of placement and of follow-up are too important,
in their relation to all aspects of the program of the junior college,
to be left to chance or to haphazard development (*111; 121*).

D. Records, Research, and Evaluation

The keeping of accurate records is one of the primary responsibilities of the student personnel service. Every student expects his
college to maintain a complete and up-to-date record of his scholarly
achievement and to be able to provide intelligible copies on short
notice at his request. For this reason, every college provides an officer
with the duties of registrar or recorder; every college, as Medsker
noted, maintains a good system of academic records, mostly with
individual student folders stored in a central location easily accessible
to faculty members (*109:162*). Three considerations deserve comment
in relation to student records: what materials become a part of the
records; what constructive use is made of these materials; and how
conveniently accessible are they for the reference of authorized personnel?

Two types of information are found in the student folder, the
academic record and additional documents from several sources. The
academic record is primarily a continuing account of the studies attempted by the student and of his success in them. It is designed in
such a way as to facilitate the recording of new information at the
end of each term of attendance; in an increasing number of colleges
it is planned to permit rapid mechanical reproduction. In general,
these records contain

1. Identifying Information
      full name
      sex
      birth date
      birthplace
      name of parents or guardian
      permanent address
2. Background Information
      summary of previous school and college record
      date of high-school graduation
      major field of study

3. Progress in College
    date of entry to college
    dates of withdrawal and re-entry
    date of graduation and degree
    semester by semester record of courses, units, grades
    cumulative summary of progress toward graduation
    notations of honors or of academic disciplinary action
    notations of institutions to which transcripts have been sent
4. Information about the College
    name
    term plan (semester or quarter)
    grading policies
    signature of issuing officer
5. Optional Features
    photograph of student
    aptitude or placement test records with norms
    record of committee action

Although this summary record, as the official evidence of the student's attendance and progress, must be guarded from every possible hazard, it contains in convenient form a wealth of fundamental information which should be readily accessible to any authorized person. It is an excellent practice, therefore, to duplicate a fresh copy of the permanent record for every student at the end of every semester, so that every counseling folder may contain an up-to-date record at the earliest possible moment. With suitable equipment and procedures, even colleges with large enrollments can make available to the counseling staff a complete report on the fall achievement of every student before classes begin in the spring. In this way, both honors earned and prerequisite courses failed may be recognized during the first days of the new semester and appropriate action taken.

The student folder, then, will include a single most recent copy of the student's permanent record. In addition, it should include such available information as will help counselors and instructors to work intelligently and professionally with the student. One school of thought would limit the contents of the folder to a bare minimum of official and quasi-public documents; at the opposite extreme are those who include every scrap of paper dealing with the student, so that the folder becomes bulky and disorganized. Some writers would restrict the use of the counseling folder to those who have extensive training in personnel work; others feel that anyone who is qualified to teach the young should be entitled to access to all pertinent information about them. The author leans toward a moderate economy of contents of the folder and the encouragement of all instructional faculty members to become acquainted with its contents. A typical student folder might include such materials as:

Application by the student for admission to the college.

A personal data sheet filled out by the student.

A four-semester educational plan, completed in conference with the counselor and adjusted at each registration period.

An up-to-date copy of the student's permanent record.

A sheet summarizing accurately the scores on any standardized tests of aptitude, achievement, interest, personality.

Summaries of important interviews, and decisions reached in them.

Notations about other information available from the counselor, if it is of a nature to require careful interpretation to instructors by means of interview.

The personnel office, ideally, should make such folders conveniently available to any instructor who asks for them. If clerical workers can collect from the files the folders of an entire class and if a suitably quiet spot is available for the instructor to look through them, the use of the folders will increase. If this service is supplemented by a continuing plan of training the faculty in the proper use of test and other personnel information, both the quality of instruction and the quality of faculty advice to students will improve.

The availability in the student personnel office of such a wealth of information about students should encourage its use in institutional research. Many writers have pointed out the folly of giving tests that were not to be used in individual counseling. Yet if facts about students are used only as a basis for counseling interviews, fully half their value is lost. Personnel workers, the faculty, the curriculum committee, and the administration of the junior college ask many questions about the characteristics of their student body. The answers are available in the personnel files, if only some worker has the responsibility and the time to assemble them. Such studies provide concrete evidence on many problems; they bring to light the successful aspects of the college and the parts that need improvement. They aid in the process of decision by substituting facts for argumentation. No college should ignore this source of insight for curriculum development and for program evaluation.

A single public junior college, in the course of one academic year, prepared a study of characteristics of entering students, including college aptitude, economic and social status, ambitions, high-school achievement, and a dozen other traits that might affect curriculum and instruction. A report on sophomore achievement, as measured by the Sequential Tests of Educational Progress, was interpreted in its

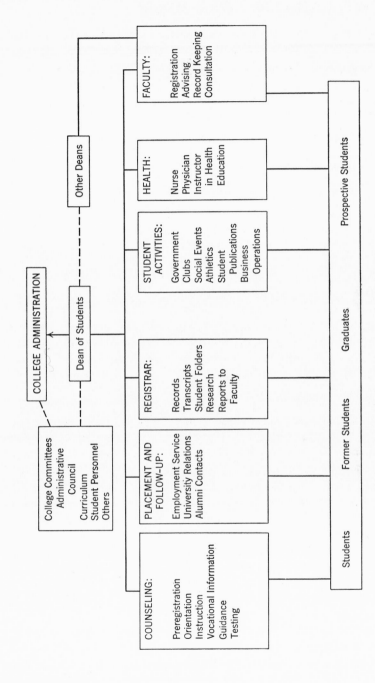

Figure 4. The organization of student personnel services.

relation to aptitude scores at entrance; the study pointed up aspects of the curriculum that needed further study. A follow-up study of students graduating over a four-year period was completed, presenting the actual comments of graduates for faculty study, as well as summaries of their evaluation of the college (*163*).

E. The Administration of Student Personnel Services

The administrative organization of student personnel services should grow out of the functions to be performed. A workable plan based on the analysis presented in the present chapter would include a Dean of Students with appropriately trained staff members in charge of the several functions of student personnel. Such an organization is similar in most details to that described by McDaniel in *Essential Student Personnel Practices* (*106*:52–53). Figure 4 concentrates on functions rather than on officers. It is quite likely that in small colleges one person will be required to administer several functions. The Dean of Students, for example, might expect to teach and to counsel students, while serving also as adviser to the student council. A counselor might be required to care for the placement and follow-up service. On the other hand, in a larger college, special titles might be assigned to the heads of the several services, such as *Associate Dean, Records* or *Coordinator, Student Activities*.

Under any form of administrative organization, it is important that the various functions be clearly defined and assigned to persons with the qualifications and with the time to accomplish them successfully. Intensive student personnel services are basic to student and faculty morale; they are an indispensable precondition of effective education.

Selected References

Black, William A. "Student Personnel Relationships of High School and Junior College," *Junior College Journal,* 19:145–150, December, 1948.

Hamrin, H. A. "Improving Student Personnel Practices for the Impending Tidal Wave of Students," *Junior College Journal,* 26:15–26, September, 1955.

Hardee, Melvene D. *Counseling and Guidance in General Education.* Yonkers-on-Hudson, N.Y.: World Book Company, 1955.

Henry, Nelson B. (editor). *Personnel Services in Education.* Fifty-eighth Yearbook of the National Society for the Study of Education, Part II. Chicago: The University of Chicago Press, 1959.

———. *The Public Junior College.* Fifty-fifth Yearbook of the National Society for the Study of Education, Part I. Chicago: The University of Chicago Press, 1956. Chapter X, "The Student Personnel Program."

Johnson, B. Lamar. *General Education in Action.* Washington: American Council on Education, 1952. Chapter IV, "The Advising, Guidance, and Counseling of Students," and Chapter XIII, "The Extraclass Program."

McDaniel, J. W. *Essential Student Personnel Practices for Junior Colleges.* Washington: American Association of Junior Colleges, 1962.

Medsker, Leland L. *The Junior College: Progress and Prospect.* New York: McGraw-Hill Book Co., 1960. Chapter VI.

Mohs, Milton C. *Service Through Placement in the Junior College.* Washington: American Association of Junior Colleges, 1962.

O'Connor, Thomas J. *Follow-Up Studies in Junior Colleges.* Washington: American Association of Junior Colleges, 1965.

Priest, Bill J. "The Most Significant Problems of Junior Colleges in the Field of Student Personnel Services," *Junior College Journal,* 29:303–306, February, 1959.

Raines, Max R. "The Student Personnel Situation," *Junior College Journal,* 36: 6–8, February, 1966.

Robinson, Donald W. "The Role of the Faculty in the Development of Student Personnel Services," *Junior College Journal,* 31:15–21, September, 1960.

Storr, J. M. "Guidance Practices in Selected Junior Colleges in the Northwest," *Junior College Journal,* 31:442–447, April, 1961.

IV

Issues and Opportunities

18

The Future of the
Community Junior College

Preceding chapters have presented the descriptive and statistical data from which an idealistic definition of the community junior college may be derived. Existing junior colleges differ widely in their characteristics; none will be found that conforms to all terms of the definition. In the future development of community junior colleges, as in the past, differences in local history, in local needs and fiscal ability, and in philosophy of education will combine to bring about adaptations and compromises within a common ideal. It is nonetheless worthwhile to state the ideal explicitly, so that the extent and the character of each departure from it may be recognized and evaluated.

A. The Community Junior College Defined

The community junior college is a free public two-year educational institution that attempts to meet the post-high-school educational needs of its local community. In achieving this objective, its faculty studies the local community in order to determine these needs and works vigorously to develop appropriate kinds of instructional organization and techniques. The emphasis in the community junior college is on providing legitimate educational services, rather than on conforming to preconceived notions of what is or is not collegiate subject matter, or of who is or is not college material.

Because its purposes are broader in some respects than those traditionally associated with the liberal arts college and the university, its educational program will differ also in significant ways. It will offer for baccalaureate degree credit the courses appropriate to the first two years of the preprofessional school, the university, or the liberal arts college. In addition, it will develop many curriculums that are not appropriate to these institutions, curriculums designed to prepare students in a period of two years or less to participate intelligently in the work of the community. For all of its students, it will offer the basic elements of general education. It will present courses of many kinds for those citizens whose major occupation is something other than student. It will provide for its community, to the extent of its facilities and the community's need, cultural opportunities in music, art, drama, and public affairs. Finally, it will provide a program of guidance to assist its students to choose wisely from among its multiple offerings and to attain maximum benefit from their studies.

Several of the terms of the idealistic definition must be explained in greater detail, because they differ widely from present practice. Certainly at present not all community junior colleges are *tuition free*. A majority of the states now provide for tuition payments by students to cover some part of the cost of their junior college instruction. The collection of tuition is justified practically on the basis of fiscal necessity and philosophically on the two premises that free public education ought to end at the completion of high school, and that education is not truly valued unless the recipient is required to pay something for it. Nevertheless, the ideal community junior college is defined as tuition free.

Practically, American society can afford to provide for its citizens the level of education that is required for employment in the economy and for participation in civic responsibility. In answer to the philosophical argument, it may be pointed out that public education in America has been continuously extended as new conditions made more schooling both possible and desirable. There is no more inherent reason to set the terminal point at high-school graduation than at eighth grade or junior college or master's degree level. In the present stage of our economy, there are many cogent arguments for planning tuition-free education for qualified students at least through the junior college years. The motivational argument for tuition charges, on the other hand, has a certain degree of validity, even though one of the effects of tuition charges is to exclude some able students from further education. Every year of school attendance is costly to the student or his parents in living expenses and in loss of earnings, and tuition charges simply add to their total burden. Present social policy should encourage the development of talent, rather than place barriers in its path. The nation can better afford the costs of free tuition than it can the loss sustained from undeveloped human resources.

The term "public" in the definition is a second factor that requires elaboration. There are almost 300 private junior colleges that provide a high quality of educational opportunity to more than 100,000 students. Their function is useful and necessary; their existence should be recognized and encouraged in every feasible manner. Some of these private junior colleges, moreover, perform many of the services of the community junior college. Yet the private junior colleges can never accomplish the entire educational task here outlined, nor should they attempt it. The majority of community junior colleges are now and probably will continue to be publicly operated and financed, whereas the community junior colleges under private auspices will continue to be valued and rare exceptions.

Even the term "two-year" cannot be proposed as an entirely unqualified attribute of community junior colleges. There are in America a number of public four-year degree-granting colleges, established by municipalities and operated truly as community-serving institutions. Yet common usage in educational literature has tended to restrict the meaning of "community college" to the kind of institution described in this volume. Another objection to the limitation of "two-year" arises from the realization that community junior colleges will organize curriculums designed to last only one semester or one year; in a very few cases three-year programs have been offered. In addition, certain single courses may attract persons who have earned college degrees or those who have not graduated from high school. The term "two-year" is included in the definition in order to differentiate the community junior college from other kinds of colleges and because of the realization that most of the effort of the typical junior college will be expended on those full-time students who are pursuing organized curriculums extending over two years of study and leading to the Associate degree.

The qualifications to the definition may leave the impression that the community junior college is an entirely amorphous institution, so fluid and adaptable as to lack character and defy consistent definition. Not so. In the early stages of their development these colleges have been progressing steadily toward a definition. They have explored various patterns of organization and experimented with types of control, concepts of function, and provisions for support. There have emerged from their accumulated experience, a clarification of their role, a comprehension of the scope of their educational responsibility, and a well-defined direction for future development. At the same time, study of their present status discloses a series of problems and issues that must be resolved as community junior colleges, fully aware of the scope of their educational tasks, progress toward the period of their most rapid development and most significant service.

B. Problems of the Open Door

The open door admission policy has been both the proudest claim and the knottiest dilemma of the community junior college. At a time when enrollments are rising annually by hundreds of thousands of students, and when junior colleges are assuming an ever increasing share of freshmen and sophomore enrollments, is it possible to accept every student who requests admission? Is it possible to develop worthwhile college curriculums for all of them? Is it reasonable to accept students who are predestined to failure? Is it wise to conserve funds by denying admittance to applicants who fail to meet minimum intellectual or educational criteria? Does the American economy, or the "American dream," require that every high-school graduate be provided opportunity for further education?

If political theory does indeed seem to justify a liberal and welcoming admission policy, what consequences ensue? Should the open door for some applicants be simply a revolving door, or an entrance to a vestibule from which all doors are closed? How much remedial work in the skills of learning should be provided by the junior college, in order to make real the opportunity promised by the open door? What limitations on study load, choice of courses, outside work, or student activities must be imposed on students who are admitted on probation?

Having admitted a student of doubtful potential, how long should the college permit him to continue in his struggle toward success in his courses? How can the distinction be made between the able idler, the slow but determined struggler, and the overly optimistic incompetent? By what means can students who are on the way to defeat in pursuit of one objective be helped to recognize and accept goals that are more realistic for them?

Alternatively, should all of these questions be evaded by abandoning any attempt to serve all post-high-school educational needs, and by establishing preconditions for admission that would eliminate many of the difficulties posed by the "open door"? If only students are admitted whose test scores and high-school grades predict acceptable chances for success, many problems do not arise. The scope of the curriculum is restricted, the task of the teacher is simplified, the costs of higher education are lower, and a high standard of scholarship is assured. On the other hand, a policy of restrictive admission would tend to diminish the total educational level of the population; it would certainly eliminate an appreciable number of applicants who would profit measurably from additional education. The benefits of a more restrictive admission policy seem to accrue more to the faculty and to the citizen as taxpayer, and to these only in the short run, than they do to the student and to the citizen as productive worker and as human being.

An open door admission policy unquestionably poses difficult problems of educational strategy that have not been faced heretofore in higher education. Difficulties, however, by no means imply that problems are impossible to solve. On the contrary, the social and economic problems that arise as a result of failure to solve these educational problems will be of a much greater order of difficulty and of long-range consequences.

C. Problems of Articulation

The transfer of credit from the community junior college to the four-year institution has been troublesome throughout the existence of junior colleges. The receiving college is concerned that the transfer student shall be fully and comparably prepared to succeed in competition with its "native" students. The junior college is equally concerned that no transfer practices seem to indicate that its courses or its students are inferior to those in the four-year colleges. Enough evidence on performance of transfer students has been gathered to enable both sides of the discussion to agree on the basic principles of transfer policies (for example, 88a), but still the debate goes on.

Developments are occurring in several of the states that will intensify the need for effective coordination of lower-division education. When a university or liberal arts college finds a greater number of transfers in its junior class than of native students, its whole concept of the four-year baccalaureate curriculum must change. To some extent, its ability to control the elements of lower-division requirements is diminished. These developments impose a new, perhaps not entirely welcome, burden on the junior college, to accept the obligation of defining and providing a lower-division education of high quality, as a basis for the specialized study at upper-division level.

A corollary of the effort to develop excellent lower-division programs is the necessity to improve the techniques of identifying and counseling the nontransfer student, and to develop appropriate curriculums for him so that he is not forced, in default of another opportunity, either to continue probation level work in transfer courses or drop out. It has been noted that two-thirds of junior college students classify themselves as transfer students, although year after year only one-third actually transfer. A large part of this discrepancy may be attributed to the fact that two-year courses simply are not available for many students. In Chapter 13, evidence was presented that half of all junior colleges offer fewer than four occupational courses; the nontransfer student who does not want any of the occupational courses offered in his junior college is forced to take a transfer course, or drop out.

The techniques of recommending transfer students require additional study (88a:89–91). There is evidence that transfers with marginal grade records in junior college are often unable to succeed in larger universities, even though similar students succeed in other institutions. Long-term persuasive counseling might help students to become aware of the differences between colleges, and aware of their own characteristics, so that they may make their choices much more realistically.

A second area of articulation concerns relations with high schools. Constant communication between high schools and community junior college faculties will help to ensure that course sequences provide for planned progress in learning and avoid gaps or repetition in presentation. The transition from high school to college may be smoothed for the student through four types of high school-junior college cooperation.

1. The junior college and other colleges can be interpreted completely and accurately to the high-school student so that he may choose intelligently rather than on the basis of hearsay or purely extrinsic criteria.

2. The transfer of appropriate parts of the permanent records of students will assist junior college counselors in continuing effective guidance procedures.

3. The two institutions can plan jointly for orientation activities for the high-school graduates, to help them become familiar with the opportunities and requirements of the local junior college.

4. Faculty groups from parallel departments of the two institutions can meet regularly to become acquainted with mutual problems and to work toward sequential organization of instruction.

D. Problems of Support

As community junior colleges assume an increasing share of rapidly growing college enrollments, their problems of adequate financial support will grow more acute. They are in competition with elementary and secondary schools for local property tax money, and with state universities and colleges for income from the state treasury. In each case, they are somewhat handicapped. At the local level, the numbers of students in the two-year community college are much smaller than in the twelve years of public schools, and so their claims for support are subordinated. In the competition for state revenues, on the other hand, they lack the prestige and the statewide appeal of the four-year institutions, and so find it difficult to secure adequate, not to say equal, appropriations.

In addition to these difficulties of the junior colleges specifically, additional financial problems face all of education in the years ahead. Enrollments in the lower schools will continue to show annual increases of more than a million pupils for at least another decade, at the same time that larger annual cadres of high-school graduates apply for admission to college. The financial difficulty is compounded by the fact that faculty members must be recruited from the comparatively small age group derived from the low birth rate of the 1930's and early 1940's; the shortage of teachers will entail increasing salaries.

Yet the burden of ad valorem property taxes on local real estate is approaching a maximum. If taxes rise too high, the homeowner cannot pay them from his annual income, and industry and commerce may intensify the revenue problem by moving away from high tax areas. Present state tax practices, although probably more elastic than local property taxes, are also subject to a law of diminishing returns. The Federal Government has enacted measures providing aid for construction of colleges, including junior colleges, and for financial aid to college students, but Congress has been unwilling to undertake a program of general support for the current expenses of education.

On the other hand, the gross national product, in real values, is higher than it has ever been, and rising annually. The nation's children must not be denied education in favor of more frivolous or more temporary investments. The nation can afford to pay for a good education for its citizens, and it cannot take the risk of denying them a high level of excellent education. The problem then is to discover how best to allocate the necessary share of the national wealth to this essential purpose.

One source of increased income for colleges is higher tuition rates for students. In independent colleges and universities this resource has been utilized increasingly since World War II, although it is likely that in many colleges costs have risen more rapidly than tuition. In state colleges and universities too, student fees have increased over the past two decades. Even in the community junior colleges, only two states specifically prohibit tuition charges to resident students; in other states tuition charges may run as high as one-third of the per capita annual operating cost.

If the community junior college is really intended to keep open the doors of educational opportunity for able youth from all social and economic levels, tuition must be free or set at a nominal rate. There seems to be no question that most elements of the higher education establishment will continue to charge tuition, and that the dollar amounts of tuition will continue to climb. All the more reason, then, that at least one segment of the system should avoid tuition, in order to permit and to encourage the nonscholarship student of good but not superior capacity to develop his talents as far as he can. This policy would work to the eventual advantage not only of the student but of the nation as a whole.

E. Problems of Control

The original ideal of the community junior college pictured a small institution, with a close personal relationship between faculty and students, and with strong ties of service and support between the institution and the community. Present realities are quite different. Faculties begin to number in the hundreds, and students in the thousands. Communities grow until the once small and personalized junior college must establish another campus, or two or three. Administrative considerations lead to the merger of several junior college districts, so that broader tax bases and some operational economies may be realized. What effects do these developments portend on the essence of the community junior college?

Control by a board of local citizens, chosen by the voters of a community, has been stated as one of the elements of the definition of a community junior college. Recent developments in district organization raise the question of the ultimate size of a community. Can either Chicago, with eight branches of one junior college, or Los Angeles, with seven junior colleges, be considered in any meaningful sense a single community? There are at least twenty similar multicampus developments in operation or in prospect. The major problems in their establishment are to retain sufficient autonomy on each local campus and to provide for sufficient sampling of local community opinion, so that the basic values of college-community cooperation are not lost in the search for bigness, administrative convenience, or fiscal economy.

A similar set of problems—perhaps, in less populous states, the same problems—arise from the establishment of state boards of control for junior colleges. There is a strong appeal in the proposal for a single state junior college board. It can exert more influence on the Legislature in its competition with the university for funds; it can assure quality of education, equal treatment of faculty, and co-ordinated statewide development of a system of junior colleges. If the board responsible for junior colleges is also responsible for all higher education, it would seem that it would lead inevitably to a thoroughly coordinated, economical, and articulated pattern of higher education for the state.

Yet the losses under a statewide system should be considered as well as the gains. Recent governmental tendencies toward centralization of support and control have not guaranteed greater economy, efficiency, or improvement in quality of service. The remoteness of control from its center of impact may protect the controlling official from criticism; but it does not assure that control will be more acceptable, more intelligent, or more humane to the subjects. There is an educational advantage in the close relationship of a community to its junior college. It is true that universities become eminent without this relationship; but the junior college is not and should not aspire to be a university. It abandons its own unique nature when it imitates a different institution. The problems of control of the junior college should be settled with reference to the essential nature of that institution, and not on the basis of a possibly false analogy to other institutions.

Another emerging problem of control concerns the role of the faculty in the internal operation of each junior college. Beginning as upward extensions of the public schools, junior colleges adopted the administrator-faculty relationships of the lower schools. The trend toward independent establishment of junior colleges, their new self-concept as truly a part of higher education, and the increasing levels of training of junior college faculty members all combine to revise these relationships. Junior college faculties feel that they have the competence and the responsibility to participate in policy formulation in the same way as the faculty senates of colleges and universities. The growth of faculty participation in policy determination seems inevitable. The problem lies in ensuring that the faculty will exert its influence toward the realization of the full set of junior college tasks, rather than seeking to shape the institution in the image of the university. Land-grant colleges have become great state universities, to the point where they are embarrassed by the original purpose. Normal schools have become great state universities, without improving their competence or pride in the preparation of teachers for the public schools. Can junior college faculties resist this emulative drive and push on toward their own excellence? Or will it be necessary in another quarter century to establish anew an institution to perform the tasks that by then the junior college will have abandoned?

F. Problems of Standards

Community junior colleges can become excellent educational institutions. In the past, too many of them have not achieved excellence. At present, conditions are favorable to their quest—growing independence, acceptance by the public and by other segments of higher education, improved preparation of administrators and of faculty, greater cooperation and articulation among educational institutions. A remaining barrier is the confusion that still persists in the definition of excellence. Once junior college workers and their several publics accept internally as well as verbally that excellence may be a quality of an educational program at any level of abstraction, the road will be open to their pursuit of excellence in the entire junior college curriculum.

One of the first steps along that road will be the establishment of a dozen or more frankly experimental community junior colleges, dedicated to providing better educational opportunities for all elements of their student bodies. There are good reasons why community colleges have not been experimental—the domination of the universities, the association with the public schools, the cost of experimentation, the local rather than universal outlook of boards and administrators. It would seem, however, that the time has now come when several communities might determine that they want the very best for their students, and work out in cooperation with an educational foundation plans for extended and fundamental controlled experiments in all areas of the curriculum. The successful techniques might then serve as models for less adventurous junior colleges.

The experimental junior college must carry its experimentation beyond independent studies in the humanities for the ablest 5% of the students. Excellence should be the goal of all faculty members, and expected of all students. Excellence in education involves a high level of expectation on the part of the college community—citizens, board of trustees, administration, teachers, students. It requires a willingness to pay for libraries, laboratories, varieties of learning spaces, and faculty time to plan for excellence. It cannot be achieved without flexibility in the use of time and space and personnel. In summation, institutional arrangements must encourage the faculty to be enthusiastic and creative about teaching, and enable the students to become actively involved as they are caught up in this enthusiasm and creativity.

Improvement of junior college standards will require increased attention to the preparation and selection of faculty members. At present, the great majority of junior college teachers hold masters' degrees; more than half of them have had teaching experience in secondary schools. Few of them have prepared specifically and during their undergraduate years for college or junior college teaching. A good deal is known of the characteristics of junior college teachers in service (135:Ch. 7), but there is no firm knowledge of what patterns of personal qualities are most closely related to stimulating junior college teaching of inspiring quality. The problem of standards will not be solved until a great deal of research is done on this subject.

Better counseling is also associated with the improvement of standards, for the student who chooses an unsuitable curriculum is not a successful student, no matter how good his grade point average. Yet the quality of junior college counseling programs is reported to be far below the ideal that is set for this function. Until competent staff are employed in sufficient numbers to be effective in junior college educational and occupational counseling, the best of junior college faculties will be hampered in their efforts.

The community junior college has successfully traversed the trials of infancy and adolescence. In its maturity, it must accept the obligation to strive for excellence at every level of its broad scope of educational tasks. High standards are possible in community junior colleges, but they are inseparable from diversification of the curriculum, exceptional teaching, and competent guidance. As these colleges dedicate themselves to these responsibilities, they will play a major part in the further evolution of American civilization.

Bibliography

1. American Association of Junior Colleges, Commission on Legislation. *Principles of Legislative Action for Community Junior Colleges.* Washington: The Association, 1962.
2. Amori, Joseph. "Why Junior College Students Withdraw," *Junior College Journal,* 21:18–24, September, 1941.
3. Anderson, H. Dewey. "Whose Children Attend Junior College?" *Junior College Journal,* 4:165–172, January, 1934.
4. *Annual Report of the Superintendent, 1963–64* (mimeographed annually). Costa Mesa, California: Orange Coast Junior College District, 1964.
5. Barzun, Jacques. *The House of Intellect.* New York: Harper and Row, 1959.
6. Bastian, Mildred E. "How We Created a Junior College District," *Junior College Journal,* 33:10–15, February, 1963.
7. Blocker, Clyde E. and Wendell Wolfe. "Academic Rank in Two-Year Colleges," *Junior College Journal,* 35:21–25, December, 1964.
8. Bogue, Jesse Parker (editor). *American Junior Colleges* (Fourth Edition). Washington: American Council on Education, 1956.
9. ———. *The Community College.* New York: McGraw-Hill Book Co., 1950.
10. ———. *The Development of Junior Colleges.* Washington: American Association of Junior Colleges, 1957.
11. ———. "Junior College World," *Junior College Journal,* 24:247–250, December, 1953.
12. Brick, Michael. *Forum and Focus for the Junior College Movement: The American Association of Junior Colleges.* New York: Bureau of Publications, Teachers College, Columbia University, 1964.
13. Brownell, Baker. *The College and the Community.* New York: Harper and Row, 1952.
14. Brumbaugh, A. J. "Better Student Personnel Services in Junior Colleges," *Junior College Journal,* 21:37–41, September, 1950.

15. Butler, Nathaniel. "The Six-Year High School," *School Review*, 12:22–25, January, 1904.
16. Butts, R. Freeman. *The College Charts Its Course*. New York: McGraw-Hill Book Co., 1939.
17. Campbell, Doak S. *A Critical Study of the Stated Purposes of the Junior College*. Nashville: George Peabody College for Teachers, 1930.
18. ———. "Graduation Titles and Academic Costume," *Junior College Journal*, 4:362–365, April, 1934.
19. Canavan, P. Joseph. "Compensations and Problems of Junior College Teaching," *Junior College Journal*, 32:509–516, May, 1962.
20. Chapman, Charles E. "Ohio Joins the Club," *Junior College Journal*, 35:8–12, October, 1964.
21. Clark, Burton R. *The Open-Door College*. New York: McGraw-Hill Book Co., 1960.
22. Cohn, Victor. *1999—Our Hopeful Future*. Indianapolis: The Bobbs-Merrill Co., 1954.
23. Cole, Charles C. *Encouraging Scientific Talent*. Princeton: College Entrance Examination Board, Educational Testing Service, 1956.
24. "College Salaries Look Better." *NEA Research Bulletin*, 42:35–42, May, 1964.
25. Colvert, C. C. "Cost per Student in the Public Junior Colleges in the United States," *Junior College Journal*, 27:396–401, March, 1957.
26. ———. "Development of the Junior College Movement," Chapter 2 in *American Junior Colleges* (Fourth Edition). Jesse P. Bogue (editor). Washington: American Council on Education, 1956.
27. ———. "Professional Development of Junior College Instructors," *Junior College Journal*, 25:474–478, April, 1955.
28. *The Community Junior College in Florida's Future*. The Report to the State Board of Education by the Community College Council. Tallahassee: The State Department of Education, 1957.
29. Conley, William H. "The Junior College Instructor," *Junior College Journal*, 9:507–512, May, 1939.
30. Cosand, Joseph and John E. Tirrell. "Flying a College on the Computer," *Junior College Journal*, 35:5–8, September, 1964.
31. Coulter, E. M. *College Life in the Old South*. New York: The Macmillan Co., 1928.
32. D'Amico, Louis A. and Marie R. Prahl. "A Follow-up of the Educational, Vocational, and Activity Pursuits of Students Graduated from Flint Junior College, 1953–1956," *Junior College Journal*, 29:474–477, April, 1959.
33. ——— and Max R. Raines. "Employment Characteristics of Flint Junior College Students," *Junior College Journal*, 28:193–195, December, 1957.
34. Dewhurst, J. Frederic, and associates. *America's Needs and Resources*. New York: The Twentieth Century Fund, 1955.
35. Diekhoff, John S. *The Domain of the Faculty*. New York: Harper and Row, 1956.
36. Drucker, Peter. *America's Next Twenty Years*. New York: Harper and Row, 1957.
37. Eckert, Ruth E. and John E. Stecklein. "Career Motivations and Satisfactions of Junior College Teachers," *Junior College Journal*, 30:83–89, October, 1959.

38. *Educational and Occupational Needs of Coastal Area, Orange County, California* (mimeographed). Costa Mesa, California: Orange Coast College, July, 1954.
39. Educational Policies Commission. *Higher Education in a Decade of Decision.* Washington: National Education Association, 1957.
40. Eells, Walter Crosby. *American Junior Colleges,* 1940. Washington: American Council on Education, 1940.
41. ———. "Junior College Terminal Education," *Junior College Journal,* 10:244–250, January, 1940.
42. ———. *Present Status of Junior College Terminal Education.* Washington: American Association of Junior Colleges, 1941.
43. ———. *Why Junior College Terminal Education?* Washington: American Association of Junior Colleges, 1941.
44. Emerson, Lynn A. "Vocational-Technical Education for American Industry," *Office of Education Circular,* No. 530. Washington: Government Printing Office, 1958.
45. Engleman, Lois E. and Walter Crosby Eells. *The Literature of Junior College Terminal Education.* Washington: American Association of Junior Colleges, 1941.
46. *Establishing Junior Colleges.* Occasional Report No. 5, Junior College Leadership Program, School of Education. Los Angeles: University of California, 1964.
47. Fariss, Gertrude Houk. "Report of Committee on Legislation," *Junior College Journal,* 17:385–387, May, 1947.
48. Fields, Ralph R. *The Community College Movement.* New York: McGraw-Hill Book Co., 1962.
49. *The Flight from Teaching.* New York: The Carnegie Foundation for the Advancement of Teaching, 1964.
50. *Florida Statutes.* Section 228.14 (3), and Section 228.16 (4), and Section 230.23 (7) (b).
51. Folwell, W. W. *University Addresses.* New York: H. W. Wilson Co., 1909.
52. French, Sidney J. *Accent on Teaching.* New York: Harper and Row, 1954.
53. Fretwell, Elbert K., Jr. *Founding Public Junior Colleges.* New York: Teachers College, Columbia University, 1954.
54. Galbraith, John Kenneth. *The Affluent Society.* Boston: Houghton Mifflin Co., 1958.
55. *General Education in a Free Society.* The Report of the Harvard Committee. Cambridge: Harvard University Press, 1946.
56. Gleazer, Edmund J., Jr. (editor). *American Junior Colleges* (Sixth Edition). Washington: American Council on Education, 1963.
57. ———. "From the Executive Director's Desk," *Junior College Journal,* 29:109–113, October, 1958.
58. Greenshields, Myrel J., Frank B. Lindsay and William H. Crawford. "Junior College Teachers as Guidance Workers," *Junior College Journal,* 29:366–373, March, 1959.
59. Hancock, J. Leonard. "Business Education: The Terminal Function," *Junior College Journal,* 2:64–73, November, 1931.
60. Harris, Norman C. *Technical Education in the Junior College: New Programs for New Jobs.* Washington: American Association of Junior Colleges, 1964.

61. Havemann, Ernest and Patricia Salter West. *They Went to College.* New York: Harcourt, Brace and World. Copyright, *Time,* 1952.
62. Havighurst, Robert J. *American Higher Education in the 1960's.* Columbus: Ohio State University Press, 1960.
63. ———— and Bernice L. Neugarten. *Society and Education* (Second Edition). Boston: Allyn and Bacon, 1962.
64. ———— and Robert Rodgers. "The Role of Motivation," Chapter VII in Byron S. Hollinshead. *Who Should Go to College.* New York: Columbia University Press, 1952.
65. Hayden, Shelden. "The Junior College as a Community Institution," *Junior College Journal,* 10:70–73, October, 1939.
66. *Health, Education, and Welfare Trends, 1963 Edition.* Washington, D. C.: Government Printing Office, 1963.
67. Hendrix, Vernon L. "Academic Rank: Mostly Peril?" *Junior College Journal,* 34:28–30, December, 1963.
68. Henry, Nelson B. (editor). *General Education.* The Fifty-first Yearbook of the National Society for the Study of Education, Part I. Chicago: The University of Chicago Press, 1952.
69. ———— (editor). *The Public Junior College.* The Fifty–fifth Yearbook of the National Society for the Study of Education, Part I. Chicago: The University of Chicago Press, 1956.
70. *Higher Education for American Democracy.* A Report of the President's Commission on Higher Education. New York: Harper and Row, 1948.
71. Hill, Merton E. "History of Terminal Courses in California," *Junior College Journal,* 12:311–313, February, 1942.
72. Hillway, Tyrus. *The American Two-Year College.* New York: Harper and Row, 1958.
73. Hollinshead, Byron S. "The Community Junior College Program," *Junior College Journal,* 7:111–116, December, 1936.
74. Hollis, Ernest V., and associates. *Costs of Attending College.* U.S. Office of Education Bulletin, 1957, No. 9. Washington: Government Printing Office, 1957.
75. Horn, Francis H. "Liberal Education Re-examined," *Harvard Educational Review,* 26:303–314, Fall, 1956.
76. Humphreys, J. Anthony. "Toward Improved Programs of Student Personnel Services," *Junior College Journal,* 22:382–392, March, 1952.
77. Hutchins, Robert. "The Report of the President's Commission on Higher Education," *Educational Record,* 29:107–122, April, 1948.
78. Iffert, Robert E. *Retention and Withdrawal of College Students.* U.S. Office of Education Bulletin, 1958, No. 1. Washington: Government Printing Office, 1958.
79. Ingles, E. T. "Criteria for Adding New Courses to the Junior College Curriculum," California Journal of Secondary Education, 32:218–221, April, 1957.
80. *Institutional Research in the Junior College.* Occasional Report No. 3. Los Angeles: Junior College Leadership Program, School of Education, University of California, 1962.
81. Johnson, B. Lamar. *General Education in Action.* Washington: American Council on Education, 1952.
82. ————. "Problems of Preparing Junior College Teachers," *Report of the*

State-wide Conference on the Preparation of Junior College Teachers (mimeographed). Sacramento: California State Department of Education, 1958.

83. Johnson, B. Lamar. *Starting a Community Junior College.* Washington: American Association of Junior Colleges, 1964.

84. Keller, Robert J., et al. *The Junior College in Minnesota.* St. Paul, Minn.: State Department of Education, 1958.

85. Kintzer, Frederick C. *Board Policy Manuals in California Junior Colleges.* Occasional Report No. 2. Los Angeles: Junior College Leadership Program, School of Education, University of California, 1962.

86. ———. *Faculty Handbooks in California Public Junior Colleges.* Institutional Report No. 1. Los Angeles: Junior College Leadership Program, School of Education, University of California, 1961.

87. ———. *President's Reports in American Junior Colleges.* Occasional Report No. 4. Los Angeles: Junior College Leadership Program, School of Education, University of California, 1963.

88. Knoell, Dorothy M. and Leland L. Medsker. *Factors Affecting Performance of Transfer Students from Two- to Four-Year Colleges: With Implications for Coordination and Articulation.* Cooperative Research Project No. 1133. Berkeley: Center for the Study of Higher Education, University of California, 1964.

88a. ———. *From Junior to Senior College: A National Study of the Transfer Student.* Washington: American Council on Education, 1965.

89. Koos, Leonard V. *Integrating High School and College.* New York: Harper and Row, 1947.

90. ———. *The Junior College.* Minneapolis: University of Minnesota Press, 1924.

91. ———. *The Junior College Movement.* Boston: Ginn and Co., 1925.

92. ———. "Junior College Teachers: Background of Experience," *Junior College Journal,* 18:457–469, April, 1958.

93. ———. "Junior College Teachers: Subjects Taught and Specialized Preparation," *Junior College Journal,* 18:196–209, December, 1947.

94. ———. "Preparation for Community-College Teaching," *Journal of Higher Education,* 21:309–317, June, 1950.

95. Kuhns, Eileen P. "Part-Time Faculty," *Junior College Journal,* 33:8–12, January, 1963.

96. Lange, Alexis F. "The Junior College as an Integral Part of the Public School System," *School Review,* 25:465–479, September, 1917.

97. Lide, Edwin S. "The Social Composition of Chicago's New Junior College Population," *School Review,* 44:673–680, November, 1936.

98. Mac Lean, Malcolm S. "Intelligences-Not Intelligence," *Education,* 73:489–495, April, 1953.

99. Martorana, S. V. "The Legal Status of American Public Junior Colleges," *American Junior Colleges* (Sixth Edition). Edmund J. Gleazer, Jr. (editor). Washington: American Council on Education, 1963.

100. ———. "Recent State Legislation Affecting Junior Colleges," *Junior College Journal,* 28:307–321, February, 1958 (also, 24:459–471, April, 1954; and 26:328–341, February, 1956; and 30:310–326, February, 1960).

101. ———. "Status of Adult Education in Junior Colleges," *Junior College Journal,* 18:322–331, February, 1948.

102. Martorana, S. V., and James K. Palmer. "Recent State Legislation Affecting Junior Colleges," *Junior College Journal,* 32:316–330, February, 1962.
102a. ——— and Robert F. McHugh. "State Legislation: 1962–64; A Survey of State Legislation Affecting Two-Year Colleges," *Junior College Journal,* 36: 27–34, March, 1966.
103. Maul, Ray C. "Are Junior College Salaries Competitive?" *Junior College Journal,* 34:20–23, March, 1964.
104. ———. "Can We Get Enough Good Teachers?" *Junior College Journal* 34:3–7, December, 1963.
105. McAlmon, Victoria. "A New Type of College Training," *California Quarterly of Secondary Education,* 6:95–101, October, 1930.
106. McDaniel, J. W. *Essential Student Personnel Practices for Junior Colleges.* Washington: American Association of Junior Colleges, 1962.
107. McDowell, F. M. *The Junior College.* U.S. Bureau of Education Bulletin, 1919, No. 35. Washington: Government Printing Office, 1919.
108. McSwain, Eunice. "Some Aspects of Status of Junior Colleges in the United States—Mississippi," *Junior College Journal,* 24:91–93, October, 1953.
109. Medsker, Leland L. *The Junior College: Progress and Prospect.* New York: McGraw-Hill Book Co., 1960.
110. Meinecke, Charlotte Drummond. "Placement and Follow-up in Junior Colleges," *Junior College Journal,* 19:59–67, October, 1948.
111. Mohs, Milton C. *Service Through Placement in the Junior College.* Washington: American Association of Junior Colleges, 1962.
112. Morris, Charles S. " 'The People's College' at San Mateo," *Junior College Journal,* 14:148–157, December, 1943.
113. Morrison, D. G., "Research and the Two-Year College," *Junior College Journal,* 29:128–132, November, 1958.
114. ———, Ken August Brunner and S. V. Martorana. *The 2-Year Community College: An Annotated List of Unpublished Studies and Surveys, 1957–61.* Office of Education Bulletin, 1963, No. 28. Washington: Government Printing Office, 1963.
115. ——— and S. V. Martorana. *Criteria for the Establishment of 2-Year Colleges.* Washington: Government Printing Office, 1963.
116. National Advisory Committee on the Junior College. *A National Resource for Occupational Education.* Washington: American Association of Junior Colleges, 1964.
117. "Need for College Teachers Grows." *NEA Research Bulletin,* 41:108–115, December, 1963.
118. *1966 Junior College Directory.* Washington: American Association of Junior Colleges, 1966.
119. Noffsinger, H. C. "One Third of a Century of Progress," *Junior College Journal,* 5:395–404, May, 1935.
120. *Occupational-Vocational Education for Contra-Costa County* (mimeographed). Martinez, California: Contra Costa Junior College District, 1958.
121. O'Connor, Thomas J. *Follow-up Studies in Junior Colleges.* Washington: American Association of Junior Colleges, 1965.
122. *Opening (Fall) Enrollment in Higher Education, 1964.* Office of Education Circular No. 762. Washington: Government Printing Office, 1964.
123. *Orange Coast College Faculty Manual, 1956* (mimeographed). Costa Mesa, California: Orange Coast College, 1956.

124. Pence, Don P. "The Oregon Story," *Junior College Journal*, 34:4–8, November, 1963.

125. Peterson, Basil H. and James W. Thornton, Jr. "Building a Functional Program for a Junior College," *Junior College Journal*, 19:119–124, November, 1948.

126. Price, Hugh G. *California Public Junior Colleges*. Bulletin of the California State Department of Education, XXVII, No. 1, February, 1958.

127. Punke, Harold H. "Ranking, Tenure, and Sex of Junior College Faculties," *School Review*, 62:480–487, November, 1954.

128. Putnam, Phil H. "Aspects of the Status of Junior Colleges in the United States—Oregon," *Junior College Journal*, 22:342–344, February, 1952.

129. Raines, Max R. "Progress Report on the National Study of Junior College Personnel Programs," in *Selected Papers from the 45th Annual Convention*. Washington: American Association of Junior Colleges, 1965.

130. Rawlinson, Howard E. "Preliminary Planning for a New Junior College," *Junior College Journal*, 29:186–190, December, 1958.

131. Ricciardi, Nicholas. "Vital Junior College Problems in California," *Junior College Journal*, 1:24–27, October, 1930.

132. Rogers, James F. *A Philosophy for the Junior College with Implications for Curriculum, Junior College Journal*, 30:125–131, November, 1959.

133. Sack, Saul. "The First Junior College," *Junior College Journal*, 30:13–15, September, 1959.

134. *Salaries Paid and Salary Practices in Universities, Colleges, and Junior Colleges, 1963–1964*. Research Report 1964-R3. Washington: Research Division, National Education Association, 1964.

135. *School Board-Superintendent Relationships*. The Thirty-fourth Yearbook. Washington: American Association of School Administrators, 1956.

136. Schultz, Raymond E. *Administrators for America's Junior Colleges: Predictions of Need 1965–1980*. Washington: American Association of Junior Colleges, 1965.

137. Seashore, Carl E. *The Junior College Movement*. New York: Holt, Rinehart and Winston, 1940.

138. Seashore, Harold. "Academic Abilities of Junior College Students," *Junior College Journal*, 29:74–80, October, 1958.

139. *Second Report to the President*. President's Committee on Education Beyond the High School. Washington: Government Printing Office, 1957.

140. Sexson, John A. and John W. Harbeson. *The New American College*. New York: Harper and Row, 1946.

141. Sheats, Paul H., Clarence D. Jayne, and Ralph B. Spence. *Adult Education: the Community Approach*. New York: The Dryden Press, 1953.

142. Simms, Charles Wesley. *The Present Legal Status of the Public Junior College*. Nashville: George Peabody College for Teachers, 1948.

143. Simon, Kenneth A. and W. Vance Grant. *Digest of Educational Statistics, 1964 Edition*. Office of Education Bulletin 1964, No. 18. Washington: Government Printing Office, 1964.

144. Snyder, William H. "The Distinctive Status of the Junior College," *Junior College Journal*, 3:235–239, February, 1933.

145. ———. "The Real Function of the Junior College," *Junior College Journal*, 1:74–80, November, 1930.

146. Spindt, H. A. "Establishment of the Junior College in California, 1907–1921," *California Journal of Secondary Education*, 32:391–396, November, 1957.
147. State Junior College Advisory Board. *Five Years of Progress: Florida's Community Junior Colleges*. Tallahassee: State Department of Education, 1963.
148. Stickler, W. Hugh (editor). *Experimental Colleges*. Tallahassee: Florida State University, 1964.
149. ———. "A Study of Florida Junior College Transfer Students in the Florida State University, Fall Semester, 1957–58." Unpublished study prepared by the Office of Institutional Research and Service. The Florida State University, March, 1958.
150. Tappan, Henry P. *University Education*. New York: G. P. Putnam's Sons, 1851.
151. *Teachers for Tomorrow*. Bulletin No. 2. New York: The Fund for the Advancement of Education, 1955.
152. Thomas, Frank W. "The Functions of the Junior College," *The Junior College: Its Organization and Administration*. William Martin Proctor (editor). Stanford, Calif.: Stanford University Press, 1927.
153. Thornton, James W., Jr. *General Education: Establishing the Program* (pamphlet). Washington: Association for Higher Education, 1958.
154. Tibbits, Fred Lyman. "Student Attitudes in Junior College," *Junior College Journal*, 2:148–151, December, 1931.
155. Tillery, Dale. "Academic Rank: Promise or Peril?" *Junior College Journal*, 33:6–9, February, 1963.
156. Todd, L. O. "Mississippi Legislation Charts a Comprehensive Program," *Junior College Journal*, 21:298–303, January, 1951.
157. *The University of Virginia Newsletter*, Charlottesville. Vol. 34, No. 9, February 1, 1958.
158. Venn, Grant. *Man, Education, and Work*. Washington: American Council on Education, 1964.
159. Vocational Education Staff. "Vocational Education in California," *Bulletin of the California State Department of Education*, Vol. XIV, No. 4, October, 1945.
160. Ward, Phebe. *Terminal Education in the Junior College*. New York: Harper and Row, 1947.
161. Watson, Fletcher G. "A Crisis in Science Teaching," *Scientific American*, 190:27–29, February, 1954.
162. Weersing, Frederick J. "Misconceptions Regarding the Junior College," *Junior College Journal*, 1:363–369, March, 1931.
163. *Who Came to Coalinga College?* (mimeographed). Coalinga, California: Office of Instruction and Records, Coalinga College, 1958.
164. Woellner, R. C., and M. Aurilla Wood. *Requirements for Certification of Teachers and Administrators for Elementary Schools, Secondary Schools, and Junior Colleges*. (Thirtieth Edition, 1965–1966). Chicago: University of Chicago Press, 1965.
165. Young, Raymond J. "Junior College Prospects and a Guide for its Legal Propagation," *Junior College Journal*, 21:444–452, April, 1951.

Index